Taking Philanthropy Seriously

Philanthropic and Nonprofit Studies

Dwight F. Burlingame and David C. Hammack, editors

EDITED BY
WILLIAM DAMON
AND
SUSAN VERDUCCI

Taking Philanthropy Seriously

Beyond Noble Intentions
to Responsible Giving

INDIANA UNIVERSITY PRESS
Bloomington and Indianapolis

This book is a publication of

Indiana University Press
601 North Morton Street
Bloomington, IN 47404-3797 USA

http://iupress.indiana.edu

Telephone orders   800-842-6796
Fax orders   812-855-7931
Orders by e-mail   iuporder@indiana.edu

© 2006 by Indiana University Press

The paper used in this publication meets the minimum requirements of American National Standard for Information Sciences—Permanence of Paper for Printed Library Materials, ANSI Z39.48-1984.

Manufactured in the United States of America

Library of Congress Cataloging-in-Publication Data

Taking philanthropy seriously : beyond noble intentions to responsible giving / edited by William Damon and Susan Verducci.
   p.   cm. — (Philanthropic and nonprofit studies)
   Includes index.
   ISBN 0-253-34772-6 (cloth : alk. paper) — ISBN 0-253-21860-8 (pbk. : alk. paper)
   1. Charities—United States. 2. Benefactors—Charitable contributions—United States. 3. Philanthropists—Charitable contributions—United States. I. Damon, William, date II. Verducci, Susan. III. Series.
   HV41.9.U5T35 2006
   361.7'40973—dc22
                                                                                              2006008082

1 2 3 4 5   11 10 09 08 07 06

For John Gardner:

May his far-sighted wisdom and generous spirit endure.

Surplus wealth is a sacred trust which its possessor is bound to administer for the good of the community.

Andrew Carnegie

The price of greatness is responsibility.

Winston Churchill

Contents

Preface

American philanthropy has a proud tradition and an uncertain future. Much like the country itself, philanthropic work in the United States always has been extraordinarily ambitious, generous, and dynamic, marked by a spirit of creativity and experimentation. This spirit endures to this day, spawning innovative approaches to "social investment" and "venture" that promise to shake the field out of its stodgy ways. Of course the field was never very stodgy to begin with—the Carnegies and Rockefellers were as venturesome and inventive in their giving as anyone who has come along since—but it is probably inevitable that those who wish to improve things will consider prior approaches to be moss-grown and ineffective.

So the field is changing, partly by intention and design. A primary purpose of this book is to examine the new currents sweeping through American philanthropy at the present time. Some of the examinations in this book are empirical, documenting recent philanthropic initiatives that the authors have investigated through observation and other social science research methods. Some of the examinations in this book are more theoretical, reflecting the insights of authors who know present-day American philanthropy intimately through their scholarship and practice. Together, I believe it is fair to say, the cases and descriptions presented across the chapters of this book add up to a portrayal of current philanthropic practice in the U.S. that has no parallel in any other published writings.

It is a portrayal that comes with some implicit concerns and leads to some questions of great consequence. For if philanthropy is changing by intent and design, it is also changing in ways that may not be under anyone's control, and in this respect perhaps not for the better. And it also may be necessary to take a critical look at the intent and design in cases where someone is in control, because not all intelligent strategies in human affairs turn out to be wise ones in the long run. The second major purpose of this book is to take a hard look at today's approaches to see how well they are serving philanthropy's essential mission of promoting the public good.

In the introductory chapter, I begin the book with the noncontroversial observation that philanthropy is a morally serious endeavor. What follows from this observation may be a bit more controversial, or at least not intuitively obvious to all who practice philanthropy: as a serious endeavor, the act of giving can cause great harm as well as important good. This claim may come as a surprise for a field imbued with generosity and good intentions. Indeed, I am certain that few who practice philanthropy are as aware as they should be of

Andrew Carnegie's old warning that most charitable acts go awry. This warning, developed at some length in the introductory chapter, is meant to provide a thematic message for the book throughout: *Generosity and noble intentions are not sufficient for successful philanthropy; its goals and practices must be taken seriously and implemented with care and strategic vision in order for good rather than harm to result.*

Of course this is true in any field of endeavor. A physician must have more than a warm heart and intention to heal in order to cure a patient, just as a scientist must have more than curiosity in order to discover a new phenomenon. Other fields long ago recognized the need to build their knowledge bases and codify their best practices in order to accomplish their own missions of serving the public good. This is what my colleagues and I have called the essential enterprise of "domain-building" that characterizes most serious professions.[1]

Philanthropy as a field has been slow to build a domain of codes and practices that extends beyond the barest legal requirements for fiscal probity. There are some understandable reasons for this. For one thing, a donor may rightly point out that "It's my money" and conclude that his or her own instincts and interests should be the sole determiner of how it should be deployed. Related to this sentiment, there is a widespread view that major giving is done out of personal passion that would shrink in the face of domain-like codes and procedures. A third point of resistance is that much philanthropic activity is highly private, lacking the kinds of transparency needed to collect reliable evidence about successful or failed practices.

Yet progress cannot be made without learning lessons from past efforts. The time is ripe for the field of philanthropy to build a domain of knowledge and practice that is commensurate with the seriousness of its ancient mission. Susan Verducci and I, along with all of our authors, intend this book to make a leading contribution to this task—a task made all the more necessary by the imminent sweeping changes the book describes.

This examination of contemporary philanthropy grew out of the Good Work Project, a broad exploration of how it is possible for professionals to acquire moral integrity and excel in their work during times of rapid change and indeterminate incentives.[2] Good work means work that is successful *and* responsible, masterful *and* moral, passionate *and* skillful. Good work resists compromises: it has a moral center. Howard Gardner, Mihalyi Csikszentmihaly, and I have examined good work in several fields, and four years ago we wrote an initial book on good work in science and journalism.[3] The present book is another step in our efforts—and those of our collaborators, many of whom are authors in this book—to identify the pathways to good work in today's complex and changing fields of work. Joining us in this endeavor for the present purposes are a number of distinguished authors from outside the Good Work Project. We hope that, with their help, we have made a contribution to an understanding of both the particular issue of how good work may be accomplished in the field of philanthropy and the general matter of how professionals in a dynamic field can reach their highest goals through mastery and responsibility.

WD

Palo Alto, California

October 2005

Notes

1. H. Gardner, M. Csikszentmihalyi, and W. Damon, *Good Work: When Excellence and Ethics Meet* (New York: Basic Books, 2001).

2. The Good Work Project (goodworkproject.org) is a collaborative research and educational venture started by Howard Gardner, Mihalyi Csikszentmihalyi, and William Damon in 1994. In addition to producing a number of books and papers on good work in today's society, the Project has designed educational workshops in professional fields such as journalism, higher education, and philanthropy. Information about the activities and publications of the Project may be found on its Web site.

3. Gardner, Csikszentmihalyi, and Damon, *Good Work.*

Acknowledgments

Many persons and funding agencies have contributed to the GoodWork Project and its present extension into the subject of philanthropy. The William and Flora Hewlett Foundation has supported the GoodWork Project since its inception, and it has provided major support to the investigations into philanthropy reported in this book. We thank Ray Bacchetti for his unflagging support as our program officer in the project's initial stages. We also thank Hewlett's president, Paul Brest, for his invaluable help, advice, and interest over the past several years. Atlantic Philanthropies also funded the philanthropy studies generously, and we especially thank Joel Fleishman for his insightful contributions to our efforts. We gratefully acknowledge financial support for related aspects of the Good-Work Project from the Carnegie Corporation of New York, the Ford Foundation, Courtney Ross (through the Ross Family Foundation), and John Bryant.

This book would not have been possible without the generosity of the many people working in philanthropy that we interviewed for our study. Their contributions to our understanding of the field form the foundation from which this book emerged.

At Stanford, research assistants Mollie Galloway and Peter Osborne contributed greatly to the interviews and analyses reported in this book. Tanya Rose, Kathy Davis, and Taru Fisher also provided skillful assistance. On a personal level, Susan Verducci thanks Tripp Sandford and William Damon thanks Anne Colby for the much-needed kinds of family dispensations required for labors such as compiling major research projects into books.

Taking Philanthropy Seriously

Part One: Defining the Problem

Introduction: Taking Philanthropy Seriously

William Damon

It is right and fitting to sing the praises of philanthropy. The generous spirit of philanthropy reflects the best part of human nature. Philanthropic gifts have filled the world with knowledge, art, healing, and enduring cultural institutions dedicated to the betterment of society. Every day, all over the world, philanthropy touches the lives of countless people, bringing them education, improved health, intellectual and spiritual elevation, and relief from misfortune. Moreover, philanthropy's full potential for improving the human condition no doubt extends beyond any contribution that has yet been realized.

With this in mind, it may seem unnecessary—indeed, a bit curmudgeonly—to dwell on the *harms* that philanthropy can bring about, as I am about to do in this chapter. Yet my focus on harms does not spring from my lack of appreciation for philanthropy's great value. Rather, my point is that philanthropy can reach its full potential only by becoming a field that scrutinizes its standards and practices more carefully than it does now. Such scrutiny should begin by confronting the harms misguided practice can cause. In philanthropy, as in any other field, the standards and practices that help guard against misguided practice also can point the way to excellent performance if properly understood and taken to their logical conclusion.

The Responsibility of Serious Endeavors

Some endeavors are more serious than others, in the sense that their consequences have especially great potential for causing good or harm in the world. Warfare, for example, inevitably leads to major changes in people's destinies. It will end some lives and alter the destiny—for better or worse—of many others. War is a *serious intervention* in the affairs of humanity, and, as such, it is an elementary matter of moral responsibility to consider the seriousness of war when it comes to making judgments about launching and conducting one.

Not all activities, of course, are serious in this way. Attending a baseball game will lead to certain pleasures (depending, of course, on how your team does) and pose certain risks (you could get hit with a flying bat or ball or the fist of a drunken fan), but its benefits are limited and its risks unlikely. It is one of many social and recreational activities with generally light consequences.

Certain professions by their very nature produce serious interventions with major benefits or harms as a matter of course. Medicine is one obvious example of this. A physician intervenes in a patient's body (and/or in the patient's behavior) after a problem is found, and the intervention can cure the patient if done well or make the patient more ill if done poorly. Medicine has a grand old tradition of recognizing the serious consequences its interventions can bring about. Hippocrates formalized this tradition in his celebrated oath that required new physicians to proclaim: "I will use my regimens for the benefits of the sick in accordance with my ability and my judgment; but from what is to their harm I will keep them."

Because medical practitioners long ago recognized that the powers they wield can have both terrible and wondrous effects, they adopted the Hippocratic oath as a universal code of medicine. The oath states that to "benefit" the sick and "keep them from harm," physicians must have not only the proper intentions but also enough knowledge, skill, careful judgment, high standards, and ethical commitment. Beneficial work in medicine does not come about casually—it requires preparation, diligence, and goodwill.

Although few professions have a code as renowned as medicine's Hippocratic oath, most do have their own agreed-upon ethical strictures, standards of excellence, and "best practices." Generally such codes are learned in professional schools and then communicated to practitioners by professional organizations such the American Bar Association, the Radio and Television News Directors Association, the American Psychological Association, and so on. Even in the field of business management (which is not really a profession), common codes of conduct are taught in virtually all business schools and publicly endorsed (at least in principle if not in practice) by business leaders everywhere. The raison d'etre for such codes is to minimize the harms that might be caused by malpractice in the field and to define the standards by which any achievement may be judged.

Philanthropy stands as an exception among the fields of highly consequential work in that it conducts its affairs without reference to common codes that are known throughout the field, learned by all new practitioners, widely accepted, and circulated by an authoritative professional association. Of course the field has basic legal statutes that almost all people working in philanthropy know and abide by. There also have been useful efforts within the field to produce materials that analyze and explain the "craft" of grant-making: for example, GrantCraft, sponsored by the Ford Foundation, has compiled cases of expert work in philanthropy and created instructional books and videos based on this practical wisdom, and the Rockefeller Foundation has sponsored an insightful examination of how social outcomes of grants may be assessed.[1] But these and other valuable instructional efforts remain isolated and little known among the vast stretches of philanthropic giving worldwide. Nor are they founded on the integrated theoretical frameworks and verified empirical databases that support virtually all other professional endeavors.

In our GoodWork Project (GWP) research in philanthropy, much of which is presented in this book, we have found that practitioners in the field of philanthropy share a sense of obligation to the public interest. Almost all practitioners in the field today acknowledge that they are stewards of resources that they are accountable for to society and that this stewardship carries a binding responsibility to act properly and avoid conflicts of interest. But beyond this general noble intention and the legal codes that enforce it, philanthropy has few agreed-upon standards of judgment or conduct and little in the way of a definitive knowledge base of proven strategies. Apart from the occasional (and far too isolated) instructional efforts of the type noted above, there is a reluctance in the field to prescribe the "best" ways of accomplishing philanthropic work or to designate an authoritative set of guidelines that people entering the field have an obligation to master. In our GWP term, the field has yet to build a core domain to guide its practice.

Domains for Guiding Practice

In our GoodWork Project, we have found that expert practitioners in most fields display mastery of their field's core "domain"—the base of knowledge, skills, standards, and best practices the field has evolved to date that is formalized in such sources as textbooks, training programs, credentialing and accreditation procedures, and ethics codes.[2] Expert mastery of the field's standards and practices no doubt takes place in philanthropy much as it does in other fields. The difference is that philanthropy has resisted the process of formal codification necessary for a field to create a domain of normative standards and practices at its center.

When a field lacks a domain of knowledge and standards to ground it, people working in the field have no means of agreeing upon what counts as success or failure, opportunity or risk, benefit or harm. They cannot learn lessons from each others' experiences, they cannot devise regular ways of training new practitioners, and they cannot establish common metrics for evaluating their practices. The result is a field that is unable to gauge its own shortcomings and to thereby lead itself toward progressive change. This is a recipe for ineffectiveness at best and catastrophic failure at worst.

Some of philanthropy's reluctance to adopt uniform codes and practices stems from the recognition that the work of philanthropy is allocating money that is—or was—a donor's and that this money carries with it the idiosyncratic stamp of that donor's intent. How, it is pointedly asked, could any general principles do justice to all the varieties of donor intent? Moreover, it is argued that donors give from a spirit of passionate concern about something meaningful to them. Surely the money is best allocated with that same subjective spirit rather than according to a set of formal or impersonal codes. Why, it is asked, should philanthropy conduct itself like a profession when it is voluntary and passion-driven at its core? These are reasonable reservations that certainly need to be taken into account in any attempt to define a domain of standards and practice for philanthropy. But similar objections could be made for any professional field: after all, doesn't medicine need to cope with an almost infinite variety of human predicaments and shouldn't doctors be encouraged to be passionate about their vocation? The nature of any field's domain of standards and practice must reflect such inevitable variations and human factors.

But philanthropy does have a special feature that poses an intransigent point of resistance to the fashioning of formal codes. Somewhat ironically, the point of resistance is the exceptionally laudatory nature of the philanthropic mission itself. Philanthropy is an exercise in giving money away without demanding any direct return (although, as we shall see, it does harbor expectations about that). It is a benevolent act of generosity. For such a generous undertaking, there would seem to be little reason to establish formal procedures to avoid harm. How could an award of debt-free (that is, nonreturnable) money do anything but help?

Here I shall quote John Gardner, the towering figure of the twentieth-century nonprofit world. In an interview I conducted with him shortly before his death, Gardner referred to the field of contemporary philanthropy with an image of an astonished pitcher watching one of his fastballs fly over the fence: "That's why I like that cartoon from Peanuts of Charlie Brown on the pitcher's mound saying, 'How can we lose when we're so sincere?'"

Now baseball has emotional ups and downs, but it is relatively light in the ultimate seriousness of its consequences: John Gardner's cartoon metaphor does not quite capture the problem I am referring to. Fields of work that are more consequential must accept greater responsibility for the results of their efforts because they intervene in people's lives in more dramatic ways. Philanthropy, like medicine and other professional activities, is a powerful intervention. It can and does change lives.

The Problem of Harms in Philanthropy

Although philanthropic interventions are implemented by gifts rather than paid services (in contrast to medicine and other professions), this does not always render them innocent in intent or harmless in consequence. Gifts may be made with impure motives for purposes of power, control, or status. They also may be made carelessly. Malevolent or careless gifts can leave recipients in worse shape than before the gifts were made. History is full of such cases, from the Trojan horse to the smallpox-ridden blankets distributed to the Sioux in the nineteenth century.

Andrew Carnegie, founder of organized philanthropy in the United States, once estimated that 95 percent of philanthropic dollars were "unwisely spent; so spent, indeed, as to produce the very evils which [the giver] proposes to mitigate or cure."[3] Whether or not Carnegie's 95 percent estimate is accurate (he probably did not mean it to be taken literally), the possibility that a well-intentioned gift could have the opposite effect from the intended one is cruel indeed. Carnegie was referring in particular to the harm of supporting habits that sustain poverty. By now, most philanthropists are aware of this danger (generally referred to as "dependency") and take steps to avoid it. But other harms too can emanate from philanthropy, as I describe below; and these harms, to use Carnegie's phrase, are at least as grave as the problems that the gifts were meant to solve. Yet the field that Carnegie founded has done little to create systematic methods for averting such potential harms.

The harms of misguided philanthropy can be subtle or shockingly direct. Many are known to practitioners in the field but are rarely discussed in open forums. Several authors in this volume discuss this problem with a candor unusual for this field. In his chapter, James Smith writes: "The greatest harms occur when gifts are bestowed haphazardly, without forethought, without regard for their effects." Smith focuses especially on ill effects that come about because recipients and donors are not always in agreement (or even in communication) about the nature of the recipient's obligation under the terms of the gift (and Smith points out that any gift, great or small, carries an obligation to respond in some way that is appropriate). As a result, the gift may not have its anticipated effect—indeed, as Carnegie warned, it may have a countereffect—and the giver's relationship with the recipient may be damaged by disappointment and mutual mistrust.

In a previous writing,[4] I have identified additional harms of misguided philanthropy, ill effects that can create serious damage to recipients, donors, and the society beyond them:

- *Direct harms to lives:* Humans have lost their lives to philanthropic interventions that were not carried out with sufficient care. At the end of the nineteenth century, a wealthy philanthropist who had made his fortune in railroads financed Rear Admiral Robert Peary's project of bringing six Eskimos from Greenland to New York for research purposes. Five of the research subjects died of pneumonia within three months. Closer to our own time, over two dozen private and public philanthropies financed the experimental gene therapy research that eventuated in the death of Jesse Geisinger, a young man who, according to his family, was never made aware of the dangers of the procedure.
- *Subverting valuable work of individuals and nonprofit organizations:* Some kinds of support end up bringing recipients farther from their goals than before the support was granted. Every philanthropic gift requires some match between the agendas of the donor and the recipient. The asymmetry of power between the two inevitably creates pressure on the recipient. Sometimes the pressure can be constructive—as when, for example, a donor has sound ideas about better ways that the recipient's agenda can be pursued. But too often the pressure forces recipient organizations to depart from their true missions. This temptation is exacerbated whenever an organization is required to go to multiple donors, all of which have their own idiosyncratic beliefs and priorities. Consider, for example, the case of a medical research lab trying to raise money for exploratory work in diagnostic testing:

> We were able to secure an initial seed grant from N.I.H. and then a larger grant from a private foundation that required matching funds. That got us entangled in a long series of conversations with smaller foundations, family-run, and then some wealthy individuals who were interested in this area. They

all wanted their own proposal in language that addressed their issues, they all had conditions and suggestions about how to go about things, but none of them knew any more than any layman about medical research. . . . They even had ideas about what to look for, sampling issues, technical stuff that they must have gotten opinions about from the press. Most of the ideas were totally unworkable, and the back-and-forth on it has been frustrating and distracting and it continues to be to this day, even from the groups who finally decided to fund us on the grounds that we laid out. We're not sure that we won't get the rug pulled out from us somewhere down the line for some arbitrary reason that will pop into someone's head.[5]

- *Destabilizing communities:* Bright ideas generated around a foundation conference table can lose their luster once put into practice. With proper experimentation, the mistake can be revealed before too much damage is done. Unfortunately, some ideas gain momentum before they can be tested or stopped. The vast urban renewal projects of the 1950s and 60s, now universally considered a disaster for every community they blighted, were designed and funded by a host of public and private agencies. The scale of these projects illustrates the tendency of many who control resources to zealously barrel ahead with well-intended but misguided plans. With the hubris that monetary power encourages, they often ignore skeptics (there were many critics of large-scale urban renewal at the time), insist on immediate action, and create damage that can take generations to undo.
- *Blocking genuine social improvements:* At any time in any society, there are people working to find solutions to social problems. Some work to develop new ideas through discovery and research, others to implement old ideas through changes in social and economic policies. Many attempts at social improvement are divergent from, indeed in contradiction to, other attempts; they are based on contrasting assumptions about the human condition. All inevitably will be subject to "market tests" of one kind or another; any approach must prove itself before it becomes persuasive enough to win a widespread following. In the natural course of events, contending approaches attract advocates and compete with one another on the basis of their validity, utility, and efficiency. Social progress can be defined as the success and survival of ideas and policies that lead to genuine improvements rather than those that lead to degradations. Indeed, historians have observed that it is those societies which encourage the unhindered generation and testing of new ideas and policies that are most likely to enjoy perpetual improvement.

Philanthropy often plays a role in determining which ideas and policies win out. In fact, this role may be philanthropy's greatest lever of influence—after all, resources available to philanthropy are not sufficient to support more than a tiny portion of the public sector, but they are sufficient to define, stimulate, and test the leading edge of social policy. Moreover, this role for philanthropy has increased exponentially in recent years, as growth in philanthropic organizations has created a philanthropic presence in virtually every effort aimed at social improvement. If applied with vigor and imagination, the resources of philanthropy can advance this essential mission in valuable ways. But it is necessary to ask whether philanthropy is prepared to play this decisive role in a responsible manner.

In order to advance the essential process of winnowing out the best approaches to social improvement, philanthropy as a field must free itself from its systemic biases and all other distortions that could impair its collective judgment. Our Good Work Project interviews with people with broad experience in philanthropy (donors, foundation board members, executives, recipients) were troubling in this regard, because they revealed a number of biases that dominate the field at this time. They include: 1) a bias toward goals of social change rather than goals of social preservation; 2) a bias toward the application of entrenched ideas rather than the testing and discovery of new ones; 3) a bias toward the judgment of experts rather than that of practitioners who have actual experience dealing with the problems addressed; and 4) a bias toward trends that have been established by others in the field, a bandwagon phenomenon that magnifies the effects of the other shared biases.

One recent example of this effect was the lockstep funding of experimental school reform efforts during the 1990s. In our interviews, we found widespread agreement among people in the philanthropic world that massive support for these efforts was driven by a trend-following mentality that led many foundations to support the same small circle of highly publicized initiatives. As for assessment, in most cases it was impossible to determine exactly what had happened because of poor documentation, and in the few cases where such identification could be made, results were disappointing.[6] Program officers commented that eventually the lack of results for these expensive initiatives cast a pall over foundations' willingness to invest in school improvement at all, resulting in a decline in philanthropic support for this key area. The irony is that all this came at a time of lively experimentation in education characterized by an energetic competition among different approaches. This competition was not left to play itself out in a normal fashion. The philanthropic efforts soaked up human and capital resources (there are only so many educators and school settings to go around, and when these resources become committed to one initiative, they become unavailable to others), crowding out other promising but less visible approaches that had not yet gathered the momentum needed to sustain attention in the face of the more publicized initiatives. It is clear that the foundation-supported efforts contributed little to this fertile movement.

Designing a More Perfect Gift

It is unfortunately the case that the act of giving is also not always able to improve the lot of those it is intended to help. More unfortunate still, the benevolence of philanthropy can manage at times to *worsen* the conditions of the intended beneficiaries. Perhaps most astonishing of all, the gift of money is not always sufficient to win even the gratitude of those who get it.

In our discussions with grantees who regularly receive philanthropic funds, we found many complaints and few accolades. Recipients rarely felt that they had been treated with respect. They felt that their efforts had been undermined by restrictions or requirements imposed on them as a condition of support, and they questioned both the priorities and strategies of the foundation world. This sense of disenchantment surprised us, because we spoke only with recipients who have led highly successful careers financed by the philanthropic organizations they were criticizing. Why were they biting the hands that have fed them? Perhaps they resented the hoops they were forced to jump through in order to garner support for their cherished causes or perhaps they really did see a more effective way of deploying philanthropic funds. Whatever the reasons behind the skepticism and bitterness of grantees, it confirms once again that giving money may not be as straightforward as it first appears.

This is why for centuries generous people have reasoned, conversed, and argued about the best way to engage in giving. One volume of insightful writings on the matter, compiled by Amy Kass, contains literally dozens of prescriptions for conducting philanthropy in the most beneficial possible manner.[7] Kass called her volume, notably, *The Perfect Gift*. Although Kass's volume refrains from coming to its own final conclusions about how to make more perfect gifts, its title suggests—correctly, I believe—the true challenge for philanthropy in this age of increasing private and decreasing public resources for societal betterment. It is the challenge, to use James Smith's paraphrase of Aristotle (in this volume), of figuring out how to "give to the right people, the right amount, at the right time, and do everything else that is implied in correct giving."

The phrase "perfect gift," which is borrowed from common occasions such as weddings and birthdays, is clarifying because it is grounded in a sense of the recipient's understanding and use of the gift. A perfect wedding or birthday gift takes into account the nature of the occasion, the nature of the recipient, the nature of the relations between giver and recipient, and the expected effect of the gift on the recipient and that relationship. The perfect gift is not, as a rule, the largest gift, nor would the gift necessarily be appropriate on other occasions or for other recipients. Rather, it is a gift that matches the requirements of the situation as well as the complexity of interests of those in that particular situation. It is well-aligned with the proper needs and expectations of both giver and recipient.

Alignment in human affairs is easy to talk about but hard to do. Different parties in any social arrangement often have divergent interests that create incentives for them to pull in opposing directions. In our GoodWork Project, we have seen how fields such as journalism have become degraded by the conflicts caused by such misalignments of interests.[8] But we have also seen how more powerful alignments can be found by building on the best traditions of the domain in creative and strategic ways.[9] For example, journalists today frequently feel pressures to abandon standards of verification and proportionality in order to compete in a market that rewards hasty reporting and sensationalistic gossip. Many cave in to these pressures, to the detriment of both the field and the public interest. But some leading journalists retain their integrity and market appeal by finding new ways of accomplishing the traditional goals of journalism and by mastering technology and other contemporary tools of their craft.[10] They have realigned their own career incentives with the public interest by strategically employing a more effective set of methods.

As Tom Tierney writes in his chapter, people will continue practicing philanthropy with or without aspirations to achieve the greatest possible impact, if only for the laudatory reason that they enjoy giving. But any endeavor with the potential to bring about serious consequences for good or for ill has a responsibility to conduct itself in a serious manner and pursue its goals with the best available tools and wisdom.

Philanthropy is such an endeavor and, like any field of serious work, it can pursue its goals most effectively by defining and drawing on a domain of standards and practices. Such a domain, if it were to exist, would reflect the field's traditional mission as well as the knowledge and strategies that have been forged by the field's most innovative and experienced practitioners. The problem in philanthropy is that it has been a field without such a domain. Progress toward designing the more perfect gift will be made only when the field of philanthropy builds a guiding domain for itself and comes to accept the implications of this domain for training and practice in the field.

Toward Responsibility and Excellence in Giving

The purpose of this book is to define the outlines of a domain that could guide practice and training in the field of philanthropy. The chapters, written by leading scholars and practitioners in the field, present a legion of strategies—some proven, some innovative—for effective philanthropic giving. In the aggregate, these strategies offer contemporary philanthropy a sound foundation for a domain to guide it toward excellent work.

If the purpose of this book is the definition of a domain for excellence, it might seem odd that one of the book's predominant themes is the problem of avoiding harms. The former challenge is a positive pursuit, the latter a defensive one. Clearly both are needed: in any challenging arena of life, one needs a good offense as well as a good defense. But are the two linked, in the senses that they draw on similar strategies and the standards and practices that serve the one also serve the other?

In my educational work with midcareer professionals, I have found that the first step in any training must be a demonstration of the need for the knowledge and skills about to be conveyed.[11] If journalists become convinced that their own unrealized biases might get in the way of accurate reporting, they want to learn methods of verification to check their biases.[12] In executive training for business, this has been called a "deficit creation" process—meaning, simply, that the executives must be shown what they don't know in order to motivate them to learn it.

My belief is that in philanthropy, raising awareness of possible harms is one route to deficit creation. It could be an especially revealing route; the idea that careless philanthropy can be worse than no philanthropy at all is far from obvious. If and when this realization sinks in, learning about responsible and effective strategies can begin.

Many pitfalls and obstacles stem directly from the nature of the pursuit of good work in philanthropy. The altruism at the center of the philanthropic mission is so praiseworthy in itself that it can lead to complacency in how the gift-giving mission is pursued. Compounding this complacency, control of significant financial resources always implies a certain power that can breed arrogance and hubris. Complacency, arrogance, and hubris do not constitute a good mindset for learning: they are more likely to foster the kind of "know-nothing" stance that can lead to unexamined failure. Not all philanthropists fall prey to such temptations, but the field as a whole has yet to establish shared strategies— the knowledge, standards, and practices of a definitive domain—for avoiding them.

The good news is that many in the field have been striving to do better, and they have been forging the essential elements of a guiding domain in their practice and their writings. This book provides an account of some of the most valuable work in this direction to date.

The book is organized in three parts. Part I presents essays, including this introduction, that define the challenges philanthropy faces as a field in building the capacity to make responsible and effective gifts. None of the essays claims that contemporary giving is generally irresponsible or ineffective, but all point to unexamined shortfalls in the way philanthropy is now practiced, and all make the case that the field can do better by building a systematic domain of proven strategies. Part II presents empirical case studies that elucidate the problem discussed in Part 1 and identify some of the strategies that could be part of such a domain. Part III presents further strategies that have been identified in other lines of work beyond the GoodWork Project. The strategies for responsible and effective giving described in Parts II and III of this book offer the field a foundation for a domain that can guide contemporary philanthropy past the harms posed by misguided practice toward its full potential to improve the human condition.

Notes

1. See the Web sites of GrantCraft (http://www.grantcraft.org) and the Rockefeller Foundation (http://www.rockfound.org).

2. Gardner, Csikszentmihalyi, and Damon (2001).

3. Carnegie (1889).

4. For a comprehensive list, see Damon (2004).

5. The interview was drawn from our GoodWork Project research (goodworkproject .org). Some details in this quote have been altered at the request of the participant.

6. Steinberg (1996). Also, see *Education Week*, 21 October 2000, for further detail

on the disappointing outcomes of the school reform movement and some rare exceptions.

7. Kass (2001).
8. Gardner, Csikszentmihalyi, and Damon (2001).
9. Damon, Colby, Bronk, and Ehrlich (2005).
10. Ibid.; see also Kovach and Rosenstiel (2000).
11. Damon, Colby, Bronk, and Ehrlich (2005); Damon (forthcoming).
12. Damon, Colby, Bronk, and Ehrlich (2005).

References

Carnegie, A. 1889. "Wealth." *North American Review* CXLVIII: 653–664.

Damon, W. 2004. *The Moral Advantage: How to Succeed in Business by Doing the Right Thing.* San Francisco: Berrett-Koehler.

———. 2006. *Recent Research on Good Work and the Development of Young Adults: Lessons for Law Schools.* Osaka, Japan: Kwansei Gakuin University Press.

Damon, W., A. Colby, K. Bronk, and T. Ehrlich. 2005. "Passion and Mastery in Balance: Towards Good Work in the Professions." *Daedalus: The Journal of the American Academy of the Arts and Sciences* 134, no. 3: 27–36.

Gardner, H., M. Csikszentmihalyi, and W. Damon. 2001. *Good Work: When Excellence and Ethics Meet.* New York: Basic Books.

Kass, A. 2001. *The Perfect Gift.* Bloomington: Indiana University Press.

Kovach, B., and T. Rosenstiel. 2000. *The Elements of Journalism: What Newspeople Should Know and the Public Should Expect.* New York: Crown Publishers.

Steinberg, L. 1996: *Beyond the Classroom: Why School Reform Has Failed and What Parents Need To Do.* New York: Free Press.

1   In Search of an Ethic of Giving

James Allen Smith

The Power of Gifts

Power is inherent in every gift. The precise nature of that power—its potential for benefit or for harm—varies from culture to culture and era to era, but its broad outlines have been understood by keen observers throughout history. "Giving and returning," said Aristotle in a succinct and penetrating insight into the societal importance of the gift, "is that which binds men together in their living" (Hands 1968, 32).[1] In the ancient Greek polis as well as in the later Roman republic, personal and political ties were created and constantly reinforced with exchanges of gifts, favors, or services. These "benefits," as the first-century Stoic philosopher Seneca would term all such exchanges, were a fundamental instrument for maintaining social and political cohesion. The ancients deemed some gift-giving, if it was on a grand enough scale, to be "magnificent" or "magnanimous." Celebrated throughout the ancient world, this was the generosity that built ancient theaters, coliseums, public baths, schools, aqueducts, and other public works; it was especially vital in societies that lacked mechanisms for raising consistent tax revenues. Whether large or small in scale, personal or public in purpose, giving in all its manifestations proved to be a worthy subject of political and ethical analysis for some of antiquity's most celebrated philosophers.

Aristotle discussed gifts in the sections of the *Nicomachean Ethics* devoted to friendship and affection and in the passages exploring such personal traits as generosity, magnanimity, extravagance, vulgarity, and stinginess. Cicero wrote sagely about gift-giving and human fellowship in his book *De Officiis (On Duties)*, which he addressed to his son, at the time a somewhat less-than-diligent student in Athens. Seneca, the prolific dramatist, philosopher, and politician and one of the wealthiest Romans of the first century, treated gift-giving in various letters and in his treatise *De Beneficiis*, still arguably the wisest and most exhaustive analysis of the subject. Each of them understood that giving and returning were not simple matters. Seneca's blunt opening observation in *De Beneficiis*, which served to justify the hundreds of pages he devoted to the subject, was an all-embracing complaint: nothing "is more disgraceful than the fact that we do not know how either to give or to receive benefits" (Seneca 1935, 3). In his advice to his son, Cicero also issued a caution: "Nothing is more suited to human nature than [beneficence and generosity], but there are many caveats" (Cicero 1991, 19).

Caveats there were and caveats there are. This chapter will examine the ways in which these and other writers have tried to understand the gift relationship. Their insights are a historical point of departure for understanding the power—and the potential harms—in gift-giving. Their observations can give us distance and thus new perspectives on how we might improve current philanthropic practices. Just as doctors still look to Hippocrates as the starting point for an understanding of the ethos of their profession, perhaps it is equally appropriate to look to ancient authors who posed basic questions and offered enduring advice about gift-giving. To be sure, there are major differences between modern philanthropic giving and the highly charged personal exchanges of benefits and services that characterized the ancient world. There are obvious and profound differences between contemporary foundations and the array of institutions, both civic and religious, that sustained charitable activities in the ancient, medieval, and early modern worlds. The contexts in which gift-giving operates have indeed changed over the millennia. But power and harm in gift-giving have been persistent topics of concern, as have the subjects of right and proper giving. If there is an ethic of giving, its origins are to be found in these classical texts. In the end, our contemporary discussions of philanthropic practice and good work in this domain will be better grounded if we pause and reflect on humankind's long experience of gift-giving. We must examine the nature of the human ties that gifts, when appropriately bestowed, can establish or, when ineptly given or denied, can rupture.

To understand why the gift relationship is so complex, so fraught with potential harms, we must first ask what makes gifts so powerful. Gifts have always enabled individuals to reinforce their personal relationships, solidifying friendships and strengthening social or political affiliations. But a gift's power can reach beyond the individuals directly involved; it can extend in many different directions. Gifts are able to exercise their force across time and generations, as in the *Iliad* when Glaukos and Diomedes ended their combat upon suddenly realizing that many years earlier their grandfathers had enjoyed a hospitable relationship, eating and drinking together and exchanging gifts (Homer 1974, 148–149).[2] Gifts also have the power to operate across geographical and political boundaries, ending violence and promoting amicable relations between hostile tribes, cities, and great empires. Anthropologists, historians, and literary scholars have found abundant evidence of gift relationships that have served to pacify warring groups; these relationships exert their power not merely upon individuals but throughout entire societies. "What was 'peace' for the author of *Beowulf*," argued medieval historian Georges Duby, "but the prospect of exchanging gifts between peoples! The risky policy of alternating raids was being replaced by a regular round of mutual offerings" (Duby 1974, 50). And, above all (indeed, very high above), there is no more conspicuous testimony to the potency of the gift than the supernatural powers that are summoned down to earth when a society's riches are offered up in prayer and sacrifice to the deities. The essence of the gift's power resides in the relationships that it either creates or sustains. As Mary Douglas has put it, "The theory of the gift is a theory of human solidarity" (Mauss 1990, x).

We should also remind ourselves that the power of a gift does not necessarily depend on its material value. As anyone who has ever opened a present from a friend or family member knows, it is not the monetary worth of a gift that matters most but rather the sentiment and intentions of the giver. In some primitive societies even the most (to us) inconsequential objects obtain power because they are thought to convey some trace of the donor's soul. In Maori practice, according to Marcel Mauss, to give a gift is to make a present of a part of oneself; the exchange of gifts thus creates a bond between souls (Mauss 1990, 12). In European feudal society a medieval lord would typically bestow a mere token, perhaps a silver knife or a white glove, on his vassal not because such gifts had great intrinsic value but because they symbolized and ceremoniously proclaimed the reciprocal obligations that bound the men together. In some societies gifts have been destined for immediate consumption or ritual destruction through elaborate feasts and ceremonies, as in the potlatch of certain Native American tribes. Even though nothing remains of the objects given and received, the gifts nevertheless establish a bond. Relationships and affiliations are also publicly proclaimed in our modern giving rituals. Indeed, some contemporary exchanges, although they may be insignificant in terms of financial value, are no less symbolic of connections created, as when a donor sends a check for $25 or $50 to a favorite charity and receives in return a coffee mug, a tote bag, or an umbrella emblazoned with a logo.

The connection created between donor and recipient is the key to understanding a gift's power. Seneca offered up an arresting visual image. He suggested that the interdependence of the gift relationship was symbolized in artistic portrayals of the Three Graces, the Greek goddesses of joy, charm, and beauty, daughters of Zeus and Eurynome. The three women were conventionally depicted with their hands interlocked in a merry circular dance: "Why do the sisters hand in hand dance in a ring which returns upon itself?" asked Seneca. "For the reason that a benefit passing in its course from hand to hand returns nevertheless to the giver; the beauty of the whole is destroyed if the course is anywhere broken, and it has most beauty if it is continuous and maintains an uninterrupted succession" (Seneca 1935, 13, 15). The image compels us to ask: What sorts of behavior might disrupt this circular dance of giving, receiving, and returning? What might threaten to disgrace the gift relationship?

Poison, Pain, and Harm

Where substantial power exists, there is also the potential for harm. As Marcel Mauss and others have noted, the old Germanic words *gift* and *gif* convey a dual and startlingly contradictory meaning: gift and poison. Similarly, the Latin *dosis*, transcribed directly from the Greek, expresses a double sense: on the one hand, the act of giving and, on the other, the administration of a lethal dose of poison (Mauss 1990, 63; Mauss 1924, 243–247). History and folklore offer plenty of cautionary tales. We should be wary of some gifts and their bearers (and we should be mindful that it is not only Greeks bearing gifts who ought to be feared). In Iceland's great literary work *Egil's Saga*, an unsolicited gift prompts the recipient to threaten vengeance upon his benefactor. Egil, the protagonist of the tale, grows angry when he returns home and learns that a magnificently bejeweled shield has been left as a thank-you gift by a young guest who had enjoyed three days of hospitality during the owner's absence from the manor hall. Egil immediately sets out to chase his visitor down, not to thank him for the gift but to murder him. The gift had placed an unexpected and unwanted obligation upon Egil, specifically that he would have to write a poem about the shield as his expression of gratitude. Egil's rage soon subsided and he composed a simple poem of thanks. In the end, the friendship was threatened by the gift but was not fatally poisoned by it (*Egil's Saga* 1976, 218–219).

Why should gifts, which are so basic an expression of human generosity and affiliation, ever be harmful? Egil's saga reminds us that gifts always place the recipient under an obligation to reciprocate in some fashion, if only to offer a verbal expression of thanks. The giver always—and immediately—turns the recipient of the gift into a debtor. As soon as the gift is received, there can be an instant of perplexity about how to respond appropriately, how to interpret the donor's motives. A potentially harmful effect is produced, if only for a passing moment. Gifts always risk being misinterpreted, thus unsettling and jeopardizing human relationships as readily as they can solidify them. As Seneca understood, for this was his core concern, the obligation to express gratitude and reciprocate appropriately could generate a host of problems.

The catalogue of potential harms in gift-giving is much lengthier. As Cicero knew, there are many caveats. He sought to overcome them by placing justice and an ever-widening circle of consideration at the center of his ethic of giving. He offered this general counsel: "First one must see that kindness harms neither the very people whom one seems to be treating kindly, nor others; next, that one's kindness does not exceed one's capabilities; and then, that kindness is bestowed upon each person according to his standing. Indeed, that is fundamental to justice, to which all these things ought to be referred" (Cicero 1991, 19). The greatest harms occur when gifts are bestowed haphazardly, without forethought, without regard for their effects. No act of seeming generosity was viewed more critically than the Roman *sparsio*, literally the sprinkling or scattering of gifts, thus the most haphazard of any form of giving. Traditionally, the *sparsio* involved throwing coins or food (perhaps figs or nuts) to the throngs that gathered to watch theatrical performances, circuses, or athletic competitions. The disorder as people fought over the carelessly tossed objects troubled some observers. Gifts so wantonly given were the source of public unrest, triggering violent brawls as the mob pounced greedily on the objects strewn at their feet. Seneca advised sensible people to run immediately from the theater before the *sparsio* began: "No one will grapple with him on the way out, or strike him as he departs; the quarreling takes place where the prizes are" (Seneca 1920, 119).

Vestiges of the Roman *sparsio* survived for centuries, especially in medieval coronation rituals when newly crowned princes tossed coins to the masses with cries of "Largesse!" Some among the nobility viewed the ensuing mob scene as a grand entertainment, and throughout the Middle Ages these callous rituals of princely benevolence took place at festivals and carnivals. Some of the most bizarre distributions, the *cocagnes*, involved setting tables with elaborate buffets and then inviting a mob (sometimes after royal guests had first dined at the table) to rush toward it and seize whatever they could in a hard-fought brawl—a culinary scrimmage.[3]

On closer examination, the *sparsio* allows us to distinguish several categories of philanthropic harm. It can supply us with a framework for thinking about the problems inherent in many other forms of giving. Harms emerge for diverse reasons:

Sometimes there are fundamental flaws in the *manner and method* of giving (when it is haphazard and dangerous, as in the *sparsio*);

The *motivations* for giving can be dishonorable, unscrupulous, or simply self-serving (in the case of the *sparsio*, the distribution was made for the donor's amusement or sometimes as a thoughtless adherence to custom);

The gift-giving might proceed despite producing *ill effects on the recipients* (the *sparsio* was physically dangerous and demeaning);

The gift itself might be of only *negligible value* and of very little benefit to the recipient (a trampled fig or nothing at all);

The *relationship* established or not established between donor and recipient can be problematic (often the gift-giving ritual is merely an assertion of the donor's power or, as in the *sparsio*, a very public manifestation of disparities of wealth and class);

The donor' *expectations for gratitude, honor, and recognition* can be unreasonable or excessive.

The mob's disorderly conduct during the *sparsio*, though it was dangerous, was not necessarily the most grievous harm. Some observers began to look beyond the act of giving to examine the larger context of such gift-giving rituals. By the seventeenth and eighteenth centuries, critics of absolutism and noble privilege regarded random acts of largesse and even the more routine charitable work of many long-established institutions as symptoms of deeper societal woes. Centuries-old monasteries and hospitals had accumulated wealth that no longer served charitable purposes, no longer circulated in productive ways. Moreover, the donors' wealth was often presumed to be ill gotten. Writers during the Enlightenment knew that terrible harms—pillage, plunder, the accumulation of war booty—had often been the source of Roman wealth; they saw that oppressive seigneurial levies and burdensome taxes continued to generate wealth in the ancien regime. Episodic largesse offered only token relief to the exploited. Charitable gestures could not hide the need for sweeping structural change. An article in the *Encyclopédie* describing the objects, the *missilia*, tossed out during the *sparsio* expressed the view succinctly: "Those sorts of largesse . . . always led to a great deal of disorder. Those who gave them ruined themselves; those herded in to participate in them sometimes lost their lives. True largesse is tax relief. Making gifts to people who are being crushed by fees is clothing them with one hand and ripping off their skin with the other" (Starobinski 1997, 36).

The greater harms, as the Stoics first hinted and as the philosophes later argued even more forcefully, resided in the social and economic structures that allowed rapacious wealth accumulation and tolerated gaping inequality of wealth. In their totality, charitable acts were harmful because they masked past crimes, holding out the mere pretense of alleviating the plight of the poor and thus impeding more meaningful change. Harms intrinsic to the gift relationship, though numerous, began to be distinguished from the larger harms inherent in the means of accumulating wealth. Gilded Age debates about "tainted money" would be a distant nineteenth-century echo of these perennial complaints.

In the catalogue of harms, yet another distinction must be made. Some harms arise from the misuse and misappropriation of charitable resources. The sad and sustained history of institutional abuses and the periodic waves of charitable reform offer another perspective on the harms inherent in charitable and philanthropic relationships. It is always harmful to divert charitable assets from their intended purposes; it is wrong for the poor or sick consigned to an organization's care to be abused or neglected; it is immoral for the administrators of philanthropic institutions to enrich themselves; it is tragic for wasteful and inefficient uses of scarce charitable resources to be tolerated. This litany of charitable abuses resonates in every era, from wealthy medieval clerics collecting illegal prebends to present-day foundation trustees or chief executives engaging in self-dealing transactions or otherwise enriching themselves. Whenever such abuses have been exposed, they have been followed by episodes of systemic charitable reform. Efforts to curtail institutional abuses have stretched across the centuries; they are reflected in Roman and Byzantine law, Renaissance juridical debates, Elizabethan statutes, and U.S. tax regulations.

There is a legal history of institutional harm, but it is much too lengthy a story to be told here. Moreover, it is not the purpose of this essay to discuss the harms that arise from patently illegal behavior and malfeasance (Geremek 1994).[4] However, it is worth pausing briefly to ask whether there is something structural within the governance of charitable institutions that has made them susceptible to such abuses. Perhaps it is the limited reach of regulation and public oversight that has left well-meaning, privately controlled philanthropic institutions uniquely vulnerable, with all-too-easy opportunities for wrongdoers to evade scrutiny. But criminal behavior and administrative negligence within charitable institutions must be distinguished from the harms that are inherent in the gift relationship. The former should be considered aberrations; they are subject to external legal remedies. The latter are subtler, harder to identify, and much more difficult to root out.

Finally we should acknowledge some effects that spill over from the gift relationship; they are felt even by those who are not directly involved in the transaction. In his treatise *On Duties*, Cicero reminds his readers that a donor must avoid harming those he seeks to help as well as those to whom he must deny assistance (Cicero 1991, 19). He elaborates on this insight: "One does not need to be warned—for it is obvious—to take care that in trying to help some people one does not upset others. For often one may hurt either those whom one should not hurt, or those whom it is inexpedient to hurt. If one does so imprudently, one shows thoughtlessness; if knowingly, rashness" (90). Cicero's advice is a timeless and well-conceived injunction for any donor: weigh the foregone charitable opportunities carefully; consider the plight of those who are not being helped. Benefiting one person or institution may well have unanticipated hurtful consequences for those who receive no assistance and whose needs remain unacknowledged. Thoughtfulness in giving is clearly the antidote to the haphazard practice of the *sparsio*; it is the first step toward mitigating the harm that accompanies every charitable act whenever a few are chosen to benefit while many more must be denied.

Ancient Advice: Correct and Noble Gifts

For the ancients, deliberation and care were the first rule of giving.[5] But deliberation about what exactly? For Aristotle, careful giving was, first, a matter of locating the mean between extravagance and stinginess; true generosity was situated at the midpoint between too much and too little. While finding the mean involved a careful calculation of the recipient's needs and an assessment of the donor's own resources, it also demanded proper motivation in giving and absolute propriety when offering the gift. Appropriately done, giving could become an ennobling act. But the donor had much to ponder: "A generous man . . . will give—give in the correct manner—because that is noble. He will give to the right people, the right amount, at the right time, and do everything else that is implied in correct giving. Moreover, it will give him pleasure to do so, or (at least) no pain; for to act in conformity with virtue is pleasant or painless, but certainly not painful. If he gives to the wrong people or for the wrong motive, and not because it is noble to give, he will not be called generous but something else" (Aristotle 1962, 84). Among the terms of opprobrium Aristotle used, especially when someone's efforts at magnanimity failed to strike the mean, were "vulgar" when it proved excessive, grandiose, or showy and "niggardly" when it amounted to too little too late.

Seneca, too, urged rational deliberation and suggested that what was needed—and what his book would supply—were "rules for a practice that constitutes the chief bond of human society; we need to be given a law of conduct in order that we may not be inclined to the thoughtless indulgence that masquerades as generosity" (Seneca 1935, 19). Throughout his lengthy treatise, Seneca made it clear that such deliberation was not to be equated with the cool financial calculations related to loans and investments. A benefit was not a business deal; gifts were to be given purely for the sake of giving. He consistently distinguished the bestowing of benefits from financial transactions. He enjoined his readers: "Let us make our benefits, not investments, but gifts" (7). Elaborating, he wrote, "No one enters his benefactions in his account-book, or like a greedy tax-collector calls for payment upon a set day, at a set hour. The good man never thinks of them unless he is reminded of them by having them returned; otherwise, they transform themselves into a loan. To regard a benefit as an amount advanced is putting it out at shameful interest" (11). Deliberation about a gift was complex, but it was markedly different from the thinking that preceded a business transaction, which concentrated exclusively on the return. Yet however complicated it might be, Seneca did not want deliberation about gifts "to narrow the bounds of liberality" or to justify hesitation and delay in giving. Sound judgment should always prevail, though never at the expense of giving in a properly beneficent spirit. "Above all," he concluded, "let us give willingly, promptly, and without hesitation" (51). Generosity must move swiftly, he said, for tardy good will smacks of ill will.

The purpose of the rules was to minimize ill will and ingratitude; this theme suffuses Seneca's work on giving. Indeed, it was ingratitude that most often threatened to poison the gift relationship. Ingratitude, he warned, "is something to be avoided in itself because there is nothing that so effectually disrupts and destroys the harmony of the human race as this vice. For how else do we live in security if it is not that we help each other by an exchange of good offices? It is only through the interchange of benefits that life becomes in some measure equipped and fortified against sudden disasters. Take us singly, and what are we? The prey of all creatures, their victims, whose blood is most delectable and most easily secured" (241). He warned that either party could be at fault in fostering ingratitude: the donor for not knowing how to give, the recipient for not knowing how to receive and reciprocate.

For Seneca, the donor should do nothing to provoke ingratitude, whether by expecting an immediate and obsequious display of gratitude, anticipating or demanding a particular favor in return, or accompanying the gift with unwanted advice and criticism. This, Seneca warned, "is grafting insult upon an act of kindness. Benefits, therefore, must not be made irritating, they must not be accompanied by anything that is unpleasant. Even if there should be something upon which you would like to offer advice, choose a different time" (61). It was no less important for the recipient to consider the timing and the propriety of a reciprocal gesture of thanks. Whether overtly and immediately expressed or not, a sincere inner feeling of gratitude was the first step toward repaying the donor's generosity. In time (but not too quickly), an appropriate return of a gift or favor could be made, even if one's benefactor were well off. In some cases, the reciprocal act need not take the form of a material gift. "How many ways are there by which we may repay whatever we owe even to the well-to-do?—loyal advice, constant intercourse, polite conversation that pleases without flattery, attentive ears if he should wish to ask counsel, safe ears if he should wish to be confidential and friendly intimacy. Good fortune has set no one so high that he does not the more feel the want of a friend because he wants for nothing" (423).

Then as now, whether the gift is from an individual or an institution, the donor's power over a beneficiary remains considerable. It is thus the inequality in the gift relationship that has always been the most intractable problem. Resentment is natural, hard to quell. Every recipient feels indebted in some way and there are almost always uncertainties about how to express adequate gratitude or to reciprocate appropriately. Sometimes the recipient might also suffer embarrassment because the gift reinforces the realities of dependency. In some cases, even careful deliberation and considerate behavior on the part of the donor will not be enough to remedy the inequality that is intrinsic to the gift relationship. Thus, another remedy, a seemingly drastic one, was sometimes proposed: the secret or anonymous gift. Anonymity has always been one of the surest ways of tempering the power imbalances inherent in the gift relationship. It deftly severs the relationship between benefactor and beneficiary. It solves many other problems, too. Anonymity liberates the recipient from reciprocal obligations and dependency. And, for better or for worse, the anonymous gift helps the donor free himself from overtly self-serving or malign motivations (or liberates him from accusations of such).

As always, Aristotle had general insights. He maintained that the only morally acceptable and truly generous gift was the one given without expectation of return. While such advice did not inevitably widen the practice of anonymous giving in the ancient world, it clearly pointed in that direction. Seneca offered the most explicit rationale for secret gifts, advising that sometimes "the very man who is helped must even be deceived in order that he may have assistance, and yet not know from whom he has received it. . . . You will be content to have yourself as your witness; otherwise your pleasure comes, not from doing a favour, but from being seen to do a favour" (65). Seneca understood that by lifting the burden of reciprocity, anonymity could prevent the recipient from being embarrassed or feeling resentment toward the giver.

For the Stoics, anonymous giving also helped remove the donor from public view, leaving him entirely free from having to weigh either public approbation or scorn when making a gift; it freed the donor to reflect on inner motivations without regard for the vagaries of public opinion. And if the donor was out of the public's eye, motives could not be questioned. But anonymity never became a general practice in antiquity, for it cut the social ties that were normally established through gift-giving and were necessary to sustain so many important relationships. Among the Greeks and Romans, anonymity was not an end in itself but simply one useful method for assuring that the act of giving would remain untainted by the expectation of a return favor. It was one way to clear the air of some of the psychological hazards that inevitably accompany gift-giving. Anonymity would become a much more powerful concept in the Judeo-Christian tradition, in which writers focused explicitly on the spiritual nature of gift-giving, the inner motivations of the donor, and the intangible or divine rewards that might be earned by the giver.

Gift versus Grant

The ancient philosophers always offered their advice on gift-giving with the understanding that giving and receiving took place within a thick web of personal obligations. Exchanges of gifts and favors sustained familial ties, solidified friendships, shaped patron-client relationships, and maintained political allegiances. Today, while friends still exchange gifts, individual patrons still support many good works, and politically active citizens donate to various causes, these practices occur in a very different, often a much less personal, context. And while our highly organized (some might even say overly bureaucratized) modern philanthropy can trace its distant origins to the charitable institutions of the ancient and medieval world and to the spirit of magnanimity that accomplished great public works, our contemporary philanthropic institutions function in a legal and professional environment that leaves little space for thinking about grant-making as an activity that might still bear some relationship to the older forms of gift-giving (Smith and Borgmann 2001, 2–34).

Many of the things that once made gift-giving such a personal matter have been shunted aside in the organized philanthropy of our own times. Some of this is clearly to good effect. Fiduciary responsibilities and charitable purposes have been explicitly defined in law. This framework of law and regulation helps assure that modern philanthropy will seek to pursue the public benefit rather than being used exclusively for personal advantage. Since the late nineteenth and early twentieth centuries, philanthropy has also become an increasingly professional affair or, at the very least, has drawn professionals from other domains into the philanthropic orbit. There are now widely accepted procedures and practices that govern many aspects of grant-making, especially in the largest foundations.[6] In those foundations we can sometimes find external peer review processes, and almost certainly we can count on an array of internal procedures to assure careful evaluation of proposals and systematic decision-making. Policies have also been implemented to forbid conflicts of interest and overt favoritism in grant-making. Formal grant agreements are also routinely required, specifying conditions for payment and performance. These practices now define the grant relationship.

But these institutional practices do not necessarily define or promote a professional ethos. They might even deter us from looking to the past—to what we have come to understand about the gift relationship—as we seek to create professional norms for modern philanthropy. Perhaps it is these bureaucratic formalities that led Mary Douglas to remark on her experience of working in a foundation that "newcomers to the office quickly learnt that the recipient does not like the giver, however cheerful he be" (Mauss 1990, vii). Why should this be so? Perhaps it is because we have ceased to think about the aspects of the gift relationship that remain deeply embedded in our grant-making activities. Douglas cautions us that foundations should never confuse their donations with *free* gifts: "There are no free gifts; gift cycles engage persons in permanent commitments that articulate the dominant institutions" (ix). If even the most successful grantees do not like donors (and certainly unsuccessful grant-seekers like them even less), it is because of the substantial imbalance of resources, power, and control in the grant relationship.

Complaints by today's grantees resound in familiar ways to any reader of Aristotle, Cicero, or Seneca. Modern grant-seeking processes can be as drawn out and humiliating as anything faced by a poor person pleading for assistance in antiquity. Indeed, speedy responses and timely help may be even more difficult to win in the modern foundation world with its well-defined grant cycles and diligent review processes. The burdens placed upon the grantee in describing a project and assessing results can be as heavy as any obligation that weighed down an ancient beneficiary. Clearly, a species of gift relationship is created when a foundation and its grantees interact. In refracting our current grant-making practices through the lens of antiquity, perhaps we can recover insights—or at least a set of relevant questions—that will prove helpful in constructing professional norms that might govern modern philanthropic conduct. However different the contexts, a few large questions might still be framed in terms that echo the language of Aristotle, Cicero, and Seneca: What now threatens to poison the gift relationship? What are the wellsprings of ingratitude?

Certainly ancient lessons about the manner and method of giving ought to be absorbed by modern grant-making institutions. The philosophers wrote often about the timing of the gift and the need to avoid hesitation and delay. This hesitancy, the seeming reluctance to give, was frequently the reason for the recipient's ill will toward the donor. Today, dilatory foundation procedures, inexplicable delays, and deferrals in making a grant are among the most annoying feature of institutionalized and professionalized philanthropy. Diligence in evaluating proposals, attention to fiduciary responsibilities, and sound evaluation processes are important—much as careful deliberation about the gift was to Seneca—but too often they can become excuses for delay. They do not necessarily lead to better or more disciplined decisions. They allow staff and boards to justify their hesitation and they show little regard for meeting the needs of the potential beneficiary in a timely manner. While donors waver and delay, grantees grow uncertain and resentful. Time and timeliness in gift-giving were subjects of keen interest to the ancients; rarely is it a significant topic of conversation today. How should those involved in modern philanthropy think about time—the timeliness of decisions, the duration of their commitments?

The ancients also were concerned about the expectations that benefactors were liable to place upon their beneficiaries. Donors were advised not to dwell upon their own expectations for gratitude or return favors; they were urged not to make their beneficiaries shoulder undue burdens. Too often a gift came with heavy expectations. Today, those expectations might take the form of detailed performance measures, the need to obtain speedy results, and prompt project evaluation. A philanthropic ethic would certainly ask what burdens ought to be born by a grantee. How should donors limit the burdens their expectations place upon a beneficiary? In this same context, ancient donors were cautioned about conveying their gifts with excessive advice or criticism, knowing that words delivered by a donor have a power, for better or for worse, that is different from counsel between equals. A donor's words can often be taken not as advice but as an order. And this advice sometimes comes from someone who has no detailed knowledge or understanding of the recipient's circumstances. This, too, is a subject rarely discussed in modern philanthropy (and when it is, it is often cast in the sterile language of technical assistance). The ancients were sensitive about offering advice. How and when is advice best conveyed? What intellectual deference is due the grantee? In what ways should knowledge become a part of the philanthropic exchange?

Aristotle was emphatic that the gift should be the right amount. In part, it had to be right in proportion to the donor's resources. More important, it had to be right given the needs of the beneficiary. A discussion of the "right" amount for a modern foundation leads in many different directions: payout levels, average grant sizes, duration of support, contributions to endowment or capital projects versus project support, loans or venture capital–style investments, among other subjects. These topics are a matter of almost constant discussion by foundation staff and board members. And they are perhaps the greatest source of tension between donor and recipient. The amount will never seem to be enough to the recipient. How can disappointment or ingratitude be assuaged? Perhaps it can be tempered when, in conveying the gift or grant, the donor demonstrates a true understanding of the recipient's needs and if the donor has responded in ways that are not merely a token show of support or sympathy. The ancients remind us that discussions of the right amount must always ask the question from both the donor's and the recipient's perspectives. In viewing the gift relationship from both vantage points, they also remind us of the importance of adhering to simple civilities.

Finally, it is by reminding us to carefully consider why we give that the ancients, especially the Stoics, have the most to teach us. The ancients focused on motivation, offering advice that tempers our impulses to be poorly motivated or unreflective about the purposes of gift-giving. They understood that a gift should be motivated not by the expectation of a return favor, not by a desire to control the beneficiary, not merely to obtain praise (though giving was certainly deemed to be praiseworthy), and most certainly not to bestow a gift that would create ingratitude. Indeed, it was ingratitude they most often sought to avoid. The gift relationship itself is harmed—gratitude suffers—when motivations are self-serving or thoughtless. And it is because the gift is such a powerful instrument that we must constantly ask ourselves why we give. We must continually subject our motives to hard scrutiny. Whether an ancient patron or a contemporary program officer, the intent of the donor ought always be to bestow a benefit that will in some manner sustain cohesive social relationships. Gifts and grants are both about human solidarity. Donors should be ever mindful of how they are sustaining the habit of giving and returning, how they will continue to allow the hands of the Three Graces to remain securely conjoined in their circular dance.

Notes

1. The quotation is from a letter attributed to Aristotle and quoted by A. R. Hands. Aristotle's principal writings on giving and receiving are in the *Nicomachean Ethics* (1962), especially Book IV, chapter 1, "Generosity, Extravagance, and Stinginess"; Book VIII, chapter 13, "What Equal Friends Owe to One Another"; and Book IX, chapter 1, "How to Measure What Friends Owe to One Another" and chapter 7, "Good Deeds and Affection."

2. In Homer, *The Iliad,* Book VI, lines 215 and following. Diomedes said on learning his foe's identity: "Why, you are my friend! My grandfather, Oineus, made friends of us long years ago. He welcomed Prince Bellerophontes in his hall, his guest for twenty days. They gave each other beautiful tokens of amity."

3. Herman Melville offers a vividly imagined account of such a melee in his 1854 short story "Poor Man's Pudding and Rich Man's Crumbs." He tells of a London banquet in celebration of the victory at Waterloo: "The yet unglutted mob raised a fierce yell, which wafted the banners like a strong gust, and filled the air with a reek as from sewers. They surged against the table, broke through all barriers, and billowed over the hall—their bare tossed arms like the dashed ribs of a wreck. It seemed to me as if a sudden impotent fury of fell envy possessed them."

4. Bronislaw Geremek (1994) provides a sweeping account of charitable reform, changing attitudes toward the needy, and social welfare policies from the early Middle Ages to the modern era.

5. The counsel of thoughtfulness has persisted. It was a bit of advice often offered by one of the most insightful observers of twentieth-century American foundations, F. Emerson Andrews (1954). His seventh and final rule for giving: "Finally, in all your giving, give thought. For with thoughtful giving even small sums may accomplish great purposes."

6. However, it is worth noting that only about 3,400 of the nation's approximately 70,000 foundations have professional staffs. They are responsible for roughly half of the roughly $30 billion given annually by American foundations. Thus, a considerable portion of American foundation decision-making remains the province of part-time board members. And total foundation grant dollars are only a fraction (10–12 percent) of all charitable giving in the United States.

References

Andrews, F. Emerson. 1954. "Private Philanthropy in Our Society." Speech to the Conference of Michigan Foundations, Ann Arbor, May 7.
Aristotle. 1962. *Nicomachean Ethics.* Translated by M. Ostwald. Indianapolis, Ind.: Bobbs-Merrill.

Cicero, Marcus Tullius. 1991. *On Duties (De Officiis)*. Edited by M. T. Griffin and E. M. Atkins. Cambridge: Cambridge University Press.

Duby, Georges. 1974. *The Early Growth of the European Economy: Warriors and Peasants from the Seventh to the Twelfth Century*. Translated by Howard B. Clarke. Ithaca, N.Y.: Cornell University Press.

Egil's Saga. 1976. Translated by Herman Pálsson and Paul Edwards. Harmondsworth: Penguin.

Geremek, Bronislaw. 1994. *Poverty: A History*. Oxford: Blackwell Publishers.

Hands, A. R. 1968. *Charities and Social Aid in Greece and Rome*. London: Thames and Hudson.

Homer. 1974. *The Iliad*. Translated by Robert Fitzgerald. Garden City, N.Y.: Anchor/ Doubleday.

Mauss, Marcel. 1924. "Gift, gift." In *Mélanges offerts à M. Charles Andler par ses amis et ses élèves*. Strasbourg: Faculté des lettres de l'université de Strasbourg.

———. 1990. *The Gift: The Form and Reason for Exchange in Archaic Societies*. Translated by W. D. Halls, introduction by Mary Douglas. New York: W. W. Norton and Company.

Seneca. 1920. "Ad Lucilium epistulae morales." In *The Epistles of Seneca*. Vol. II. Translated by Richard M. Gunmere. Cambridge, Mass.: Harvard University Press.

———. 1935. *De Beneficiis*. In *Moral Essays*. Vol. III. Translated by John W. Basore. Cambridge, Mass.: Harvard University Press.

Smith, James Allen, and Karsten Borgmann. 2001. "Foundations in Europe: The Historical Context." In *Foundations in Europe: Society, Management and Law*, edited by A. Schlüter, V. Then, and P. Walkenhorst, 2–34. London: Directory of Social Change.

Starobinski, Jean. 1997. *Largesse*. Translated by Jare Marie Todd. Chicago: University of Chicago Press.

2 Philanthropy and Its Uneasy Relation to Equality

Rob Reich

There is a standard story about philanthropy and its relation to liberty and equality. Indeed, it is likely told in some version or another in this volume. The story is this. Philanthropy is tightly connected to liberty. This is so for two reasons. First, philanthropy is voluntary. Whereas the state can mandate and coerce behavior, activity within the philanthropic sector is not compelled. Indeed, philanthropic or charitable actions that are coerced are often thought not to be instances of philanthropy or charity at all. It is no coincidence that philanthropic organizations are part of what is typically called "the voluntary sector." Second, the exercise of liberty includes freedom to associate, which, famously in the American context, has resulted in a strong inclination for people to join together to address and solve social problems. Philanthropy is not just an activity of free persons; when the state protects the freedoms of individuals, it becomes a group activity. To illustrate this latter point, any number of Tocqueville citations can be produced.[1]

Philanthropy is also tightly connected to equality. This is so because the quintessentially philanthropic act—and the virtue in the philanthropic act—is generally thought to consist in providing for the poor or disadvantaged or attacking the root causes of poverty or disadvantage. Certainly this is historically true of the world's various traditions of charity—think of alms-giving in various religious traditions and the famous 1601 Elizabethan charity law. And many believe it is true today: that the philanthropic sector in modern society is justified at least in part because of its redistributive or eleemosynary aims. Philanthropy results in the lessening of inequality between rich and poor, either through direct transfers from the rich to the poor or through efforts to improve structural conditions so the poor will no longer need to rely on charity for basic sustenance.

This story, which links philanthropy to both liberty and equality, is an attractive one. And it contains some truth. My aim in this chapter, however, is to complicate this rosy story. I hope to show how the rosy story holds perhaps less than we ordinarily think it does and that philanthropy has an especially rocky relationship with equality. Befitting the theme of this book—showing how philanthropy is capable of good as well as harm—I shall argue that philanthropy is not always a friend of equality; it can be indifferent to equality and sometimes even a cause of *in*equality. When philanthropy causes or worsens inequality, it can be harmful and at odds with social justice. This is no decisive objection to the existence of a nonprofit and philanthropic sector in society in general, for there are a variety of justifications for philanthropic endeavors, some of which do not depend at all on philanthropy being redistributive or eleemosynary. But when philanthropic activity actually worsens inequality, any justification for the state's provision of special tax treatment to philanthropic organizations is considerably weakened and perhaps entirely eroded.

In some sense I hope to make a familiar point about liberty and equality and apply it to philanthropy. The conventional account about liberty and equality sets these two ideals in tension with one another. On the one hand, protecting the liberty of individuals will result in social inequalities. When people are free to lead their lives as they please, the cumulative impact of the choices they make will leave them in unequal positions. On the other hand, promoting social equality will require wide-scale interference with the liberty of individuals. To make people equal with respect to some opportunity or outcome, the state needs either to redistribute goods from some people to others (e.g., through taxation) or curtail the liberty of some for the benefit of others. (Many believe that the former is tantamount to the latter; philosopher Robert Nozick infamously described taxation as "on a par with forced labor" [Nozick 1974, 305].) If the tension between liberty and equality is unavoidable, then philanthropy cannot unproblematically embrace both liberty and equality. The familiar story about philanthropy I began with must be more complicated.

I write as a political theorist and therefore my focus is on the political institutions in which philanthropy takes place rather than on the actions and motives of individual philanthropists. I am inclined to think that the actions and motives of individuals cannot be properly understood or evaluated outside the political institutions that currently structure philanthropy. (Can the motive of the philanthropist be understood apart from the tax incentives that reward philanthropic behavior?) But such a claim is not necessary for my argument here. I want simply to recognize that though philanthropy may be as old as humanity itself, its setting in modern society embeds it firmly within the political institutions of the state. Laws govern the creation of foundations and nonprofit organizations and they spell out the rules under which these organizations may operate. Laws set up special tax treatment for philanthropic and nonprofit organizations and they permit tax concessions for individual and corporate donations to qualifying nonprofits. In this sense, philanthropy is not exactly an invention of the state but can be viewed as an artifact of the state; we can be certain that philanthropy would not have the form it currently does in the absence of the various laws that structure it and tax incentives that encourage it.[2] The goods and harms of philanthropy can be products of, or at least can be promoted or diminished by, the policies of the state that are designed to encourage or reward philanthropic behavior. The basic argument I shall advance is that public policy does not do enough to encourage philanthropic behavior that aims at greater equality. Worse, public policy currently rewards some philanthropic behavior—in the form of tax concessions—that worsens social inequalities and causes harm. The state is therefore implicated in these philanthropic harms, and unjustifiably so.

The chapter proceeds as follows. The first section offers a short consideration of the potential harms of philanthropy, distinguishing between individual and institutional harms. A brief treatment of the complex interplay between philanthropy and the tax code follows. I then turn to the variety of institutional harms that public policies governing philanthropy can inflict, focusing special attention on the ways in which philanthropy is indifferent to equality. I then provide an illustration of how philanthropy can be causally implicated in the worsening of inequality: the case of private donations to public schools. I conclude with a few gestures toward policy recommendations aimed at making the outcome of philanthropic endeavors more egalitarian.

One terminological note merits a comment. Though many people seek to distinguish philanthropy from charity, usually on the ground that philanthropy seeks to attack the root causes of social problems and charity is the provision of direct assistance or on the ground that philanthropy refers to foundation activity and charity refers to individual donations, I shall use the two here relatively interchangeably. The reason for doing so is not because I think the putative distinctions between the two are faulty. The reason is that, however distinguished, both philanthropy and charity are activities regulated and governed by a common institutional framework of laws and public policies. When distinctions between philanthropy and charity are necessary in order to account for differences in institutional treatment, I indicate so below. Otherwise readers can assume that when I write about philanthropy I am also including activities that more typically go under the name of charity.

Philanthropic Harms

Philanthropists seek to intervene in the lives of others, or in the institutions that structure the lives of others, in order to improve their lives, create innovative solutions to problems—to create public goods. As an intervention, philanthropy is therefore capable of harm as well as good. The notion that philanthropy can cause harm is perhaps at odds with popular conceptions about what philanthropy is and does, but even philanthropic practitioners recognize the potential for harm. Writing about the array of private philanthropic foundations in the United States, for instance, former foundation executive and current Duke University scholar Joel Fleishman opines, "I believe deeply that foundations do far more good than harm, and that such harm as they do can be attributed mostly to operating inefficiencies and the consequent waste of assets, assets which they are morally obligated to steward wisely" (Fleishman 2004, 112).

Fleishman's statement is not incorrect but it is Pollyanna-ish. Philanthropic acts can cause harms in a number of ways that go far beyond the failure to steward assets wisely. We can divide these harms into the two broad categories, individual harms and institutional harms. Individual harms are the product of the actions, motives, and behavior of individual philanthropists; philanthropic endeavors sometimes harm the people they were meant to benefit. Institutional harms are the product of public policies and incentives that set the framework within which philanthropy takes place; public policy can cause and exacerbate harms itself, apart from the motives or actions of individuals. Obviously individuals and institutions interact with and affect one another. Institutional structures are set up by individuals and these structures in turn have effects on the behavior of individuals. So the two categories cannot be completely walled off from one another. Nevertheless, the division between individual and institutional harms is a helpful way to demarcate the kinds of harms worth worrying about.

This book concerns itself primarily with individual harms: the dangers of philanthropic behavior that stem from moral dogmatism (e.g., imposing one's values on others); the perils of poor planning and execution in philanthropy (e.g., worsening problems that one intended to ameliorate); the damage that arrogance, hubris, and vanity can inflict (e.g., being patronizing or paternalistic). My concern is with the institutional harms of philanthropy—how the public policies that guide philanthropy or the very structure of philanthropy itself can be harmful.

In some respect, this is an old criticism. Left-wing critics, especially those of a Gramscian bent, have long suggested that philanthropy is but another self-interested way for the powerful to continue their dominion over the poor and entrench the ideological interests of the wealthy in all of society.[3] To the extent that the state is involved in supporting philanthropy, the state would merely be abetting the philanthropic actions of the powerful and reinforcing their already dominant position. But one needn't be a foe of capitalism to see how philanthropy can be harmful. Contemporary political philosopher Will Kymlicka argues, for instance, that justice supersedes charity in importance and that our obligations as citizens to fulfill and realize social justice through political institutions effectively subsume any reasons we might have to perform acts of charity (Kymlicka 2001).[4] Kymlicka's argument raises the basic question of why the state should be involved in any way whatsoever in subsidizing, through tax incentives, philanthropic activity. Philanthropy existed long before the state decided to become involved, so it is surely not true that philanthropy would disappear without the state's involvement. These are important critiques that cut to the heart of the very legitimacy of philanthropic and charitable activities and organizations in a democratic society. But for purposes of this chapter, I shall sidestep the important issue of justifying the "intervention" of the state in legitimizing, regulating, and providing incentives for philanthropy and instead simply assume, with the weight of longstanding practice as a provisional warrant, that such state involvement can be justified. The relevant question here is:

If the state will be involved, what are better rather than worse public policies for philanthropy, policies that will encourage goods rather than harms?

Leaving aside, then, radical broadsides against philanthropy and worries about whether the state should be involved at all in philanthropy, what are the institutional harms about which we should be concerned? To answer this question we first need a better understanding of the particular manner in which modern philanthropy is not the sum total of individual philanthropic decisions but rests in a web of public policies, mainly in the tax code.

Philanthropy and Tax Policy

Nonprofit organizations and philanthropic foundations enjoy an array of substantial tax benefits at the federal level. The details and levels of these benefits have changed from time to time, either when Congress passed legislation directly affecting nonprofits and foundations or when it passed legislation making changes in the rates of taxation for individuals, estates, and corporations. The rules are often very complicated, but the underlying mechanisms that supply the tax advantage are simple and have always been the same.[5] First, nonprofit organizations, including philanthropic foundations, which are a specific kind of nonprofit organization, are tax-exempt entities. They are not subject to tax on income (e.g., donations or grants made to the organization or fees collected in the performance of their function, such as tuition payments to universities). Second, for a specific and large class of nonprofit organizations (those called 501(c)(3)s after the section of the tax code that defines them), contributions of cash or property to the nonprofit organization are tax deductible for the individual or corporation making the contribution. This latter provision is perhaps the most well-known institutional incentive for charitable activity, and some version or another of this incentive has existed since the creation by the U.S. Congress of a federal income tax in 1917. In addition to these two basic mechanisms, nonprofit organizations are exempt from tax on investment income; private foundations pay a small 2 percent excise tax on net investment income, which generally comes from endowments. Finally, nonprofit organizations of all kinds are generally exempt from property taxation at the state and local level.

When they are expressed in the abstract language of the tax code, it is hard to appreciate just how significant an intervention into charitable and philanthropic behavior these tax laws are. To get a better picture, consider what the tax laws mean in concrete terms for a would-be donor. The mechanism of a tax deduction for a donation creates a subsidy by the government at the rate at which the donor is taxed. So a person who occupies the top tax bracket—currently 35 percent—would find that a $1,000 donation actually "cost" her only $650. The government effectively pays $350 of her donation, subtracting this amount from her tax burden. Similar incentives exist for the creation of private and family foundations and for contributions to community foundations, where donations and bequests to a foundation are deducted from estate and gift taxation.

In permitting these tax incentives, federal and state treasuries forego tax revenue. Had there been no tax deduction on the $1,000 contribution, the state would have collected $350 in tax revenue. Or to put it differently, tax incentives for philanthropy constitute a kind of spending program, or "tax expenditure."[6] Just as a direct spending program has an effect on the annual budget of the United States—congressional allocation of funds for defense spending, for example—so too does a tax deduction affect the national budget. In fact, the fiscal effect of a direct spending program and a tax expenditure is exactly the same. Seen in this light, tax incentives for philanthropy amount to massive federal and state subsidies, or tax expenditures, for the operation of philanthropic and charitable organizations and to the individuals and corporations who make charitable donations. These tax policies have been described as "the world's most generous tax concessions" (Clotfelter 1988/1989, 663). One economist observes that "no other nation grants subsidies at such a high level or across so many types of activities" (Weisbrod 2004, 45).

Just how large are these subsidies? It is surprisingly difficult to put a precise dollar figure on the total. Evelyn Brody estimates that the charitable contribution deduction in the federal income tax code alone cost the U.S. Treasury nearly $26 billion in 2000 and the charitable contribution deduction in the estate and gift tax code deprived the treasury of more than $6 billion (Brody 1999, 695). These already large figures omit tax concessions on income earned by nonprofit organizations and on property taxes that would be paid by nonprofits and foundations, so they considerably understate the total subsidy. But focus just on the charitable contributions deduction in the income tax code. According to the U.S. federal budget for fiscal year 2005, estimated tax expenditures in 2005 on charitable contributions total more than $36 billion, a sharp rise (38 percent) from Brody's calculation in 2000. Measured against other tax expenditures given to individuals in the federal tax code, the charitable contributions deduction is the fourth largest of more than 130 such tax expenditures, ranking only behind the mortgage interest deduction, exclusions of pension contributions to 401(k) plans, and deductibility of state and local taxes (Office of Management and Budget 2004, 287–294).

This short overview of tax policy and philanthropic activity does not do justice to the complexity of the rules that divide kinds of nonprofit organizations or to the different tax treatment and regulation of these entities or even to the intricate debates about how to specify the total cost of the tax expenditures to the federal and state treasuries. Moreover, as I mentioned earlier, whether the state should provide these tax concessions is not a question I will take up here. Presumably the state believes that in extending advantageous tax treatment to charitable and philanthropic behavior, it is rewarding and providing incentives for such behavior.[7] It will suffice for my purposes here merely to have shown how significant and wide ranging these tax policies are for nonprofit organizations and philanthropic foundations. I wish now to turn to questions about the potential harms these tax policies—the political institution that channels and shapes philanthropic behavior—can inflict.

Public Policy and Institutional Harm

Let us note first a range of arguable harms, or at the very least unfairnesses, that inhere in the current structure of the preferential tax treatment of nonprofits and philanthropies. First, the charitable contribution deduction is available only to those individuals who itemize their deductions, people who opt not to take the so-called standard deduction on their income tax. This effectively penalizes, or fails to reward and provide an incentive for, all people who do not itemize their deductions, a group that constitutes roughly 70 percent of all taxpayers.[8] Thus, the low-income renter who does not itemize her deductions but makes a $500 donation to her church receives no tax concession, while the high-income home owner who makes the same $500 donation to the same church can claim a deduction. One might think that it is predominantly high-income earners, and therefore itemizers, who make charitable contributions, but this is false. A remarkable 89 percent of American households made a charitable contribution in 2000 (Independent Sector 2001). The consequence is that a great many people are capriciously excluded from enjoying the tax deduction simply because they do not itemize deductions on their return. Why should the benefit of the charitable contribution deduction turn on this contingency?

Second, the tax subsidy given to those who do receive the deduction possesses what is known as an "upside-down effect." The deduction functions as an increasingly greater subsidy and incentive with every higher step in the income tax bracket. Those at the highest tax bracket (35 percent in 2005) receive the largest deduction; those in the lowest tax bracket (10 percent in 2005) receive the lowest deduction. As two scholars wryly noted long ago, in such a system "the opportunity cost of virtue falls as one moves up the income scale" (Musgrave and Musgrave 1984, 348). Table 2.1 illustrates how the progressivity of the tax code translates, perversely, into a regressive system of tax deductions: the wealthiest garner the largest tax advantages. Compounding this oddity is a variant of the objection offered above. Identical donations to identical recipients are treated differently by the state depending on the donor's income: a $500 donation by the person in the 35 percent bracket costs the person less than the same donation by the person in the 10 percent bracket. Since the same social good is ostensibly produced in both cases, the differential treatment appears totally arbitrary. The upside-down phenomenon is not specific to the tax deduction for charitable donations, of course. Deductions in general massively favor the wealthy. In 1999, 50 percent of all tax deductions were claimed by the wealthiest decile of earners.

Both of these features of the tax code arbitrarily and unfairly benefit the well off. In the process, the structure of the tax code's treatment of philanthropy, it could be argued, harms low-income earners, who are either excluded from the benefit of a deduction or who receive a smaller subsidy for the same charitable contribution. This is so because the tax code, as applied to charitable and phil-

Table 2.1. Cost per Dollar of a Charitable Contribution for Married Taxpayers Filing Jointly, 2005

Source: Adapted and updated from Clotfelter (1988/1989).

Taxable Income	Itemization Status	Tax Bracket	Net Cost of a Dollar Donation
$ 14,300	non-itemizer	10%	$1.00
$ 50,000	non-itemizer	15%	$1.00
$ 60,000	non-itemizer	25%	$1.00
$ 60,000	itemizer	25%	$0.75
$125,000	itemizer	28%	$0.72
$200,000	itemizer	33%	$0.67
$319,500	itemizer	35%	$0.65

anthropic donors, arbitrarily discriminates between individuals on the basis of a characteristic—status as itemizers or tax-bracket position—that is unrelated to the purpose of the preferential tax treatment in the first place. Happily, it would be quite simple to remedy this unfairness and remove the harm. Congress could allow those who do not itemize to deduct their charitable contributions from their income. Better, since this solution would still leave the upside-down effect in place, Congress could allow all donors a non-reimbursable tax credit, rather than a tax deduction, for donations that would be capped at a certain level. This fix would be of the greatest marginal value to lower-income individuals but would still be an equivalent subsidy for all persons. Congress has at times debated versions of both remedies, but neither has ever become law.[9]

Even if Congress were to pass legislation that eliminated these unfair and harmful aspects of the tax code, important questions about the structure of tax policy would remain. The focus would turn from evaluating whether tax laws treat the supply side of philanthropy—the donors—in a fair and justifiable way to whether the incentive of a state subsidy works in a way to encourage the good we wish philanthropy to accomplish and deter the harms we wish to avoid. This is important for more than the obvious reason that we wish for public policies of any sort to bring about good rather than harm. It is also important because in providing tax concessions to philanthropy, the state is not merely permitting and setting guidelines within which philanthropy takes place—offering the state's imprimatur to every charitable nonprofit and philanthropic foundation and charitable donation and bequest—but is actively participating in what nonprofits and foundations and donors do. If the state is actually funding, through a tax expenditure, some philanthropic harm, it makes the state complicit in the harmful action of the philanthropist. It is no exaggeration to say that as philanthropy is currently structured, when philanthropists do harm, so too does the state.[10]

This is what lies behind Joel Fleishman's observation, cited earlier, that philanthropy is harmful when philanthropic foundations fail to steward their assets wisely and instead waste them without benefit to anyone. It is false to say of such a situation that a wealthy individual or foundation simply squanders its assets and to remark, "Too bad for the donor or the foundation but no loss to the rest of us." Instead, we should recognize that the individual or foundation squandered assets that, had there not been tax concessions, would have been the public's in the form of tax revenue. The wasting of philanthropic assets is the wasting of assets that belong partially to the public.

But, as I have asserted, the potential harms of philanthropy go beyond poor management of philanthropic dollars. When our focus is on institutional rather than individual harms, our attention necessarily moves from the motives and actions of the individual to the effects of the public policies that structure the philanthropic sector. Do the public policies encourage good or cause harm? In focusing on the potential harms, there are a great many ways to proceed. One might examine how public policies create a regional bias in philanthropy that favors parts of the country with concentrations of wealthy people (see Clotfelter 1988/1989). One might examine how public policies systematically favor certain kinds of nonprofits, especially those that save money and earn endowment income. Here the very large beneficiaries are private foundations and major universities (see Brody 1999, 696). One might also examine why public policy should ignore gifts of time and labor and instead reward gifts of cash or assets. The list of potential institutional harms is lengthy.

In keeping with the initial question of this chapter, I shall focus on whether and how public policies strengthen or weaken the connection between philanthropy and equality. Do public policies governing philanthropy contribute to activities in the form of direct assistance or structural reform that benefits the poor and disadvantaged? Do public policies direct or provide incentives for philanthropic dollars to flow in a redistributive direction, from rich to poor? Can public policy help vindicate the claims of philanthropy that it is tightly connected to equality?

On the one hand, public policies in the nonprofit and philanthropic world appear to take account of the likely distributional flow of dollars. Most significant, in order to qualify for 501(c)(3) status as a nonprofit—the status that permits organizations to receive tax-deductible donations—an organization must serve, according to the tax code, religious, charitable, scientific, testing for public safety, literary, or educational purposes. This large group of 501(c)(3) organizations is usually referred to as the "public charities," distinguishing them from other nonprofit organizations that are primarily mutual benefit societies (e.g., unions, private membership clubs, veterans' organizations, etc.) For certain nonprofit organizations that compete with for-profit organizations in the marketplace for business, such as day care centers and hospitals, there are additional rules that the nonprofit organization must serve poor or disadvantaged communities. In the world of foundations, there is a long history and set of social expectations that philanthropists work to improve society and benefit the least advantaged. In addition, the public policies regulating foundations subject them to more stringent controls than public charities in order to help ensure that foundations produce benefits that are public rather than private. Thus, for instance, since 1969, foundations have been subject to a minimum 5 percent payout rule and must have a board of governors that is not controlled by the donor.

On the other hand, public policy seems remarkably indifferent to equality and redistributive outcomes. One of the oldest objections to the provision of tax-deductible donations to qualifying nonprofits is that the policy fails to differentiate between the social benefits produced by various nonprofits. Thus, from the perspective of the state, assuming we are in the same tax bracket, the $1,000 donation that you make to a contemporary arts museum to underwrite a video installation is worth exactly the same as the $1,000 that I give to tsunami or hurricane Katrina relief. Are these of equal social value? That social policy should be indifferent between these two kinds of goods and provide equivalent subsidies to their respective donors seems quite odd. Yet so long as the recipient organization is a qualifying 501(c)(3), the state grants a tax deduction.

More damning, if we move away from the treatment of individual contributions and consider the total distribution of charitable dollars, we find a pattern of giving that appears hard to reconcile with redistributive outcomes. As Figure 2.1 shows, the great majority of charitable donations by individuals go to religion. Note too that the "Other" category includes giving to private and community foundations, which constitute a comparatively and perhaps surprisingly small portion of the charitable universe. The unexpected elephant in the room, the subject so often overlooked in discussions of philanthropy, is the dominant presence of religious groups as recipients of charitable dollars. Is giving to a religious group a redistributive or eleemosynary enterprise? It might be thought so, if contributions to religious organizations included gifts to religious schools and faith-based social services. But gifts to these religious enterprises have been sectioned off and assigned to their appropriate categories of education and human services, respectively. Gifts to religious organizations can only be understood as predominantly for the operation and sustenance of the religious group, and in this sense, religious groups look more like mutual benefit societies than public charities. It appears very difficult, then, to construe giving to religion as redistributive.[11] Even if we ignore the elephant in the room and focus instead on the other recipients, we find that social welfare groups receive only 2 percent of charitable dollars and human services only 9 percent. A larger amount goes to education, health, and science (13 percent), which is potentially redistributive but not obviously so.

Clotfelter (1992) examines the distributive benefits of nonprofits and concludes, optimistically, I think, that "no overarching conclusions about distributional impact can be made" and that while "in no subsector is there evidence that benefits are dramatically skewed away from the poor and toward the affluent," there is also evidence "that relatively few nonprofit institutions serve the poor as a primary clientele" (22). Based simply on examining the distribution of charitable dollars, then, it is at best very difficult to claim that charitable con-

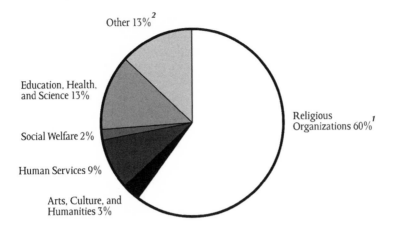

Other 13%[2]

Education, Health, and Science 13%

Social Welfare 2%

Human Services 9%

Arts, Culture, and Humanities 3%

Religious Organizations 60%[1]

1 The "Religious Organizations" category does not include giving to religious schools or faith-based social services; these dollars are tallied in education and human services, respectively.
2 The "Other" category includes giving to international aid and development, private and community foundations, recreation, and other charities.

Source: Independent Sector (2002).

Figure 2.1. Distribution of Charitable Dollars by Type of Charity, 1998
Source: Independent Sector (2002).

tributions benefit the poor. Of the possible redistributive and eleemosynary aims of public charities, Murphy and Nagel (2002) conclude:

> The word charity suggests that this deduction is a means of decentralizing the process by which a community discharges its collective responsibility to alleviate the worst aspects of life at the bottom of the socioeconomic ladder. Since there is disagreement about what the exact nature of that responsibility is, and about which are the most efficient agencies, it is arguably a good idea for the state to subsidize individuals' contributions to agencies of their choice rather than itself making all the decisions about the use of public funds for this purpose. But even if that is so, the existing deduction cannot be defended on those grounds, because many currently deductible "charitable" contributions go to cultural and educational institutions that have nothing to do with the poor, the sick, or the handicapped. State funding of such institutions may or may not be desirable, but the argument would be very different, and "charity" is hardly the right word. (127)

Does the picture change if we limit ourselves to the world of philanthropic foundations? Though these constitute a relatively small part of the charitable universe (gifts from individuals and their bequests accounted for roughly 85 percent of all private giving in 2004; the remaining 15 percent comes from foundations and corporations; *Giving USA 2005*, 18), foundations might be more straightforwardly redistributive for three reasons. First, the funds that create them almost always come from the very, very wealthy; it would be difficult for the money to flow upward to the even wealthier. Second, whereas the charitable giving of individuals is directed very heavily toward religion (60 percent of all charitable contributions), foundations direct only 2.6 percent of their grant dollars to religion (*Giving USA 2005,* 83). Third, at a conceptual level, to the extent that our focus should be on philanthropy as an activity separate and distinct from charity, we would have good reason to believe that philanthropic endeavors, conceived as large-scale interventions with the goal of social melioration, would be more likely to be redistributive in outcome than the aggregation of charitable contributions to all nonprofit organizations described above. The eye-popping growth of foundations in the past fifteen years also warrants special attention. According to figures produced by the Foundation Center, almost half of the largest foundations in the United States were created after 1989 (Renz and Lawrence 2005, 9).[12] An even more explosive growth pattern can be seen in the subsector of community and family foundations. Can foundations lay a greater claim than nonprofits more generally to the embrace of equality?

Figure 2.2 displays the distribution of foundation dollars in 2002. The grant dollars are certainly distributed more evenly than is the case with the charitable contributions of individuals. But the grant categories tell us relatively little about whether the grant dollars are redistributive or not. Take the education category, for instance. Almost half of foundation dollars to education go toward higher education. But we have no way of knowing if these dollars are funding boutique centers for research, the endowment of a professorial chair, or scholarships for disadvantaged and poor students. Julian Wolpert's extensive analysis of the redistributional effects of foundations notes a host of other complex issues, including how to account for the time horizon of foundation activities, which are often directed at long-term rather than short-term change, and the scope of foundation activities, some of which are very local (community foundations) and others of which are global in reach (e.g., the Gates Foundation; Wolpert 2006). There are both technical and conceptual issues that are related to efforts to measure redistribution.

Wolpert concludes that available data demonstrates that foundations are at best "modestly redistributive" (Wolpert 2006). Let us assume that he is correct and that, contrary to the evidence in the nonprofit sector more generally, we are on firmer ground in believing that the grants of philanthropic foundations enhance equity. We may nevertheless not yet conclude that philanthropic foundations are redistributive in outcome because we must still account for the tax concessions to philanthropy and the counterfactual scenario in which the money flowing into philanthropic foundations would have been taxed and become public revenue. The relevant question is not merely, Are philanthropic foundations redistributive? but rather, Do foundation dollars flow more sharply downward than government spending does? In order for the return, so to speak, on the public's investment in philanthropy to be worthwhile, philanthropy must do better than the state would do had it taxed the philanthropic assets.

Answering this counterfactual question is even more difficult than determining whether philanthropic foundations are redistributive. We are forced to speculate about how the state might spend the tax revenue it could have col-

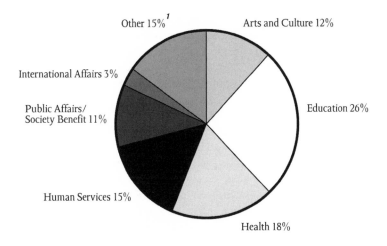

Other 15%¹   Arts and Culture 12%

International Affairs 3%

Public Affairs/
Society Benefit 11%

Education 26%

Human Services 15%

Health 18%

1 *The "Other" category includes giving to environmental and animal rights groups, to research in science and technology, to research in the social sciences, and to religious institutions or for the purpose of forwarding religion.*
Source: The Foundation Center (2004).

Figure 2.2. Distribution of Foundation Dollars by Subject Category of Recipient, 2002
Source: The Foundation Center (2004).

lected if it had not extended the tax concessions to philanthropists for their gifts to foundations.[13] I will not make any such speculation here. Instead, I wish to note that anyone who seeks to ground the special tax treatment of philanthropy on the sector's redistributive outcomes must confront at least three reasons to be suspicious that any such redistribution actually occurs. There is the first and obvious difficulty that a motley assortment of nonprofit groups all qualify for 501(c)(3) status, puppet theaters and soup kitchens alike. There is the second difficulty that religious groups dominate the beneficiaries of individual charitable dollars. And there is the third difficulty that the burden on the sector's advocate is to show not merely that philanthropy is redistributive but that it is more redistributive in its actions than the government would be. In short, we have some good prima facie reasons to doubt that philanthropy is redistributive in effect or eleemosynary in aim. Philanthropy's supposed tight connection to equality looks more and more dubious.

If we accept these prima facie reasons, we must conclude that the very large tax expenditures of the American public on charitable and philanthropic giving result in subsidies for the activities of individuals that, in the aggregate, bear no discernible relationship with equality, conceived of as money that is redistributed from rich to poor or that is directed at the needy. Public policies governing charity and philanthropy appear to be indifferent to equality, and what redistribution occurs is the effect of happenstance or the fortunate predilections of individuals rather than the incentive effects of public policy. Let it be clear: one might still find reasons to justify the existence of nonprofits and philanthropies, resting the justification on the importance of decentralized authority, the creation of a set of mediating institutions in civil society, the desire for the production of public goods to be sensitive to local demand, the fact that non-profits reflect and generate the pluralism of a diverse democratic society. But the public policy framework that gives preferential tax treatment to donors will be more difficult to justify. Though pursuing greater equality is not the only aim of social policy, it is certainly one of the central aspirations of social justice. If the massive tax subsidies given to philanthropy do not serve to enhance equality, the justification will have to lie elsewhere.

And what if the effect of public policies governing philanthropy is to contribute to inequality? In this case, certainly, the extraordinarily generous tax concessions would be even more difficult, perhaps impossible, to justify. Yet in some cases, philanthropy actively exacerbates social inequalities in a way that seems fundamentally at odds with the appropriate egalitarian aims of social policy. Here, public policy does active harm. And I turn now to an illustration of exactly this phenomenon.

Generating Inequality:
Private Funding for Public Schools

Private funding for public schools is a very old practice. Think of bake sales, car washes, and spaghetti dinners. What is new is the scale and professional organization of the effort and the total dollars being raised. Where once it was the wide-ranging activities of Parent-Teacher Associations (PTAs) that were the organizational hub of fund-raising, today many schools and school districts have created independent entities known as local education foundations (LEFs) whose main or sole purpose is to raise private money to supplement public funds. In some places, the local foundations resemble university fund-raising offices more than volunteer-driven PTAs. New York City famously hired Caroline Kennedy, the daughter of former president John F. Kennedy, to lead its education foundation, the New York City Fund for Public Schools. LEFs are almost always 501(c)(3) organizations. Individuals and corporations make tax-deductible contributions to the LEF, which in turn funnels and disburses the money to the school or district.

School and district policies determine whether private funds can be collected at the school or at the district level (or at both) and whether there are limits on how private funds can be spent (on core academic activities or only on extracurricular activities). Very frequently these donations are earmarked for particular activities—for extracurricular events or materials, for additional school supplies, for field trips—giving the donors a nontrivial amount of input or leverage on how the school or district operates. While parents cannot suggest to the district that a special aide be hired with their privately donated funds to shadow their own child around, there are many circumstances that would permit parents collectively to get the district to hire art and music teachers, additional teacher aides, sophisticated technological equipment, and so on that would targeted to benefit their own children.

In the context of ever-tightening state budgets and a general reluctance in many states to increase funding for education, LEFs have grown exponentially in recent years. They exist in almost every large urban district, but they are also increasingly common in smaller and comparatively well-off suburban districts. For most LEFs, especially those in suburban districts, the potential donors are parents of the children in the school district or citizens of the town or city in which the district is located.

It is difficult to fault the motives of parents and townspeople who respond to efforts to fund-raise for public schools. Parents seek to do the best by their own children. Townspeople support their local public institutions. Everyone can lay claim to a public-spiritedness in contributing to public education. Yet the distributional consequences of private funding for public schools are not hard to intuit. Wealthy schools and school districts can raise substantially more money than can schools that have high concentrations of poor students. The effect will be that the savage inequalities of school funding that Jonathan Kozol described fifteen years ago—in which towns with high property wealth spend much more per pupil on education than do poor towns and cities (Kozol 1991, 2005)—will be compounded by the philanthropic and charitable undertakings of local education foundations. In short, local education foundations worsen inequalities in funding between schools and between school districts. And they do it with the active support of the state in the familiar form of tax subsidies for charitable contributions.

Private giving to public schools is a nationwide phenomenon, but it is perhaps most prominent in California, a state that has experienced a long decline in public school funding in the wake of the 1971 *Serrano* decision, which mandated much more equal spending across districts in California, and the 1978 passage of Proposition 13, which capped property taxes at 1 percent of assessed value and severely limited the amount of money that could be raised from property taxes for education. According to the California Consortium of Education Foundations, more than 500 LEFs are operating in California. In an ongoing project, I have been collecting data on the amount of money raised by LEFs and all other 501(c)(3) school organizations (primarily PTAs) in California, and though the project is not yet complete, I report some results below.[14]

Figure 2.3 shows the distribution of expenditures from LEFs, grouped by district, on a per-pupil basis from the years 1997 to 2002. What stands out immediately is the large group of districts that have LEFs raising more than $200 per pupil per year, represented by the bar on the far right of each graph. This contrasts with the massive clumping of districts that receive private funds at a rate of between $5 and $25 per pupil each year. The overall picture of private dollars for public schools is clear. Most districts are not raising appreciable amounts of private money, but a small and growing percentage are raising $200 or more per pupil.

What districts are these, and just how much money are they raising each

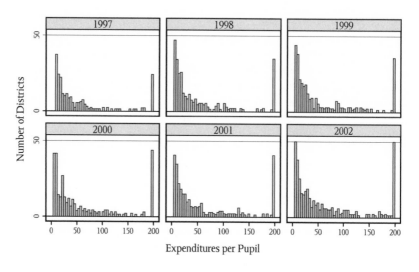

1 *Values <= $5 not shown; all values above $200 are shown as $200*

Figure 2.3. Distribution of Expenditures per Pupil, by Year, 1997–2000[1]

year? Tables 2.2 and 2.3 give a good illustration of the winners and losers in the private fund-raising campaigns. Table 2.2 lists the top fifteen LEFs in California in 1998, ranked by revenue. Two things immediately stand out. First, we are talking about massive fund-raising campaigns; each of the top fifteen LEFs receives well over $1 million in revenue. Second, we see that when the revenue available to the respective district is calculated on a per-pupil basis, the list divides sharply into two groups, suburban and urban districts. The italicized rows represent suburban LEFs, each of which raised at least $100 per pupil. The top performer, Woodside Elementary School District, a district with a single elementary school, raised more than $7,000 per pupil in 1998. By contrast, the urban districts raised far less.

Table 2.3 lists the top fifteen school districts in California in 1998 ranked by the aggregated revenue of all LEFs and other 501(c)(3)s that raise money in the district. The trend seen in Table 2.3 is even more pronounced. Suburban schools enjoy a massive private fund-raising advantage over urban schools, and the top-performing suburban districts in private fund-raising have an exponential advantage.

Those who have examined the phenomenon of private fund-raising have sought to explain it as the effort of parents to avoid court-mandated or legislative efforts to equalize public school funding at the state level (Brunner and Sonstelie 2003). Or they have sought to celebrate and expand the practice, seeing it as the virtuous effort of parents and local citizens to support their public schools. The lesson I wish to draw from the phenomenon is not a strictly educational one, however. I believe that the existence of private fund-raising for

Table 2.2. Top 15 California Education Foundations Ranked by Total Revenue, 1998
Source: Author's dataset.

Foundation Name	District	Revenue	Revenue per Pupil
Brea Hope, Inc.[1]	*Brea-Olinda Unified*	*$5,857,630*	*$982*
Project Seed	Oakland Unified	$5,671,750	$106
LA Educational Partners	Los Angeles Unified	$5,258,200	$8
Woodside School Foundation	*Woodside Elementary*	*$3,384,390*	*$7,065*
Manchester Gate	Fresno United	$2,707,400	$35
Irvine Public Schools Foundation	Irvine United	$1,776,590	$77
Ross School Foundation	*Ross Elementary*	*$1,700,590*	*$4,168*
Cupertino Education Endowment	*Cupertino Union*	*$1,672,670*	*$111*
Newport-Mesa Schools Foundation	Newport-Mesa Unified	$1,603,400	$79
New Haven Schools Foundation	*New Haven Unified*	*$1,302,190*	*$92*
Hillsborough Schools Foundation	*Hillsborough*	*$1,240,820*	*$932*
Palos Verdes Penninsula Education	*Palos Verdes Unified*	*$1,234,820*	*$133*
Portola Valley Schools Foundation	*Portola Valley Elementary*	*$1,111,010*	*$1,603*
Berkeley Public Education Endowment	Albany City Unified	$1,105,970	$373
Telacue Education Foundation	Los Angeles Unified	$1,057,000	$2

1. Names of suburban districts are italicized.

Table 2.3. Top 15 California Districts in Private Fundraising,
Ranked by Total Revenue, 1998
Source: Author's dataset.

District Name	Total Revenue	Pupils	Revenue per Pupil
Los Angeles Unified	$12,507,000	680,430	$18
Oakland Unified	$7,377,082	53,564	$138
Brea-Olinda Unified[1]	*$5,983,699*	*5,965*	*$1,003*
Newport-Mesa Unified	$3,948,777	20,241	$195
Woodside Elementary School	*$3,384,390*	*479*	*$7,065*
Fresno Unified	$3,091,884	78,166	$39
San Francisco Unified	$3,090,717	61,007	$51
Irvine Unified	$2,826,291	23,061	$122
Palos Verdes Peninsula Unified	*$2,676,578*	*9,285*	*$288*
Cupertino Union Elementary	*$2,402,372*	*15,024*	*$160*
San Diego Unified	$2,398,120	136,282	$17
San Ramon Valley Unified	$2,265,910	19,526	$116
Los Altos Elementary	*$1,952,226*	*3,618*	*$540*
Hillsborough City Elementary	*$1,864,189*	*1,332*	*$1,400*
Ross Elementary	*$1,841,586*	*408*	*$4,514*

1. Names of suburban districts are italicized.

public schools is but one illustration of the fact that the public policies which guide philanthropy give much greater deference to liberty than to upholding or promoting equality. And in the case of school funding, we should not at be surprised. Public policy does much the same thing with respect to parents and their children. We know that parents are a main cause—from their genetic endowments, from their parenting styles, from their socioeconomic standing—of inequalities between children when they show up for the first day of kindergarten. Yet public policy is right not to promote equality between children at the expense of the liberty of parents to raise their children as they see fit. A democratic society would not countenance a "parenting police force" that would, say, limit the number of bedtime stories that parents read to their children to two. Liberty has a special place in the domain of the family.[15]

Yet for the phenomenon of private money for public schools, we are not talking about interventions in the family. It is the public institution of the schoolhouse that is the focus of the money and of public policy. The relevant question is not about limits on parental liberty within the family but whether public policy should not merely permit but provide incentives for parents to give money to public schools so that their children can receive a better education than they otherwise would without the private funds. For many, the function of public schools and the very reason why society invests so much money in them and compels children to attend them is to try to *remedy* some of the inequalities children bring with them into the first day of kindergarten. We would think very poorly of the school system if the effect of public schools was to exacerbate the inequalities between children in kindergarten. Yet the institutional structure of philanthropy not only permits charitable giving to exacerbate the vastly different levels of public funding between schools, it also subsidizes the charitable giving of those who, in seeking to support their own children's or their own town's schools, worsen the inequalities between schools. Rather than rewarding virtue, public policy rewards what from the perspective of the public must be considered a vice. The state is implicated in the creation of harms that it is ostensibly charged to eliminate.

To see the problem more vividly, consider a hypothetical case—call it the police department case—that is analogous to the phenomenon of private giving to public schools. Let's say that the block on which you live has been victimized in recent months by a crime wave. The incidence of break-ins, vandalism, and theft has increased. You and your neighbors attribute the crime wave to lower funding of the police department, whose resources have been stretched thin as a result of budget cuts. Attempting to come up with a solution, you and you neighbors pool together some money and offer to make a $100,000 donation to a local police foundation that is set up to provide additional financial support to the local police department. You offer the donation only on the condition, however, that the money be used to hire a new officer whose only patrol will be your block. You fully expect to take a tax deduction for your donation.

Note that in both the school and the police cases there is an exit option. Parents could choose to send their children to private school, but they would not receive any tax deduction for their tuition payment. Similarly, you and your neighbors could hire a private security officer, but this would not qualify for any deduction either.

Should you be permitted to make the donation to the police department? I believe that our intuition runs firmly against any such donation for most people. And public policy tracks our intuitions here. Not only does public policy forbid anyone from taking a tax deduction for donations to police departments, it strictly forbids the donation in the first place. With more space, I would take the opportunity here to draw several lessons from this hypothetical case—lessons about the importance of not allowing public institutions to be deployed in the interest or at the behest of private individuals, lessons about the need for public policy to help set the incentives for citizens to participate in the messiness of democratic politics rather than seek private solutions to their problems, lessons about how the public's interest in schooling has waned in comparison to the public's interest in security. I restrict myself, however, to only one lesson, one that is germane to the general thesis of this essay. In the police case, the liberty of individuals is constrained in the interest of equality. Private individuals are not permitted to make charitable contributions to a public institution in which all citizens are thought to have an equal stake. Note that nothing less than the U.S. Constitution enshrines a version of this principle. Only Congress can appropriate funding for federal branches of the government. Beyond making a donation to the U.S. Treasury, individuals are not permitted to direct funds to a particular federal agency or organization. This is not a denial of a tax benefit; it is a blanket prohibition on giving.

Conclusion

I hasten to add that making a blanket prohibition on private giving to public schools is not necessarily the most justifiable public policy with respect to philanthropy and public education. The aim, it seems to me, should be to have policies that make the effect of philanthropy egalitarian rather than inegalitarian, to provide incentives in the case of education for private giving to disadvantaged students, schools, and districts. In other words, the aim should be to make good on the promise of the old story about philanthropy with which I began—that philanthropy is tightly connected to both liberty and equality.

Such policies are far from utopian. Institutional design here is key, and there is much to learn from other societies that are far less generous or much more stringent in their tax treatment and regulation of philanthropy. When we think about philanthropy and the nonprofit sector, the aim cannot be, as is so often the case in writing about philanthropy, to justify the current arrangements that we have in the United States. Rather, the aim must be to identify what role the state ought to play in the creation and operation of a philanthropic and nonprofit sector.

It is at this point that an examination of philanthropy becomes an exercise in political philosophy. There will be no final and definitive answer in any such exercise, but it is important nevertheless to recognize the potential injustices—*the potential harms*—of current public policy. Public policy creates the institutional context in which philanthropy exists. Laws license and regulate the operation of nonprofit organizations and philanthropic foundations. Laws also provide significant tax concessions for the charitable donations of individuals and the activities of charitable and philanthropic organizations. The public policies designed to create a favorable environment for nonprofits and foundations and offer incentives for people to make charitable donations represent a wide-scale governmental intervention within the charitable and philanthropic sector. As things currently stand, these policies do not do much, if anything, to enhance equality. Instead, they systematically defer to the liberty of individuals to make philanthropic decisions of their own. At worst, public policy is not merely indifferent to whether philanthropy enhances equality. As the phenomenon of private funding for public schools shows, public policy is sometimes causally implicated in the creation of greater inequalities. This is something we should worry about.

I wish to emphasize that the rocky relationship between philanthropy and equality and the data I have presented about private funding for public schools does not shake the legitimacy of philanthropy, charity, nonprofits, and foundations. But it should shake any conviction or belief we might have that their legitimacy and the public policies that give incentives for their activities might rest on their connection to equality. In the end, when assessed as an institutionally sanctioned, encouraged, and rewarded activity, philanthropy is much more tightly connected to, or systematically favors, liberty rather than equality.

Notes

1. The most frequent invoked and justly famous Tocqueville reference is almost certainly this passage: "Americans of all ages, all conditions, and all minds are constantly joining together in groups. In addition to commercial and industrial associations in which everyone takes part, there are associations of a thousand other kinds: some religious, some moral, some grave, some trivial, some quite general and others quite particular, some huge and others tiny. Americans associate to give fêtes, to found seminaries, to build inns, to erect churches, to distribute books, to send missionaries to the antipodes. This is how they create hospitals, prisons, and schools. If, finally, they wish to publicize a truth or foster a sentiment with the help of a great example, they associate. Wherever there is a new undertaking, at the head of which you would expect to see in France the government and in England some great lord, in the United States you are sure to find an association" (Tocqueville 2004, 595).

2. For an economist's perspective on how tax policy creates "distortions" in the philanthropic sector, see Clotfelter 1988/1989.

3. For an analysis of the content and historical trajectory of these left-wing critiques in the American setting, see Karl and Katz (1987). For a classic exposition of the Gramscian critique, see Fisher (1983).

4. Kymlicka operates with a limited definition of charity—gifts of money to other people in need—and he specifically separates out donations to organizations that promote activities enjoyed by the donor (e.g., cultural groups) or causes preferred by the donor (e.g., environmental groups or gun lobbies). Nevertheless, Kymlicka's argument undermines any account of philanthropy or charity whose aim or justification is redistributive or eleemosynary. His conclusion: "Once we accept a modern conception of social justice, our first obligation must be to ensure that social institutions fulfil principles of justice. And then . . . justice will crowd out charity, both in theory and in practice. It is only by radically curtailing obligations of justice that earlier religious traditions were able to make significant space for charity" (Kymlicka 2001, 115).

5. For a detailed overview of the tax treatment of nonprofit organizations, see Simon (1987).

6. The "tax expenditure" concept was pioneered by Stanley Surrey in the late 1960s, and it applied to every tax concession in the tax code. Surrey equated tax expenditures with direct spending programs in terms of their respective impact on the federal treasury. For a comprehensive overview, see Surrey and McDaniel (1985). The concept has had practical effects: the U.S. government and many state governments now publish an annual list of actual and estimated tax expenditures in their annual budgets.

7. Whether the existence of the deduction actually has any effect on rates of participation in giving and levels of giving is a matter of debate. The conventional view is that the tax subsidy has an effect only on those who earn very high incomes. In explaining why people make charitable donations, Evelyn Brody concludes that "tax considerations are not paramount" (1999, 714–715).

8. Calculated from Internal Revenue Service (2004).

9. For a review of various reforms, some implemented, some not, see Brody 1999.

10. This remark suggests that a two-stage justification is needed to explain and support the current organization of the nonprofit and philanthropic sector, a fact that I believe is insufficiently recognized in discussions about philanthropy and the voluntary sector. The first stage of justification grants a license to philanthropic organizations to operate; the state permits individuals to create foundations that will give money away with fidelity to donor intent and without state interference. A second stage of justification is needed to underwrite the existence of the generous tax concessions designed to spur philanthropic behavior. The second stage is independent of the first; it is possible to decide that while the state rightly permits a nonprofit and philanthropic sector, there should be no tax incentive for its operation. I do not explore the implications of this two-stage process of justification here; a full theory of philanthropy would need to do so.

11. Jeff Biddle presents some interesting though inconclusive evidence that 70 percent of giving to religious congregations is for operation of the congregation and 30 percent for philanthropic undertakings. He also suggests that religious giving might be understood as redistributive since it is possible, and perhaps likely, that "wealthy members subsidize the spiritual consumption of less wealthy members" within congregations (Biddle 1992, 125). On this view, charitable contributions to religion are redistributive when the scope of analysis is confined to the flow of dollars within religious groups themselves. This is by no means irrelevant, but to understand redistribution in this sense is to depart from the spirit of the idea that charity is connected to equality because charitable dollars go to help the needy and flow from rich to poor.

12. Despite the growth in large foundations, total foundation giving actually declined in 2002 and 2003 (Renz and Lawrence 2005, 1–2).

13. Ken Prewitt notes that western European governments have been historically

more redistributive than the United States and that the counterfactual question presented here has correspondingly greater bite than the more redistributive a government is with its taxpayers' dollars (Prewitt 2006).

14. Economists Eric Brunner and Jon Sonstelie have undertaken similar research and were kind enough to share with me their database of 501(c)(3) school organizations in California. See Brunner and Sonstelie (2003) for their conclusions.

15. Parents possess great liberty indeed within the family, but it is not absolute and can still be curtailed under certain circumstances, the most obvious and uncontroversial of which are when parents abuse or neglect their children.

References

Biddle, Jeff E. 1992. "Religious Organizations." In *Who Benefits from the Nonprofit Sector?* edited by Charles Clotfelter, 92–133. Chicago: University of Chicago Press.

Brody, Evelyn. 1999. "Charities in Tax Reform: Threats to Subsidies Overt and Covert." *Tennessee Law Review* 66: 687–763.

Brunner, Eric, and Jon Sonstelie. 2003. "School Finance Reform and Voluntary Fiscal Federalism." *Journal of Public Economics* 87: 2157–2185.

Clotfelter, Charles. 1988/1989. "Tax-Induced Distortions in the Voluntary Sector." *Case Western Law Review* 39: 663–694.

———, ed. 1992. *Who Benefits from the Nonprofit Sector?* Chicago: University of Chicago Press.

Fisher, Donald. 1983. "The Role of Philanthropic Foundations in the Reproduction and Production of Hegemony: Rockefeller Foundations and the Social Sciences." *Sociology* 17, no. 2: 206–233.

Fleishman, Joel. 2004. "Simply Doing Good or Doing Good Well." In *Just Money: A Critique of Contemporary American Philanthropy,* edited by H. Peter Karoff, 101–128. Boston: TPI Editions.

The Foundation Center. 2004. *Foundation Giving Trends: Update on Funding Priorities.* New York: The Foundation Center

Giving USA 2005. Researched and written by the Center on Philanthropy at Indiana University. Glenview, Ill.: American Association of Fundraising Counsel, 2005.

Independent Sector. 2002. *The New Nonprofit Almanac and Desk Reference : The Essential Facts and Figures for Managers, Researchers, and Volunteers.* San Francisco, Calif.: Jossey-Bass.

Internal Revenue Service. 2004. "Table 1: Individual Income Tax Returns: Selected Income and Tax Items for Specified Tax Years, 1985–2002." *Statistics of Income Bulletin* (Fall). Available online at http://www.irs.gov/pub/irs-soi/02in01si.xls.

Karl, Barry D., and Stanley N. Katz. 1987. "Foundations and Ruling Class Elites." *Daedelus* 116, no. 1: 1–40.

Kozol, Jonathan. 1991. *Savage Inequalities.* New York: Crown Publishing.

———. 2005. *Shame of the Nation.* New York: Crown Publishing.

Kymlicka, Will. 2001. "Altruism in Philosophical and Ethical Traditions: Two Views." In *Between State and Market: Essays on Charity Law and Policy in Canada,* edited by Jim Phillips, Bruce Chapman, and David Stevens, 87–126. Toronto: McGill-Queen's University Press.

Murphy, Liam, and Thomas Nagel. 2002. *The Myth of Ownership: Taxes and Justice*. Oxford: Oxford University Press.

Musgrave, Richard A., and Peggy Musgrave. 1984. *Public Finance in Theory and Practice*. 4th ed. New York: McGraw Hill.

Nozick, Robert. 1974. *Anarchy, State, and Utopia*. New York: Basic Books.

Office of Management and Budget. 2004. *Budget of the United States Government: Fiscal Year 2005*. Washington, D.C.: U.S. Government Printing Office.

Prewitt, Kenneth. 2006. "Modern Philanthropic Foundations and the Liberal Society." In *The Legitimacy of Philanthropic Foundations*, edited by Kenneth Prewitt, Mattei Dogan, Steven Heydemann, and Stefan Toepler. New York: Russell Sage Foundation.

Renz, Loren, and Steven Lawrence. 2005. *Foundation Growth and Giving Estimates 2004*. New York: The Foundation Center.

Simon, John G. 1987. "The Tax Treatment of Nonprofit Organizations: A Review of Federal and State Policies." In *The Nonprofit Sector: A Research Handbook*, edited by Walter W. Powell, 67–98. New Haven, Conn.: Yale University Press.

Surrey, Stanley S., and Paul R. McDaniel. 1985. *Tax Expenditures*. Cambridge, Mass.: Harvard University Press.

Tocqueville, Alexis de. *Democracy in America*. 2004. Translated by Arthur Goldhammer. New York: Library of America.

Weisbrod, Burton. 2004. "The Pitfalls of Profits." *Stanford Social Innovation Review* 2, no. 3 (Winter): 40–47.

Wolpert, Julian. 2006. "The Redistributional Effects of America's Private Foundations." In *The Legitimacy of Philanthropic Foundations*, edited by Kenneth Prewitt, Mattei Dogan, Steven Heydemann, and Stefan Toepler. New York: Russell Sage Foundation.

3   The Politics of Doing Good: Philanthropic Leadership for the Twenty-First Century

Leslie Lenkowsky

In his *Discourses* on the work of Livy, Niccolo Machiavelli recounted an episode from the history of Rome. It concerns a famine that had struck the city and the donation by a citizen named Spurius Melius of a "private stock of grain and feed" to the hungry. In return, "fearing the evil consequences that might arise" from this act of generosity, Machiavelli wrote, the Roman Senate created "a Dictator" who put this early philanthropist to death. Notwithstanding the old saying that no good deed goes unpunished, that would seem to be a bit excessive.

However, in his commentary, Machiavelli leaves no doubt that he believes the Senate was right. A republic that has "no distinguished citizens," he wrote, cannot be well governed, but at the same time, the influence of such citizens often causes the public to surrender their freedoms to those who promise them great rewards. To avoid that fate, Machiavelli advised, a "well-regulated" government should offer many opportunities for such citizens to serve the public through the state. But if it allows its distinguished citizens to obtain "reputation and influence" through private means, it is asking for trouble. Indeed, warned Machiavelli, "if one such transgression were allowed to go unpunished, it might lead to the ruin of the republic, for it would then be difficult to force back the ambitious to the true path of duty" (Machiavelli 1950, 490–493).

The lesson of this story might be, to paraphrase William Shakespeare, "First, kill all the philanthropists." And if we have not yet heard a state attorney general go quite that far, we have seen no less than the former head of the Council on Foundations, the premier association of the nation's grant-making bodies, quoted as saying that sooner or later, she expected to see one of her members paraded before television cameras in a "perp walk." Moreover, many legal experts, such as well-known television commentator Jonathan Turley, a professor at the George Washington University law school, have argued that the time has come to extend the corporate-governance laws prompted by the scandals at Enron, Tyco, and other companies—and presumably, the penalties for breaking them as well—to large not-for-profit corporations (Turley 2004).

In a country long accustomed to holding philanthropy and charities in high regard, such proposals—and Professor Turley is by no means alone in making them—strike a discordant note. Between 1995 and 2002, a period in which the size of the nonprofit sector expanded greatly, a survey of newspaper reports by Marion Fremont-Smith and Andras Kosaras found 152 reports of criminal and civil wrongdoing (Fremont-Smith and Kosaras 2003). In the years that followed, spurred particularly by reporters for the *New York Times,* the *Boston Globe,* and the *Washington Post,* the "bad news" continued and perhaps even increased as Congress held several widely publicized hearings to examine abuses by tax-exempt organizations and their supporters. What has happened? And what will happen? Obviously, some questionable practices have now come to light which, if not always strictly illegal, are less tolerable than they were before the corporate scandals.

But where there is smoke, there is not necessarily fire. The scandals that have recently engulfed the philanthropic world are not a sign that legal and ethical transgressions are rampant in philanthropy. But they do reveal the growing importance of philanthropy in American life—and the resulting political questions about doing good through private means.

Indeed, in light of the magnitude of the alleged transgressions (of the more than $350 billion the Internal Revenue Service [IRS] estimates is lost to the U.S. Treasury because of illegal tax avoidance, only about $6 billion might be realized by curbing the misuse of charitable organizations), the amount of attention the nonprofit world has been receiving from government has been striking (Everson 2005; Joint Committee on Taxation 2005). In the name of increasing foundation payouts, Congress considered—and will undoubtedly do so again—a bill that would disallow certain administrative expenses—especially high salaries and excessive travel expenses—from the required spending amount (which is currently 5 percent of asset values, averaged over several preceding years). Sponsored by an unusual coalition of liberals and conservatives, the proposals resulted in the kind of lobbying effort by the philanthropic world that is generally associated with advocates for tariffs and highways, a campaign which itself became something of an embarrassment, though for now, at any rate, it has been successful.

The 2002 Bipartisan Campaign Finance Reform Act opened the door to regulating political advertising near federal elections by ostensibly nonpartisan nonprofit groups that are supported by donations. During the 2004 campaign, the Federal Election Commission considered actions to regulate contributions to issue-oriented nonprofit organizations established under Section 527 of the tax code, and rules for 501(c)(3) and 501(c)(4) groups—public charities and social welfare organizations—may come next. The PATRIOT Act, passed in the wake of the 9/11 terrorist attacks, gave broad new powers to the Departments of Justice and Treasury to monitor the flow of money to organizations suspected of supporting terrorism, including supposedly charitable ones. Several foundations and the Combined Federal Campaign (the "United Way" for federal employees) adopted rules aimed at preventing such gifts, leading to protests from groups such as the American Civil Liberties Union and higher education institutions, which regarded them as too intrusive and burdensome.

Following the United States Supreme Court's decision in the case of *Ryan v. Telemarketing Associates,* the Federal Trade Commission and over three dozen state attorneys general have become more aggressive in pursuing cases of alleged fund-raising fraud. California, Minnesota, New York, Indiana, and other states have enacted new laws that give officials expanded powers to regulate charities, including, if necessary, replacing their boards of trustees if they have misused or improperly solicited gifts. Still under consideration are proposals to extend the so-called Sarbanes-Oxley rules on corporate governance to nonprofits, including by making financial records more transparent to stakeholders, curtailing conflicts of interest, and imposing greater penalties for misdeeds.[1] Legal advisors and groups such as Independent Sector are urging charities to get ready for the changes likely in store and to preempt new mandates through greater self-regulation.

High-profile lawsuits, such as one accusing Princeton's Woodrow Wilson School of Public and International Affairs of ignoring the intent of a major donor, are becoming more common, as are challenges to trustee decisions by public officials, including governors. Following court injunctions requested by the Pennsylvania attorney general, the trustees of the Milton Hershey Trust cancelled a planned sale of the stock it owned in the Hershey Foods Corporation, which comprised the bulk of its assets and 77 percent of the shares with voting rights, lest the company's operations be moved out of the state. And under pressure from state and local officials, as well as other philanthropists, the trustees of Philadelphia's Barnes Foundation successfully petitioned a court to relocate its multibillion-dollar art collection to a new locale, despite concerns that the move might be at odds with the donor's intent.

Following a widely publicized series of articles in the *Washington Post,* the IRS launched an audit of The Nature Conservancy, the largest environmental organization in the world, which led to major changes in its governance and procedures to prevent accusations of favoritism toward board members and large donors in sales of property under the organization's control. After a report by the General Accounting Office and a legislative hearing, President George W. Bush proposed and Congress enacted new rules for calculating the amount of the charitable deduction for gifts of used cars to keep donors from overvaluing them. Similar changes for other contributions of property are also under consideration.

As the *Washington Post*'s exposé of The Nature Conservancy demonstrated, far from still being a spin-off of reporting in society pages on fund-raising galas, "needy cases," and heart-warming philanthropic projects, covering charities has become a focus for investigative reporters, especially at major national and regional dailies, such as the *Boston Globe,* the *San Jose Mercury News,* and the *New York Times.* Specialized publications, such as *The Chronicle of Philanthropy,* have been doing more in-depth reports too, such as examining loans and other forms of compensation to key executives of charities.

To be sure, the developments of the past two years—and others could be listed—are not unprecedented. The 1980s and 1990s also saw a number of high-profile episodes of misbehavior in the nonprofit world: among others, the fraudulent investment practices of the Foundation for New Era Philanthropy; excessive expenditures by executives of the Freedom Forum Foundation; improprieties by the trustees of Hawaii's largest philanthropy, the Bishop Estate; and misuse of funds by the head of the United Way of America, the umbrella organization for over 1,000 employee-giving campaigns in the United States. At a 1998 American Assembly gathering on "Philanthropy in a Changing America," Duke University's Joel L. Fleishman, a veteran participant in and observer of the nonprofit world, used instances such as these to argue for the creation of a new government regulatory body to oversee charities. "The truth is," he wrote, "that there is no entity at present . . . which has the authority to establish and police standards of compliance on a national scale, yet the existence of such standards and both actual and perceived compliance with them are essential if the public is to continue to feel justifiably comfortable in trusting not-for-profit organizations." While meant as a "strategy of last resort," the new agency would be designed not to replace the efforts of the IRS or state attorneys general but to add to them (Fleishman 1999, 186).

Though it attracted considerable attention, Fleishman's proposal garnered very little support. (The American Assembly's final report called merely for strengthening the existing oversight agencies.) This may have been partly because the scandals were largely perceived as isolated incidents that did not reflect any deep-seated problem with philanthropy in general. They could cause—and may indeed have caused—damage to the organizations involved. They may also have produced greater public skepticism about nonprofit organizations in general. But even so, a 1994 Independent Sector poll found that more than one-third of the American public still had "a great deal" or "quite a lot" of confidence in nonprofits (even if religious groups are not counted), nearly double the level expressing such views about federal and state government (Independent Sector 1995).

The most urgent challenges facing the philanthropic world appeared to be external more than internal. Cutbacks or policy changes in government funding in "areas of concern to nonprofits" (to use Lester M. Salamon's phrase) were putting increasing pressure on donors to "pick up the slack" (as President Ronald Reagan's advisor, Michael K. Deaver, reportedly said). At the same time, reductions in tax rates seemed likely to reduce some of the economic advantages of charitable giving. For-profit companies, such as Fidelity Investments, were establishing tax-exempt "donor-advised" funds that threatened to draw money away from more traditional forms of philanthropy, such as foundations and local branches of the United Way. And as the Baby Boom generation achieved greater financial success, its apparent preference for "bowling alone" (in political scientist Robert D. Putnam's words) and disinclination to support charities as their parents had boded ill for the likelihood they would be generous with their new wealth. Nonetheless, when, on occasion, questions were raised about the health of philanthropy (for example, the issues the Bradley Foundation's National Commission on Philanthropy and Civic Renewal raised in 1997), they were largely ignored.

And why not? Despite the scandals and challenges that beset it, the 1990s were a pretty good decade for the nonprofit world. Charitable giving kept pace with a rapidly growing economy and at times exceeded it. The number of nonprofit organizations grew, as did the number of and assets held by foundations. (By the end of the decade, holdings of $1 billion were barely sufficient to place an organization among the top fifty grant-makers in the United States.) Because of growing student interest, programs to prepare them for careers in the nonprofit sector were started or expanded. The Clinton administration sponsored what was billed as the first White House Conference on Philanthropy, and in the 2000 campaign, both Vice President Gore and Governor George W. Bush promised, if elected, to rely more on what the latter called "the armies of compassion."

Writing early in the new millennium, Salamon (2002) called "nonprofit America" the "resilient sector." In the face of challenges and opportunities in the 1980s and 1990s, it had responded, he wrote, by "strengthening its fiscal base, upgrading its operations, enlisting new partners and new resources in its activities, and generally improving its reputation for effectiveness" (45). It still faced "risks," including the "*potential* loss of public trust," Salamon said (48; emphasis added). But while he called for some changes in public policy, mostly aimed at distinguishing the charitable from the commercial activities of nonprofits, there was little suggestion of the intense public scrutiny about to come.

How much difference a short amount of time can make is apparent in a report from The Brookings Institution entitled "To Give or Not to Give: The Crisis of Confidence in Charities." In it, Paul Light notes that public opinion of the job nonprofits were doing sank in 2001 and has not recovered much since. Especially striking, he adds, is that confidence in other civic institutions went up during this period (though it has since gone down again). "Whether correctly or incorrectly," Light concludes, "the public has come to believe that substantial numbers of charitable organizations are not doing well enough or not doing enough good" (Light 2003, 8).

Light attributes this largely to the aftermath of the 9/11 terrorist attacks and the criticisms leveled against the American Red Cross and other nonprofit groups for mishandling relief contributions. Undoubtedly, reports that the large sums of money Americans donated were slow in getting to the victims of the attacks (or were slated to be used for other purposes altogether) were an embarrassment for the nonprofit world. But how valid the criticisms were and what effect they really had is open to doubt. A careful review for The Century Foundation by Paula DiPerna concluded that much of the press coverage was inaccurate or incomplete and that the successful efforts of charities to respond innovatively in the face of an unprecedented disaster went virtually unnoticed (DiPerna 2003). In any case, Light notes that public confidence in the Red Cross rebounded and surpassed that for charitable organizations in general (before a new round of criticisms were directed at its performance after Hurricane Katrina). If the negative publicity really did have a harmful effect, the fact that the respect of the Red Cross did not have more of a positive impact on the rest of the nonprofit world is puzzling.

By the same token, despite all the charges that have been leveled in the past two years, the extent of misbehavior in the philanthropic world still appears to be small. For example, of the 152 instances of wrongdoing Fremont-Smith and Kosaras found in their survey of newspapers, less than one-fifth involved foundations or giving federations such as the United Way. Donations of property—whose overvaluation, according to the congressional Joint Committee on Taxation, costs the U.S. Treasury about $2 billion annually (Joint Committee on Taxation 2005)—comprised less than a quarter of the contributions taxpayers who itemized their deductions reported in 2002; most of what Americans—especially non-itemizers—give is in cash, the value of which is indisputable (Parisi and Hollenbeck 2004). Even the much-criticized used-car donations involved just 4,300 of the 160,000 charities with revenues over $100,000 and less than 1 percent of taxpayers (General Accounting Office 2003).

Excessive foundation staffing and administrative expenses, the target of the threatened congressional action, are mostly an issue for larger grant-makers. Smaller ones, which make up the bulk of the foundation world (but account for only a small share of its spending), are apt to be leaner, though not meaner. According to a survey of its 2,900 members by the Association of Small Foundations, the median administrative expense for those with paid staff was three-quarters of a percent of their assets; for those without staff, the figure was just one-quarter of a percent. By contrast, the median grant payout came to 5 percent of their holdings, and judging from the average of 8.5 percent, many give more, which is exactly what Congress intended when it established a rate in the 1969 tax act (Association of Small Foundations 2002).

These figures agree with those compiled by the IRS. The smaller the foundation, the more generous it is likely to be. But even the largest ones consistently give a substantial amount to charities. Between 1985 and 1997, a panel study conducted by the IRS determined, the 100 wealthiest "non-operating" (i.e., mostly grant-making) foundations "consistently" allocated about 90 percent of their expenditures to grants and other kinds of gifts. They spent just 5 percent on salaries, benefits, and other forms of compensation for their officers, directors, and staffs (Whitten 2001).

Few accusations are more likely to prompt outrage (and attract the attention of enforcement officials) than claims of excessively generous compensation payments and excessively stingy grant payments. Yet apart from egregious (and often-cited) examples, such as the foundation that gave more to its directors and staff than to its grantees or the fund that did nothing with its assets except give its donor a large charitable tax deduction, the evidence that such practices are the norm—or are even growing—in the philanthropic world is nonexistent. Such misbehavior deserves to be punished when it occurs (and the IRS catches it), and new laws should be enacted if the current ones are insufficient to deal with new problems. But the necessity for taking such steps should not lead to the conclusion that instead of trying to do good, the philanthropic world is bent on doing bad unless it is subjected to more stringent oversight and control.

In any case, some of the practices that are now being criticized were not long ago being praised (or at least encouraged) as ways of improving the effectiveness of the nation's charities. As Peter Frumkin has pointed out, in response to the message of the 1969 tax act that they needed to become more serious about grant-making, foundations increased the size and professionalism of their staffs, thus opening themselves to attacks today for devoting too much of their budgets to personnel (Frumkin 1999). To prevent good intentions from being mistaken for good results, grant-makers have been urged to devote more attention to evaluation, which inevitably adds to their administrative costs. In order to expand the diversity of their grantees, funders have been asked to invest more of their resources in outreach and in providing assistance to new applicants; neither is inexpensive. And in the name of fostering "high-performance grant-making," venture philanthropy gurus advised donors to become closely involved with their grantees rather than maintain an arm's-length relationship, which is likely to invite criticism in the post–Sarbanes-Oxley world of heightened sensitivity to potential conflicts of interest in corporate activity.

Good practices can, of course, be carried to such excess that they become abuses. (Whatever they might do to improve donor accountability, the demands for greater "transparency" in grant-making that are part of the current reform proposals are all but certain to increase the amount funders will have to spend on lawyers and accountants.) On the public stage, a juicy anecdote will trump a dry statistical report every time, especially for officials who pride themselves on being guardians of the public treasury. Nor have foundations (or, for that matter, government) provided the kind of support for data-gathering and research that could shed more light on the kinds of charges leveled against philanthropy. (Ironically, just as the nonprofit world was becoming the object of policymaker attention, several underwriters of research on the sector announced plans to focus their grants elsewhere.) But while philanthropy should not be immune from criticism or, when necessary, stricter rules and tougher penalties for acting improperly, the costs of such actions also need to be kept in mind.

No one in the United States Senate (or elsewhere in Washington or in state capitals) is seriously entertaining the idea of killing philanthropists nowadays. To the contrary, all who propose new laws or call for tightening the enforcement of existing ones invariably preface their remarks by claiming that their intent is to ensure that Americans will continue to trust—and thus give generously to—charities. However, if they will not kill them, new laws and regulations have the potential to curtail the independence of philanthropists. That could be nearly as deadly.

Is it entirely coincidental that this latest round of criticism—which includes the first major congressional investigations since the 1960s—comes at the end of a decade of extraordinary growth for philanthropy and just before an impending intergenerational transfer of wealth is expected to send trillions of additional dollars in gifts to foundations and other nonprofit groups? And is it a coincidence that these criticisms are being made during a period in which the public philosophy of the United States—even if not always mirrored by its actions—has grown increasingly skeptical about the value of government-run programs? In other words, could it be that the scandal-mongering of the past few years has more than a little to do with the greater size and visibility of philanthropists in American society as well as expectations of them?

As a case in point, consider a controversy that recently occurred in Colorado. The Daniels Fund was created by cable television magnate Bill Daniels, and after his death in March 2000, it became the largest foundation in the Rocky Mountain region. On the recommendation of its president, former U.S. senator Hank Brown (now University of Colorado president), the trustees approved a plan to eliminate the fund's offices in New Mexico, Utah, and Wyoming as a way of reducing administrative costs and increasing the amount available for grants. Criticisms ensued, led by the governors of New Mexico and Wyoming and New Mexico's lieutenant governor, who was a niece of the late Mr. Daniels and a trustee of the fund, one of two board members to object to the reorganization. They claimed that closing the offices would mean fewer grants for their states, though fund officials argued that the opposite was as likely, since under the new arrangement, applicants could apply to any of the grant-maker's programs, not just those designated for grants in their states. The fund was also accused of paying Brown an excessive salary and moving into a lavish new office building in Denver, just as it was supposedly trying to economize elsewhere (Gose 2004).

Whatever the truth of such claims (and they were disputed), the central issue was essentially one of governance. Traditionally, directors and trustees of foundations and other nonprofit groups have been empowered to make decisions about the use of charitable resources. The results have not always been to everyone's liking, but they did receive deference, unless they were patently illegal or improper. (Even then efforts at oversight tended to give a wide berth to private discretion.) The controversy that erupted over the Daniels Fund is just one sign—and there are others—that in an era of philanthropic growth, the public impact of such decisions will not go uncontested, especially if, as in this case, those responsible for making them are divided.

Moreover, this era is still in its early stages, as University of Southern California historian Kevin Starr observed in the *Los Angeles Times*. Noting that The David and Lucile Packard Foundation had recently completed a project to set aside 342,000 acres of picturesque California landscapes for conservation, an amount about the size of Sequoia National Park, Starr envisioned a future in which more foundations would take on more and more of what had been regarded as government's responsibilities. "In the years to come," he wrote, "as governmental resources remain scarce and foundation assistance grows increasingly necessary, Californians might be expected to regard foundations as established governance structures" (Starr 2004).

Starr is only partly correct. The developments he foresees will affect not only Californians but all Americans. They will be obvious not just in the years to come—they are already obvious and they have led to a view of foundations as institutions that are open to questioning.

Starr understands that the entry of philanthropy into the public sphere on the scale he envisions is a recipe for contention. Whose interests are really being served when private donors set aside land for public use? Or sponsor a variety of educational and social services? Who does not have an opinion about how someone else's funds should have been spent in any of these or other areas? In public life, such disputes are usually resolved—even if only temporarily—through the political process. But how can they be settled when the key decision makers are philanthropists outside of government? And since the United States is still a nation which believes that private donors and nongovernmental organizations have at least some right to use their funds as they see fit, is it surprising that concerns about what they do are often expressed in seemingly legalistic ways, such as by faulting the accountability, governance, or administrative policies of grant-making organizations rather than faulting how the money is actually spent?

That is why, at root, the scandals engulfing the philanthropic world are about the politics of doing good through private means. The kinds of reforms now being considered—improving ethical standards, restricting the ability of donors to use charities for their own benefit, adopting "best practices" in corporate governance, and reporting to the public more adequately about the work of the nonprofit sector—might be helpful, though obtaining voluntary compliance will always be a challenge. However, they are not likely to be sufficient for those whose ultimate concern is with what philanthropic groups do, not how they operate. To the extent that the challenge is a political one, the problems facing philanthropy are likely to get worse before they get better as foundations and other grant-makers continue to grow in activity and influence.

Paul Light and others believe that if charities want to deal with the accusations that have been made against them and regain public confidence, they need to show that they are "spending money wisely, helping people, and running their programs and services effectively." To do this, Light argues, both philanthropists and their grantees should invest more in what he calls "capacity building" measures, such as strategic planning, board development, and employee training (Light 2003, 5, 7). But useful as such steps might be, they might not be enough.

In addition, leaders of the nonprofit world ought to pay more attention to how their actions are perceived by the public, whether they can be justified in terms of the charitable purposes of their organizations, and, ultimately, what impact they have. One of the putative virtues of philanthropy is its potential to be independent of public opinion, to take risks that democratically accountable officials might hesitate to embark upon or ordinary citizens might regard as dubious, if not peculiar. Yet when practiced immoderately, this virtue, like any other, can become a vice. That may be particularly likely when the distance between grant-makers and the communities in which they work grows too wide.

Useful as it has been in many respects, the professionalization of the non-profit world has probably had that effect. Projects that seem compelling to well-educated foundation officers who are seeking new solutions to urgent problems may come to look very different to those whose welfare is apt to be affected by them. Indeed, from the very beginnings of foundations in the United States, this has been a source of concern. The advent of the Rockefeller Foundation early in the twentieth century was greeted not by praise for its donor's magnanimity but with suspicion about what the oilman and his associates were really up to (Bremner 1988, 112–113). A few early successes, mostly in addressing medical and public health problems, were required to put these doubts at least partly to rest.

Today, foundations are far more numerous and wealthy than they were a century ago, and perhaps more ambitious too. The largest have developed highly trained staffs with considerable grant-making experience (and often, as well, a commitment to what are now called "progressive" principles that a substantial portion of the public may not share). They are engaged in a variety of issues, such as reforming schools or health care, which are important and inseparable from American political and ideological disputes. Not least important, they generally work closely—in "partnership"—with public officials (especially civil servants), whose own standing in the eyes of the public is much lower than it used to be.

From one vantage point, these changes might seem to be positive ones. But from another, their very growth, expertise, aspirations, and proximity to the levers of power inevitably make philanthropists forces to be reckoned with. And if that reckoning is now under way, as it appears to be, foundations need to do much more than get their legal and financial affairs in order or even become more effective grant-makers. They need to reexamine what they are trying to accomplish with their funds and what their relationship to government in the American political system ought to be.

Machiavelli's warning about the threat to republican government posed by those who aim to do good by private means was taken seriously by this nation's founders. Indeed, early in the history of the United States, Virginia, Pennsylvania, and other states tried to abolish charities or at least any special treatment of them. James Madison expressed such fears in his famous warning about the dangers of "faction" in *The Federalist Papers: No. 10:* "The friend of popular governments never finds himself so much alarmed for their character and fate," he wrote, as when he thinks about "the violence of faction." Left unchecked, such private interests can be responsible for "many of our heaviest misfortunes," Madison added, and "particularly, for that prevailing and increasing distrust of public engagements and alarm for private rights" (Hamilton 1961, 130).Or, as a more contemporary observer, *National Journal's* Jonathan Rauch, has put it, they can cause "demosclerosis," a hardening of the arteries of democratic government (Rauch 1999).

But Madison understood that eliminating factions was not only impossible (since they sprang from human nature) but would also require unacceptable restrictions on individual liberty. He turned to the design of government as a way of controlling their effects, a "republican remedy" of allowing factions to contest with other factions within rules established by the Constitution and the laws derived from it, a formula that has generally served us well.

Instead of killing philanthropists, the United States took the path of encouraging them, within some minimal restraints. But if the nonprofit sector is now moving into an era where its role and influence will loom large and the reliance of the public on its actions will grow, the delicate balance struck between doing good through the state and doing good through private means will come under increasing stress. As in Madison's day, adding to the legal restrictions placed upon donors—even the relatively innocuous ones under consideration in Congress—risks being ineffective and counterproductive, insofar as the result will be less philanthropy. But how to produce a healthier outcome is a challenge facing philanthropic leaders in the twenty-first century, not only to protect themselves but, at least as important, to maintain the equilibrium of public and private organizations that is so vital to the preservation of democracy.

Note

1. The Sarbanes-Oxley rules of the Public Accounting Reform and Investor Protection Act of 2002, which was co-sponsored by Senator Paul Sarbanes (D-Maryland) and Representative Michael G. Oxley (R-Ohio), require business corporations to adopt stricter procedures for financial reporting and assure that directors provide auditors with certain information about the financial operations of the corporation.

References

Association of Small Foundations. 2003. *Foundation Operations and Management Survey.* Bethesda, Md.: Association of Small Foundations.

Bremner, Robert H. 1988. *American Philanthropy.* 2nd ed. Chicago: University of Chicago Press.

DiPerna, Paula. 2003. *Media, Charity, and Philanthropy in the Aftermath of September 11, 2001.* A Century Foundation Report. New York: The Century Foundation. Available online at http://www.tcf.org/Publications/HomelandSecurity/diperna.pdf.

Everson, Mark. 2005. "The $350 Billion Question: How to Solve the Tax Gap." Written testimony before the Committee on Finance, U.S. Senate, April 14. Available online at http://finance.senate.gov/hearings/statements/metest0411405.pdf

Fleishman, Joel L. 1999. "Public Trust in Not-for-Profit Organizations and the Need for

Regulatory Reform." In *Philanthropy and the Nonprofit Sector,* edited by Charles T. Clotfelter and Thomas Ehrlich, 172–197. Bloomington: Indiana University Press, 1999.

Fremont-Smith, Marion R., and Andres Kosaras. 2003. *Wrongdoing by Officers and Directors of Charities: A Survey of Press Reports, 1995–2002.* Working Paper No. 20, The Hauser Center for Nonprofit Organizations. Cambridge, Mass.: John F. Kennedy School of Government, Harvard University.

Frumkin, Peter. 1999. "Private Foundations as Public Institutions: Regulation, Professionalization, and the Redefinition of Organized Philanthropy." In *Philanthropic Foundations: New Scholarship, New Possibilities,* edited by Ellen Condliffe Lagemann, 69–98. Bloomington: Indiana University Press.

General Accounting Office. 2003. *Vehicle Donations: Benefits to Charities and Donors, but Limited Program Oversight.* Report to the Committee on Finance, U.S. Senate. Washington, D.C.: U.S. General Accounting Office. Available online at http://www.gao.gov/new.items/d0473.pdf.

Gose, Ben. 2004. "Changes at Denver's Daniels Fund: Politics or Prudence?" *The Chronicle of Philanthropy* 16 (February 5): 16.

Hamilton, Alexander, James Madison, and John Jay. 1961. *The Federalist,* edited by Benjamin Fletcher Wright. Cambridge, Mass.: Belknap Press of Harvard University Press.

Independent Sector. 1995. *Giving and Volunteering in the United States.* Washington, D.C.: Independent Sector.

Joint Committee on Taxation. 2005. *Options to Improve Tax Compliance and Reform Tax Expenditures.* Report JCS-2-05. Washington, D.C.: U.S. Congress. Available online at http://www.house.gov/jct/s-2-05.pdf.

Light, Paul C. 2003. "To Give or Not to Give: The Crisis of Confidence in Charities." Policy Brief #7-2003. Washington, D.C.: Brookings Institution.

Machiavelli, Niccolo. 1950. *The Prince and the Discourses.* Translated by Luigi Ricci and Christian E. Detmold. New York: Random House.

Parisi, Michael, and Scott Hollenbeck. 2004. *Individual Income Tax Returns, 2002.* Washington, D.C.: Internal Revenue Service. Available online at http://www.irs.gov/pub/irs-soi/02indtr.pdf.

Rauch, Jonathan. 1999. *Government's End: Why Washington Stopped Working.* New York: Public Affairs Press.

Salamon, Lester M. 2002. "The Resilient Sector: The State of Nonprofit America." In *The State of Nonprofit America,* edited by Lester M. Salamon, 3–61. Washington, D.C.: Brookings Institution, 2002.

Starr, Kevin. 2004. "Foundation of a New Kind of Governance?" *Los Angeles Times,* January 4.

Turley, Jonathan. 2004. "Non-Profits' Executives Avoid Scrutiny, Valid Reforms." *USA Today,* February 13.

Whitten, Melissa. 2001. "Large Nonoperating Private Foundations Panel Study, 1985–1997." Statistics of Income Bulletin. Washington, D.C.: Internal Revenue Service, U.S. Department of the Treasury. Available online at http://www.irs.gov/pub/irs-soi/97pfpanl.pdf.

4 Toward Higher-Impact Philanthropy

Thomas J. Tierney

Philanthropy is a growth business. Over the past two decades the number of foundations has increased nearly threefold; some 3,000 were established in 2002 alone. Donor-advised funds now constitute over $11 billion in assets, up from $2.4 billion in 1985. Single gifts exceeding $5 million used to be unusual; in the past five years there have been at least 963 such "big bets." Total foundation assets in America now top $435 billion, and this is just the beginning.

The healthiest and wealthiest generation the world has ever known is now entering philanthropic prime time. As the baby boomers age, they will be part of a massive onetime wealth transfer estimated to amount to at least $40 trillion (with a possible upside of $88 trillion). This wealth can flow to only three possible destinations: family members (through inheritance), the government (through estate taxes), or nonprofit organizations including foundations (through gifts and bequests). So there will surely be even more philanthropists and more foundations, with even greater assets, giving away more money. Will this influx of philanthropic capital yield dramatically more social impact?

Considering that most donors already want their dollars to make a difference (and certainly don't want to see their hard-earned money go to waste), it's reasonable to wonder why such a question even needs to be asked. After all, leading foundations have long invested in formal evaluations to assess the impact of their grant-making. Today, more and more grant-makers (individuals and institutions both) are pressing their grantees to develop metrics to quantify the results of their programs. Grant-makers themselves are wrestling with what it means to give "strategically." Nevertheless, this question holds for two reasons.

First, and perhaps most obvious, not all philanthropic giving is motivated purely by the desire to achieve results. Donors often make gifts based on perceived community obligations ("doing my share"), personal relationships ("can't say no"), giving back, returning a favor, or felt responsibility ("we need 100 percent participation from the board"). Such gifts may be relatively small (given one's circumstances), as in purchasing a table at a charitable event. Or they may be enormous, as evidenced by the large number of seven- and eight-figure gifts given to universities each year. Either way, the motivation behind the gift is primarily personal. Impact matters, of course, but impact is not the driving force.

Second, achieving and measuring impact is exceptionally difficult with certain types of philanthropy. In the complex world of giving away money, tangible philanthropy—constructing a new medical center, preserving acres of wetlands, endowing a senior center—is as simple as it gets. As donors, we can take pride in our contributions without the nagging suspicion that somehow we didn't get exactly what we paid for.

In contrast, the direct impact of other philanthropic endeavors—funding community health initiatives, sponsoring research on global warming, funding preschool literacy programs—is defiantly difficult to measure. We bet that such gifts and grants will "make a difference," but unlike a construction site, we cannot easily see that difference as it is being made, nor can we be certain that whatever consequences we do see were indeed a direct result of our intervention. This ambiguity and complexity heighten the risk that these philanthropic initiatives will fall short, risk that can be mitigated only through thoughtful and disciplined decision making.

This chapter is directed to philanthropists, be they individual donors or foundation executives, whose efforts are focused on endeavors in which the ambiguity between cause and effect is inescapable and who are nonetheless motivated, first and foremost, by the desire for impact. My hope is that these grant-makers will strive to create a philanthropic analog—call it higher-impact philanthropy—to the continuous improvement so common in the for-profit sector. Successful businesses increase their impact and financial returns by continuously striving to achieve better results with the same or fewer resources. Imagine if, in aggregate, philanthropic grant-making were to become 10 percent more effective? Or 30 percent? By business standards, such ambitions would by no means be considered "stretch goals." Yet for philanthropy's ultimate beneficiaries—children and communities in need, education, the arts, the environment—such an improvement would convert the emerging wealth transfer into a social watershed.

What follows are a few thoughts about how we can begin to capture some of this philanthropic upside. Let me state at the outset that this is very much a work in progress. Unlike other contributors to this volume, I am neither an accomplished philanthropist nor an expert in the field of philanthropy. My perspective derives from my observations and experiences, first with Bain & Company and more recently as the co-founder and chairman of The Bridgespan Group. What I bring to this conversation is a passion for results, a desire to help others succeed, and a willingness to speak frankly about the obstacles to achieving impact that are inherent in philanthropy itself.

A Businessman's View of Philanthropy

Business is the engine of our society's wealth. Business success in turn relies on disciplined, quantifiable, and financially centered bottom-line thinking —crunching numbers and keeping score. Businesspeople adore data: customer data, competitor data, marketplace data, financial data, even data on their own performance from bosses, peers, and direct reports. Mountains of solid data combined with thoughtful, rational decision making are essential to achieving results. The right numbers, correctly crunched, provide a source of competitive advantage, which explains in part why so much time and money is wisely invested in sophisticated information systems and strategic planning exercises.

Not surprisingly, businesspeople-turned-philanthropists often want to apply a similar sort of analytical thinking to their gift-giving. Some have gone as far as investing in research and writing that explain how business principles can be applied to philanthropy (for example, creating quantitative measures to calculate the social returns that nonprofit organizations generate). At the same time, more and more top-ranked MBA programs are developing content related to social enterprise, essentially designed to explore the application of business means to philanthropic ends. So it is fair to assume that as philanthropy continues to grow, fueled by businesspeople and their wealth, there will be more and more momentum to make giving more businesslike and to push foundations to be run more like businesses.

Is this a realistic approach toward higher-impact philanthropy? Yes—and no. There is no question that philanthropy, like all decision making, requires and benefits from the application of good data and sound analysis. But philanthropists motivated primarily by the desire for impact also need a realistic view of the environment in which they and their grantees interact, beginning with the fact that all philanthropy is personal.

It's "My" Money: All Philanthropy Is Personal

No laws mandate generosity. Giving away something that you own is a deeply personal decision based on private beliefs and individual priorities. When people choose to donate their time by volunteering, they are allocating a scarce resource to a cause or organization they care about. The same is true when they give away money (although, for many, time is the more scarce resource). America's 1.4 million nonprofit organizations provide ample evidence of philanthropy's individualistic nature. People give to every conceivable cause, from saving sea turtles to curing cancer. Determining whether youth development initiatives are more important than cultural institutions is up to each individual donor. No such decision is inherently "right" or "wrong."

Because all philanthropy is personal, donors generally want to decide themselves which organizations will receive their gifts. Years ago, most United Ways across the country were forced to introduce donor choice to allow workplace contributors the option of specifying the causes, or even the particular charities, that would receive their money. Growing numbers of community foundations are also discovering the importance of offering donor-advised funds, which allow wealthy contributors to retain significant control over their grant-making. The Fidelity Charitable Gift Fund, launched in 1991, now has almost $3 billion in assets, all under the personal control of individual donors (Fidelity Charitable Gift Fund 2004, 8). In contrast, the total assets of venture philanthropy organizations, which pool funds from wealthy donors and re-grant them to qualified nonprofits, amount to less than $400 million (Community Wealth Ventures, Inc. 2002, 33). Apparently donors are not lining up to outsource their philanthropic decision making, however much merit this approach to giving may have.

When institutions replace individuals as the source of funds, philanthropy's personal taproots do not disappear, even though they are seldom discussed publicly. In family-dominated foundations, for example, directors naturally feel a certain sense of ownership of the institution's assets, and their interests and worldviews are likely to influence the focus and nature of its grants. Professionally staffed foundations typically have well-defined institutional priorities and processes, yet their program managers often have considerable discretionary latitude in proposing grants, as do the executive directors who ultimately decide what will go before the board. Since many of these officers are recruited on the basis of their expertise and experience, this institutional confidence in their judgment is not at all surprising. But neither should it be surprising that many day-to-day decisions about how much to give, and to whom, naturally bear the stamp of the decision makers themselves.

One could argue that the authority vested in program officers and foundation executives and their boards is similar to that vested in business leaders. However, there is one profound difference: unlike businesses, foundations exist largely in a world of self-imposed accountability and limited consequences.

Structural Realities: A School without Grades

Business executives are accountable to their stakeholders for delivering both short- and long-term results. These results take many forms, most of them quantifiable. Financial results encompass measures such as earnings per share, return on assets, and revenue growth. Strategic results may include market share gains, customer loyalty, and the relative price and quality of competing product lines. Operational results include everything from employee retention to research and development productivity to cost performance. A corporation may have dozens of such metrics, subsumed within one another, which cascade down from the chief executive's office through various layers of management. If, over time, individual executives "make their numbers," they are rewarded with money and promotions. If they continually fall short, they are eventually replaced. Human resource professionals, financial departments, and strategic planning units assist this process by collecting and organizing useful information. Managers cannot hide from the facts (at least not for long).

Nor can they escape the harsh realities of the marketplace. If they do not satisfy their customers, they lose them to competitors. If their prices are too high for the value delivered, they lose. If they cannot attract and retain top talent, they lose. If they cannot innovate, they lose. Winning and losing have a direct impact on both the company and its executives; the two are highly correlated. Business leaders make decisions, take risks, and learn from their mistakes. The "invisible hand" of capitalism drives toward continuous improvement, whether or not organizations and their managers want to change.

None of these dynamics apply to the world of philanthropy.

In philanthropy, accountability for delivering results is not imposed by the external pressure of customers, competitors, or marketplace dynamics. Most foundations are established in perpetuity; unlike businesses, they literally cannot fail. The only requirements they must satisfy are to give away a minimum amount of money each year (5 percent of assets) and to maintain a "reasonable" cost structure. Any further accountability is entirely self-imposed. If grantors want to pursue excellence, fine. If they become satisfied with mediocrity, that is also fine. Performance objectives, if any, are established on the basis of internal motivation rather than external forces, which, again, tends to make even institutional philanthropy highly personal.

Self-imposed accountability is not a natural act. It requires extraordinary determination and discipline to pursue outstanding results year after year when those results are not, in fact, being demanded by the surrounding environment. Such behavior is like striving for straight A's in a school without grades or exercising aggressively every day simply because you know it is the right thing to do. And it is especially unnatural in the absence of data. Imagine working your heart out to achieve straight A's (in that school without grades) and then discovering that all your report cards read "Incomplete: Inadequate Information." This is the world in which much of philanthropy takes place: grant-making results are extremely difficult to measure. The impact of those grants may not be evident until years later, and even then causality may be hard to determine. For example, suppose a youngster enrolled in an inner-city mentoring program becomes a successful pediatrician. It's likely that the mentoring program contributed to this outcome, but how much it contributed and whether it was the critical factor and whether the outcome would have been the same had the youngster not been enrolled are questions impossible to answer.

While philanthropists may experience a dearth of hard facts, however, there is no shortage of feedback. The old saying that once a person becomes a philanthropist or foundation executive he has had his last bad meal and told his last bad joke has more than a kernel of truth. When you are in the business of giving away money, people have a tendency to tell you what they think you want to hear. Surrounded by smiling faces and awash in reassuring rhetoric, it's natural for even the most objective and disciplined grant-makers to begin to feel important, to think they really are achieving outstanding results. Personal incentives are surreptitiously aligned: grant-makers want to feel good about their activities, and current and potential grantees need to be liked if they hope to secure future funding. Without hard facts to intrude, the insidious nature of feel-good philanthropy can overwhelm the most well-intentioned individuals.

The result of these structural forces is a profound disconnect between grant-makers and the consequences of their decisions. On the downside, extraordinary philanthropic achievements are rarely identified, much less rewarded. On the upside, failures appear to be almost nonexistent. How many foundations identify failures, much less analyze the root causes of failure and actively communicate that understanding to various constituencies? When did you last hear about a program manager or foundation executive being fired because the impact of her grant-making fell below expectations? Or rewarded because he achieved exceptional results? Individuals may strive diligently for A's, but the consequences are often the same whether the ultimate grade is an A or a D.

Moreover, the absence of direct consequences undermines the potential for learning. Many people (and especially businesspeople) learn through the compounding experience of trial and error. In the 1990s, the advent of so-called learning organizations illustrated the importance of designing feedback loops within businesses that would nurture learning and thereby improve performance. While consequences motivate learning, information and feedback enable it. The shortage of both undermines the ability of philanthropists and foundations to systematically improve the effectiveness of their grant-making.

Behavior that Undermines Results

The consequences of these philanthropic realities—the primacy of personal beliefs and values, the absence of external marketplace disciplines, the dearth of reliable feedback—are both understandable and unfortunate. On the one hand, they reinforce some perfectly natural assumptions and behavior on the part of grant-makers. On the other hand, those assumptions and behavior often lead to grant-making practices which diminish the grantees' ability to achieve results. The net effect is that many philanthropists and foundations inadvertently undermine the social impact they set out to achieve.

Role Confusion: Acting Like a Principal

Achieving social impact requires a complex network of players that includes direct service organizations, their constituents, and the sources (public, private, or both) from which they receive their funding. Philanthropic gifts and grants help supply the raw material that fuels this system, but with few exceptions (for example, operating foundations that deliver programs themselves), foundations and individual philanthropists are not principals, but intermediaries whose impact depends almost entirely on the impact of the organizations they choose to fund. Nevertheless, most grant-makers think of themselves as principals. They have their own priorities and points of view. They have their own goals bolstered by their knowledge of the fields in which they give. And it is *their* money. They may even use the language of principals, calling themselves "investors," which implies legal ownership, or "partners," which implies co-ownership and shared destiny with the grantees.

This role confusion often gets played out in common grant-making practices. For example, many foundations focus their grant-making on specific program goals and provide restricted grants with only minimal support, at best, for overhead costs. They have their own strategies with their own objectives, and their grants often contain explicit milestones independent of those of their grantees. This behavior is perfectly natural, and yet implicit in it is a handful of dubious assumptions: that the foundation is more knowledgeable than the grantee and can therefore add significant programmatic value; that the foundation's strategy is more important and better designed than the grantee's; and that the foundation's behavior will in no way undermine the effectiveness of the grantee.

In some situations, these assumptions may be entirely valid, but often they are unwarranted. For example, when a wealthy new foundation was launched a few years back, it recruited a cadre of very bright people, all of whom lacked deep knowledge or experience in the fields to be addressed. Over the course of a year, the foundation executives designed a "breakthrough" strategy and then identified potential grantees who they thought might execute their objectives. Prospective grantees were asked to explain what they could do to serve the foundation's needs, independent of their own strategic ambitions or cumulative knowledge. The nonprofits, chronically in need of funding, went along, creating compelling proposals even when those initiatives conflicted with their existing priorities. The unstated message from the foundation was clear, and clearly received: "If you want any of our money, you'd best do things our way."

By insisting on acting like a principal with control rather than an intermediary with influence, this foundation diminished its own impact. The foundation's executives were not more knowledgeable than its grantees, who had hundreds of years of cumulative experience in the field. The foundation's strategy was both untested and lacking in clarity. Worst of all, by demanding that grantees conform to its needs (as opposed to supporting its grantees' capabilities), the foundation actually undermined the strategies of the organizations it was trying to support. This was not a "partnership" of equal players with aligned incentives. It was money throwing its weight around to the apparent detriment of the causes it was hoping to serve.

Going It Alone

Given its inherently personal nature, it is not surprising that philanthropy is seldom a team sport. Or that the benefactors of newly formed foundations tend to want to do things "their way." When one billionaire established his foundation, for example, he was convinced that many of the current approaches to helping disadvantaged young people were flawed and that he could come up with a better idea. Nothing could be as natural as a confident, successful, and wealthy executive believing in the potential to innovate and add value. But the lack of data, tremendous complexity, long time frames, and absence of market forces can easily confuse the boundary between "breakthrough" ideas and "broken" ideas.

Rarely does a new entrant to philanthropy take the time to leverage the experience of others by assessing, rigorously and objectively, what has worked in a particular field and what has not. Not only would such an exercise be costly, it might be inconclusive—and conflict with the grantor's personal beliefs or desires. The result seems to be a natural tendency to reinvent the wheel rather than seek out and support those wheels that are more or less proven to deliver impact.

This country's collective love affair with charitable start-ups is evident in the statistics: on average, about 30,000 new nonprofit organizations are established in the United States each year (The Independent Sector 2001). On one hand, this offers wonderful evidence of civil society in action; on the other, it is unlikely there are 30,000 new social problems each year—much less tens of thousands of brand new, never-tried-before breakthrough ideas. The bias toward entrepreneurship has driven the reported number of nonprofit organizations from 800,000 in 1980 to about 1.4 million today (ibid.). And while those numbers are certainly overstated (since nonprofits with annual revenues below $25,000 are not required to file forms with the IRS and can therefore remain on the registry of tax-exempt organizations even if they are inactive or defunct), the increase is considerable.

The irony in this behavior is unmistakable. In business, everyone recognizes that it is much riskier to invest in start-ups than in proven entities: just compare the relative economics and performance measures of venture capital with those of private equity. It is hard to see why the same principle wouldn't apply in the nonprofit sector, indicating that the riskiest grants—that is, those with the lowest probability of impact—are the ones that go to unproven, early-stage organizations.

For their part, foundations seem to be as independent-minded as individual philanthropists. They may convene, but they rarely collaborate. When asked why he wouldn't contribute to an outstanding potential grantee which clearly fit with his foundation's priorities, one well-respected program officer replied, "Well, that's not my deal; it's being led by another foundation." The foundation world has many examples of reciprocity: "You contribute to my grantee and I'll contribute to yours." However, there are few examples of genuine collaboration: foundations joining forces to address a problem that requires more resources than any one of them alone can possibly provide. Even knowledge that might inform others' efforts (such as program evaluations and reports) tends to be shared only rarely.

Underestimating and Underinvesting

The old saying that "everything in life takes longer and costs more than you expect" should resonate particularly strongly for philanthropists. And yet the median grant made by America's larger foundations is less than $50,000, while the average duration is less than eighteen months (although many are renewed; The Foundation Center 2004).[1] How many social problems can be solved with $50,000 over eighteen months? Not many, I would venture to say. Small grants can certainly create social impact: consider the value of a college scholarship to a deserving youth. But problems arise when complex social problems are confronted with what, in context, are relatively tiny resources.

Consider the Annenberg Challenge. In 1993, Ambassador Walter Annenberg committed $500 million to help transform America's public schools. His unprecedented gift produced more than $600 million in matching funds from foundations, businesses, governments, and others. It also supported a host of reforms ranging from the creation of new urban schools to increased professional development opportunities for teachers. But in 2002, in a commentary as courageous as it was candid (given how tempting it is for philanthropy to declare victory and move on), the Annenberg Foundation itself described the results of the challenge as mixed. While $500 million was a gigantic sum in the world of philanthropy, it paled in comparison to the budgets of the large urban school districts (such as New York City's $11.4 billion) it sought to transform.

This mismatch between the resources that are required to get the job done and the grant-making dollars that are actually available is far from atypical. Save the oceans for $5 million per year. Change national technology policy for $1.5 million per year. Transform the K–12 education system for $3 million per year. The problem is neither the objective nor the resources but the mismatch between the two. In the absence of a rigorous understanding of the problem, clarity about the impact they intend to achieve, and a pragmatic understanding of how that impact will be accomplished, philanthropists can easily fall prey to wishful thinking and the seductive allure of feel-good philanthropy, which is all the more alarming given the propensity of foundations to go it alone.

Philanthropy's natural tendency to underinvest in programs (or to overreach one's resources) is complemented by pervasive underinvestment in capacity-building. In the business world, it is widely understood that the effectiveness of an organization depends on the capacity of its people (their mutual commitment and capability), its processes and systems (from financial management to human resources to technology), and the resources at its disposal. In *Good to Great,* Jim Collins (2001) rigorously analyzed thousands of corporations to uncover the ingredients that permitted a few "good" companies to become "great" companies. He concluded that no single element of success is more important than the quality and fit of the individuals in the organization. Average performers, it turns out, deliver average results; great results demand more.

Collins articulates an insight that is often repeated in business schools, boardrooms, and private equity firms. Achieving excellence requires an excellent organization. In most businesses, most of the time, people matter most. Or, as I observed in *Aligning the Stars* (Lorsch and Tierney 2002), "The people you pay are more important than the people who pay you" (64). This may be the one business principal that transfers directly from the for-profit to the nonprofit world.

Yet it is a principle that philanthropists (most of whom earned their money in business) generally ignore. Only 20 percent of foundation grants are unrestricted, available to support whatever costs (organizational and programmatic) the grantee thinks are necessary. The vast majority of grantees strive to limit "overhead" (that is, organizational) expenses, in part because nonprofits are penalized if their overhead burden appears out of line. Grant-makers send an unambiguous signal (backed up by money): do not invest to recruit, retain, and develop the best people. Do not invest in the infrastructure necessary to support those people. Do not focus executive time and energy on management and organization-building. In other words, deliver exceptional programmatic impact on the cheap—and do it year after year.

Does this make sense if you genuinely want to pursue higher-impact philanthropy? I think not. But there is a natural tendency to try to avoid "wasting" scarce philanthropic assets on "overhead." And because we can evaluate a nonprofit's costs far more definitively—and easily—than its actual results, we resort to measuring and minimizing inputs rather than maximizing the outputs those inputs create.

The Added Costs of Philanthropic Capital

Just as businesses incur a "cost of capital," nonprofit organizations pay a price for the money they raise. The true costs of fund-raising, however, are rarely as modest as the 20 cents (or less) on the dollar that many of the better nonprofits report. Under certain selected circumstances, such figures may reflect reality. More often, they provide only a baseline of direct and measurable costs onto which must be added the indirect costs that philanthropists and foundations (despite their generally good intentions) often impose. These indirect costs, registered in the form of management disruption, organizational constraints, and strategic distractions, are never quantified, much less reported. Yet they erode the value of each philanthropic dollar, just as water flowing through a corroded pipe imperceptibly seeps away. And whereas a nonprofit may be able to reduce the direct expenses associated with development (for example, by attracting, inspiring, and retaining wealthy board members), these indirect costs are far less tractable because of the imbalance in power between those who have money and those who need it.

Grantees are seldom in a position to negotiate aggressively with potential contributors the way a business would with its capital providers. Their unending need for charitable funding generally requires them to accept whatever terms and conditions major contributors impose, even if those demands are costly and disruptive. Because these burdens are invisible to the grant-maker, however, few foundations strive to mitigate the unintended costs of their dollars. On the contrary, what is costly to the grantee is free to the philanthropist, which provides little incentive for behavior modification.

The tragicomedy that played out when a small but growing nonprofit approached a well-endowed foundation for a "significant" grant vividly illustrates the cost of management disruption. The program manager was encouraging, assuring the executive director that the foundation respected her organization and that its mission was congruent with the foundation's program priorities. Enthused, the executive director scheduled additional meetings and prepared pitch materials, actively involving the two other members of her senior team, who were equally excited about the $250,000 they desperately needed and hoped to receive.

Months went by, during which foundation staff cancelled and postponed meetings while the nonprofit responded to a barrage of requests ranging from evaluation reports to rewritten grant proposals. Fourteen months later, the final proposal was submitted. As the foundation's board prepared to meet, the friendly and supportive program manager called the executive director and said that things were "going well," although "it doesn't look like we will be able to come up with the full $250,000 during this grant-making cycle." Heartbroken, but still hopeful, the executive director had no choice but to go along.

Two months went by without a word, and then a letter arrived, promising "exciting" news: the foundation's board had unanimously supported an initial grant of $50,000 and "was open to entertaining additional requests once the nonprofit was able to demonstrate results." The letter went on to request detailed annual evaluations of the programs, ongoing financial reports to ensure that overhead costs were being contained, and semi-annual progress reports. The executive director didn't know whether to laugh or cry.

Aside from money, senior management time is a nonprofit's most scarce resource. Small executive teams, limited infrastructure, and modest staff levels place enormous daily burdens on executive directors and their direct reports—burdens that the most well-intentioned foundations can unwittingly exacerbate. Grant proposals are written and rewritten, while grant-making decisions stretch over multiple quarters (and even years). In an effort to measure program results, funders impose elaborate systems to complement existing forms of compliance, but measuring the immeasurable can become quite time consuming. Meetings are called and groups are convened to discuss progress. Foundations generously pay for their grantees' travel expenses but overlook the cost of all those hours. The grantees' payroll accounting systems never report the true cost incurred, and because these hours are "free" to foundation executives, they are easily taken for granted. Nonprofits are in no position to complain, however, even if they are forced to invest massive amounts of time to comply with the demands of multiple donors, because those relationships are essential for future funding.

In addition to depleting management time, foundations often impose constraints that hamstring the entire organization. As noted earlier, foundations strongly prefer funding specific programs to providing unrestricted operating support, and as a general rule, grant-makers prefer that their grantees minimize overhead costs. Even when these preferences are not explicitly stated, they have a profound impact on nonprofits and their boards, who automatically assume that any costs not directly associated with programs are undesirable and, as such, ought to be minimized. For example, many nonprofits, perhaps most, would view the addition of a chief operating officer as a discretionary overhead cost that increases staffing levels. Yet that "cost" might well yield a significant net benefit if, as a consequence, the organization becomes more productive and efficient—freeing up more of the executive director's time for fund-raising, for instance.

Grant-makers' intense bias against "overhead" costs reinforces the natural inclination of nonprofit leaders to concentrate on service delivery rather than management and organizational capacity-building (or what one executive director disdainfully referred to as "administrivia"). Taken together, the absence of both funding and attention from leaders means that expenditures associated with people, systems, and internal management processes are kept to bare minimums. Bookkeepers are hired when chief financial officers are required. Individuals rarely receive regular performance reviews, much less development and training. With limited recruiting budgets, organizations are forced to hire whomever they can and then hope that each person can be motivated and capable enough to perform well. So-called capacity-building is viewed as an unaffordable luxury rather than what it is—an undeniable necessity.

Strategic distraction is the last but not least of the indirect costs of philanthropic capital. Strategy is the allocation of scarce resources to achieve desired results. Like foundations, which attempt to use their assets in ways that will lead to certain desired outcomes, nonprofits also have strategies (although these are often not as rigorous or explicit as they might be). Nonprofits almost always confront severe financial and organizational constraints to pursuing their strategies, however. And unlike endowed foundations, they have to both raise annual funds and implement programs. A foundation can "waste" resources without any direct consequences to the institution or its executives (and quite possibly without even knowing that the resources were indeed wasted). But if a nonprofit wastes its resources, it not only impairs its ability to attract future funding but also handicaps its ability to serve its constituents. The more a nonprofit's strategy is disrupted, the less likely it is that it will deliver impact.

Whenever grant-makers impose their strategic imperatives on grantees, they run the risk of eroding impact. Given limited resources, organizations must make choices about what they will do and what they *won't* do. Saying "no" is as important as saying "yes." Because the top priority of most nonprofits is funding, however, they find it impossible to say "no" to funders, even if a particular grant is somewhat inconsistent with their strategy. In fact, in order to appeal to the widest possible set of funders, a broad (or sometimes even ill-defined) strategy can be helpful, because it allows donors with different priorities to add their own pieces to the organization's crazy quilt of activities. Focus may be essential for allocating resources and delivering results, but it can complicate fund-raising; and ultimately fund-raising effectiveness is even more essential, because without money there are no programs.

The fundamental illogic of this approach emerges sharply when you contrast it with private equity investing. A private equity firm's most valued asset is its deal flow, its access to top-notch investment opportunities. Private equity partners build networks of relationships designed to attract outstanding companies. What matters to the company's owners are the deal terms, the potential value added by the private equity firm, and the personal chemistry that is essential for an effective partnership. It is inherently a sellers' market: everyone's money is green. Imagine if a private equity firm in pursuit of high returns imposed significant indirect costs on potential portfolio companies. Imagine if its partners disrupted the management teams, directed their invested funds away from organizational expenses, and imposed their strategic perspectives on the company's management. With behavior like that it would not be long before the best deals went elsewhere. In a dynamic market, costly behaviors lead to undesirable outcomes.

In contrast, philanthropy is a buyers' market. Philanthropists and foundations hold all the cards; nonprofits must comply with whatever indirect costs are imposed upon them. Of course, they can always seek other sources of funding. Yet the prevalence of small short-term grants (and the unlikely odds of generating truly sustainable fee-related income) leaves most nonprofits ready to pay whatever price is necessary to raise the cash required to cover annual expenses and deliver much-needed services. An exorbitant cost of capital becomes simply business as usual.

Moving toward Higher-Impact Philanthropy

Anyone can give money away. The simple act of writing checks or approving grants demands no particular skill, rigor, or accountability, yet it is virtually guaranteed to generate recognition, praise, and goodwill. Thankful beneficiaries need their benefactors to feel appreciated; hopeful beneficiaries need to position themselves for future grants. So the cycle of high-cost, feel-good philanthropy is perpetuated, occasionally netting social results but often falling short.

Breaking this cycle begins at home: in a sense, motive matters most. Philanthropists who are genuinely committed to increasing the impact of their grants and gifts accept that *how* they give is as important as *what* they give to. They supplement their own opinions and perspectives with the best facts available and (if need be) pay more attention to the latter than the former. They place their grantees' needs and strategies ahead of (or at least on par with) their own. They subordinate the understandable inclination to act like principals to playing the less-glamorous role of financial intermediary. They combine the excitement and appeal of supporting programs with the more mundane activity of building capacity. Such logical (but by no means natural) acts are essential if higher impact really is the primary objective.

A commitment to higher-impact philanthropy also requires a willingness to bet on future outcomes, outcomes over which the donor has limited control. The bigger the bet (in the context of one's overall resources), however, the greater the risk; so, not surprisingly, some donors try to reduce the risk by making relatively small grants to numerous grantees. The implicit premise is that by spreading resources this way, donors will minimize the downside of any particular bad bet. In actuality, small tentative commitments may often be the riskiest bets of all, because they sustain chronically undercapitalized organizations, which, in turn, underperform and struggle to deliver results.

In contrast to this "peanut butter" approach to philanthropy, donors committed first and foremost to impact are likely to make fewer, bigger grants over longer periods of time. Such grant-making is grounded in the belief that focus matters and that enduring impact cannot be achieved overnight. For example, the Edna McConnell Clark Foundation devotes its resources to a relatively small network of high-potential youth development organizations. Ray Chambers has concentrated his Amelior Foundation for years on revitalizing Newark, New Jersey, and expanding youth mentorship nationwide. Mario Marino has focused the portfolio of Venture Philanthropy Partners on a handful of promising nonprofits in Washington, D.C. The Pisces Foundation has concentrated on developing and expanding KIPP academies. Variances in scale notwithstanding, all these philanthropists are big bettors.

Mitigating the risks inherent in big bets like these requires a rigorous approach: strategy, anchored in objective facts, is essential to guiding resource allocation and decision making. So is the discipline to say "no," repeatedly, to enticing possibilities that don't fit the strategic imperatives. Intensive (and relatively costly) due diligence is necessary to vet opportunities before bets are placed. There is no free lunch: generating above-average impact requires an above-average investment of time and money in the grant-making process. Instead of considering these costs as a necessary evil, however, it is more useful to think of them as assets—essential inputs designed to maximize returns. Spending more time on due diligence is wise as long as such incremental investment generates better decisions with a higher probability of future impact.

That brings us to a final issue: the chronic philanthropic conundrum of measuring impact. As noted earlier, in many philanthropic endeavors, measuring the direct impact of a particular grant is virtually impossible. Established foundations spend millions of dollars on sophisticated assessments that attempt to evaluate the efficacy of particular social programs and still the findings are often ambiguous. Just because a direct return on investment cannot be quantified, however, doesn't mean the investment should be foregone. It simply requires developing approaches that address the inherent ambiguity in measuring results.

For an analogy, consider television advertisements. Each year U.S. companies spend billions of dollars on television ads. Marketers can crunch numbers that provide approximate indications of how many people saw a particular advertisement. Detailed sales tracking can identify purchasing patterns before, during, and after the ad campaign. Sophisticated mathematical models can calibrate "spend effectiveness." Yet despite a degree of precision which would have been unimaginable twenty years ago, measuring the effectiveness of advertising is still something of an art.

Philanthropists can also use imperfect proxies—and judgment—to assess impact. An organization's strength, reputation in its field, quality of services, and cost per unit of service can all be calibrated on a relative basis—relative to similar organizations and/or relative to the organization itself over time. Likewise, while we may not be able to measure precisely the return on investment for a particular grant, we can certainly develop an informed point of view about whether an organization is—or is not—performing well. The bigger the bet, the more important such performance indicators become.

Moving toward higher-impact philanthropy is challenging but not impossible. After five years of experience in this arena, my own understanding of these dynamics is at best incomplete. Nevertheless, I am certain of one truth: society deserves, and desperately needs, philanthropists and foundations to increase the real impact of our giving. Satisfactory underperformance, complacency, and "feel-good" philanthropy notwithstanding, our own lives will be just fine. It is others who will suffer unnecessarily as a consequence of philanthropy as usual. This is our opportunity. And because all philanthropy is personal, it is also our choice.

Notes

This chapter is based on a presentation to the Philanthropy Discussion Series organized by the Center for Social Innovation at Stanford University in May 2004.

1. Based on grants of $10,000 or more awarded by a national sample of 1,005 larger U.S. foundations (including 800 of the 1,000 largest ranked by total giving). For community foundations, only discretionary grants are included. Grants to individuals are not included in the sample.

References

Collins, Jim. 2001. *Good to Great.* New York: HarperCollins.

Community Wealth Ventures, Inc. 2002. *Venture Philanthropy 2002: Advancing Nonprofit Performance through High-Engagement Grantmaking.* Washington, D.C.: Venture Philanthropy Partners.

Fidelity Charitable Gift Fund. 2004. *Annual Report, 2004.* Boston: Fidelity Charitable Gift Fund.

The Independent Sector. 2001. *The New Non-Profit Almanac in Brief.* Washington, D.C.: The Independent Sector. Available online at http://www.independentsector.org/PDFs/inbrief.pdf.

Lorsch, Jay W., and Thomas J. Tierney. 2002. *Aligning the Stars.* Boston: Harvard Business School Press.

5   The Lonely Profession

Laura Horn and Howard Gardner

Grantmaking seems like the ideal job. You earn a comfortable living by distributing large sums of other people's money. You work in a plush office with resources to fly around the world collecting the information you need to carry out your responsibility. People hang on your every word, laugh at your jokes, and treat you like royalty because they want the funds that you control. You don't have to raise money or worry about the bottom line, and, barring gross malfeasance, there is little risk of being fired. You work on difficult social, political, or scholarly problems from a place of relative luxury and can feel good about yourself at the end of the day for your efforts to change society. Framed in this way, the job of a grantmaker sounds idyllic.

In truth, the life of the professional grantmaker is not as serene as it sounds. Our study has concluded that the current environment in organized philanthropy makes it difficult to find lasting satisfaction from one's philanthropic work. Professional grantmakers support other people's work by giving away other people's money and cannot legitimately take credit for the work they fund or for the generosity of the philanthropic donor. Many grantmakers feel isolated from the public, their grantees, and their professional colleagues. The structure of philanthropy as a whole provides little grounding for its professional grantmakers.

Perhaps as a result of these conditions, most program officers and foundation executives do not approach philanthropy as a career. They do not plan to work in philanthropy, and once they are there, they do not plan to stay forever. Rather than allowing philanthropy alone to define their professional lives, the grantmakers and executives we interviewed take three different stances toward the field. They view philanthropy as a continuation of their established career, an opportunity to pursue a specific agenda of personal importance, or an opportunity to take a broad look at the world. Philanthropy does not define their work; under optimal conditions, philanthropy enhances it.

This characterization cries out for a comparative perspective. Typically, professionals in other domains feel called to enter their respective fields and work hard to get there. They go through a period of training to develop the competencies required to be accepted as members of the profession. In contrast to grantmakers, most of whom maintain a sense of professional identity independent of philanthropy, doctors, lawyers, journalists, and scientists typically view their chosen professions as a lifelong career, feel passionate about their work, and—under normal circumstances—remain committed to carrying out the mission and upholding the standards of the profession throughout their working lives. While each profession inevitably presents obstacles that professionals must overcome to do work that they feel good about, practitioners normally stay rooted in the ideals of their professions, even in the face of these challenges (Gardner, Csikszentmihalyi, and Damon 2001).

Our assertion that grantmakers do not identify with philanthropy in the way that other professionals identify with their respective fields stems from research conducted at the GoodWork Project. For the past decade, researchers at the project have studied workers in a variety of professions. Through in-depth interviews with leading professionals, the investigators have probed the psychology of those who strive to carry out work that is both excellent and ethical and the circumstances under which this dual sense of good work can best be achieved. We asked about the goals of these individuals, the obstacles they regularly confront, the strategies they have developed to deal with these pressures, and their perspectives on the field in general. So far, we have conducted interviews with approximately 1,200 leading practitioners in genetics, journalism, law, business, higher education, theater, medicine, and philanthropy.

In what follows, we take a detailed look at a cross-section of those involved with philanthropy: program officers and executives employed by medium to large private foundations. Throughout this chapter, the term "grantmaker" refers specifically to this group of philanthropic professionals. Our analysis draws primarily from interviews with seventeen leading figures in traditional organized philanthropy. It is informed as well by the large sample of data collected in our recent study of good work in philanthropy and by our interviews with professionals in other realms.

Evidence of Professional Identity

In comparison with those in other professions, we noticed distinct features in the way grantmakers talk about themselves in relation to the field as a whole. In stark contrast to the doctors, lawyers, journalists, scientists, and actors for whom entering their professional fields often represents the fulfillment of a dream and a source of pride, grantmaking is typically an unplanned occupational shift rather than a career decision.

For many professionals, the formation of a professional identity begins when they choose to pursue a specific profession, well before they become members of their chosen profession. Many describe their professional work as a calling, much like this lawyer's explanation of his choice to go into criminal law:

> I didn't know there was anything else. . . . It was just not something I ever really thought hard about. . . . It was not even something I would have given a second thought to. . . . I think I was born to be a defense attorney. . . . It's just, I think, part of my personality.

Grantmakers and foundation executives do not plan to go into philanthropy, as do their counterparts in other professions. They describe "backing into" the field or ending up in philanthropy by "accident."

> I would say time out of mind, people who go into philanthropy not only weren't prepared for it, but weren't even thinking about it. They were running their deanship or their department chairmanship or doing something, running a little nonprofit, and some foundation taps them on the shoulder and says, "We want you to come in and join us."

None of the program officers or foundation executives that we interviewed planned a career in philanthropy; rather, the opportunity to enter the field presented itself unexpectedly as they were pursuing other work. A well-known foundation executive describes his entry into the field of philanthropy.

> I stumbled into this. I only had the vaguest understanding that there was even such a profession as philanthropy when I was going to graduate school. Of course I'd heard of the Ford Foundation and a few other foundations, but I had only a dim understanding of what in fact they did. . . . It's the sort of thing when you do a lot of other things and then an opportunity arises and you can go into it.

A few of the grantmakers we interviewed framed their unexpected encounter with philanthropy as a lucky turn of events.

> What I find interesting is the idealistic sense of trying to make the world a better place. And I never dreamed I would be doing it from [name of foundation]. I always thought I would be doing it as an activist in the community. And then I just got terribly lucky and ended up here.

More commonly, however, grantmakers accepted positions in philanthropy with some reluctance, like the following three grantmakers.

> I wasn't sure about coming to the [name of foundation]. I had not dealt much with foundations. I didn't have a very high opinion of foundations. I mean, in the issues I cared about . . . they were not necessarily working in some of the concerns that I had. . . . I didn't necessarily want to be here; it was not my ideal to come here.

Another said:

> Well, I was a really hard sell, as the story goes around here, because I turned them down a couple times. I had always wanted to be a professor. . . . I had an endowed professorship with tenure and a young family . . . and that's what I wanted to retire doing.

A third grantmaker said:

> I had never had an ambition to become a foundation person. While I had been successful at raising foundation money, it was not a world that I knew well or admired

particularly. The opportunity to head this foundation came along at a time when I was ready for a move.

Professional Stance

Most grantmakers do not identify with philanthropy as a career in itself. They approach philanthropy on their own terms, with an independent sense of how philanthropy fits into their identity as professionals. We found three common stances that grantmakers take toward the field. They view philanthropy as a continuation of their established career, as an opportunity to pursue a specific agenda of personal importance, or as an opportunity to look broadly at the world.

An Established Career

Some grantmakers have a career identity in a different field before entering philanthropy and regard philanthropy as a variation on their previous work rather than a different profession altogether. These individuals view their grantmaking work as one phase of their career in a different field such as academia, law, education, or public policy.

Some of these grantmakers work in philanthropy as a hiatus from their primary career. They either work in philanthropy temporarily before moving back to the field in which they were trained or they work in philanthropy at the end of their career as a way to influence their field more broadly before retiring. Consider one participant, who spent most of her professional life at a liberal arts college as a professor and administrator before accepting a grantmaking position in a foundation.

> I think that philanthropy in general probably wouldn't have attracted me. It was what this foundation did. . . . I've been trying to do good within the liberal arts college sector for all of my life because I deeply believe in it as the very best way to educate the young. And I just see this as an extension of that work. It's just that I'm able to do it more broadly.

Others in this group work in philanthropy indefinitely but remain strongly grounded in their previous career.

> There is, I think, a strong connection between what I did before and what I do now. I was an educator for 25 years before I started doing foundation work, and for the first dozen years here, in addition to being the president of the foundation, I was also the higher education program officer. . . . I don't do that anymore, but that was obviously a very nice thread from my career in education through my work in philanthropy.

Later in the interview, he said:

> I think it helps to have had another career before you do this work so that this does not become your identity. . . . [I have] a pretty healthy sense of self that if I

couldn't do this tomorrow, that would be fine. I'd go do something else. I don't need [name of foundation] to define who I am.

Another participant presented a model of what he thinks a philanthropic career should be. His ideal captures the professional stance of grantmakers in this first group.

> I don't think [philanthropy] should be a career track. The career should be the content of what you're doing. And one of the roles that you can play in it, one of the jobs you can have, is in philanthropy. Let me use an example here. . . . I don't think a person should come to a foundation to be a program director in philanthropy. Somebody should come to the foundation to be a program director in health. And through that, they continue their commitment to their career goals of improving health practices, or whatever they are, and they play a role from the perspective of philanthropy. So to make my case the strongest is to say that a person should not come to philanthropy too early because you do need an experience base and to have chosen a career and have found those commitments and the path you want to pursue. And secondly, you should not stay that long. You either come into your career and retire, or somewhere in the middle of your career, and then take all of what you've learned in philanthropy and go back to, say, another role in the field. . . . And if a person's well-grounded in their field through doing their work, then they have a chance to broaden their view significantly for a decade in philanthropy, he may be better positioned to go back and provide leadership to that field.

A Specific Agenda

Other grantmakers dedicate their professional lives to pursuing a personal mission and approach their work in philanthropy as one of many ways to advance that mission. They come to philanthropy with a specific agenda such as "encouraging youth involvement in communities" and act as if they could leave philanthropy at any time to pursue their agenda elsewhere. A grantmaker illustrates this type of professional stance in the following passage:

> My work is an expression of what I believe and what I value. That's what guides me. In other words, like I said earlier, if I weren't doing it here, I wouldn't have the [name of foundation] money to do it, but I would find another way to do some version of what I'm doing. It's a privilege to have this opportunity, but it's my values that are guiding that. . . . So wherever I wanted to work, I wanted to do something for those who were . . . dispossessed, if you will, who have been left out.

For these grantmakers, philanthropy serves as an opportunity to enact values or carry out goals that are not directly related to philanthropy.

> The way the [name of foundation] works is that they bring in program officers to help shape the priorities, not just to carry out some already shaped priorities. So I had a chance to emphasize things that I thought were important. . . . And the whole notion of an experimentalist world of solving problems, of being eternally optimistic, of being committed to democratic processes, that's who I think I am. And this was an opportunity. Being in the foundation was an opportunity to put those values into programmatic form.

A Broad Perspective

In a third approach to philanthropic work, grantmakers enter philanthropy because it allows them to apply their ability to think broadly and pursue wide-ranging interests. They see themselves as generalists, and philanthropy allows them to maintain a broad perspective on the world. Some have been trained in a specific discipline and want to widen their focus. They use philanthropy as a way to step back from their narrow discipline, to "see across the fray" and take a broad look at the world before moving on to other work.

> I had intended to become an academic. And then for one reason or another, I decided I didn't want to be an academic. I wasn't all that interested after a certain age in disciplinary research, which was—I felt that was what you had to do. Now if I had any sense, I can see now that you can make your way [in academia] without necessarily doing narrow disciplinary research, but I didn't understand that at the time. . . . So I stumbled into this.

Philanthropy allowed this participant to look at the world through a wide lens to gain a perspective that he couldn't see during his previous, narrowly focused work. He plans to return to writing and teaching in academia once his tenure at the foundation expires.

Another participant described a similar approach to the field of philanthropy:

> Before the war, World War II, I had been an intensely focused faculty member, psychologist. My world was psychology—my research, my students—I wasn't even interested in faculty meetings. . . . But when I came back, I was determined to find work that exposed me to a broader range of social issues, social problems, the way the world functioned. And it was just extraordinary luck that [name of foundation] was holding a spot which they did not intend to fill until they interviewed me. . . . So you can see it was a job that fit my general sense of where I had to go. . . . I had been much too narrow in my interests. And the foundation, the big general purpose of the foundation provides an extraordinary opportunity to look down into the plans of human beings.

After working in philanthropy for a while, this participant moved on to start a nonprofit organization and to work in government. Philanthropy represents not a permanent shift for these participants but rather a unique opportunity to widen their previously narrow focus.

Others who approach philanthropy with this generalist stance have a broad education. They highlight their ability to see across different realms of life and synthesize complex information. Philanthropy is a way to exercise these skills without narrowing their professional focus.

> I have a Ph.D. in American Political Thought, which equips me to do little else than to make judgments about broad and general ideas of political thought. And this is a way for me to exercise that particular training—that particular talent.

Another participant developed an ability to understand and synthesize concepts from a variety of domains early in life. She identifies with this type of thinking as an important and unusual skill and is determined to use it in her work to help make the world a better place, whether through philanthropy or social reform activism.

> Anything I was interested in to the best of their ability, [my family] helped me learn. If it was lessons in something, I was encouraged to do that. If it was meeting someone, they did their best to arrange that. If I never became really good at any one thing, nobody ever criticized me for that. . . . And I think it gave me a confidence that you can enter fields you don't quite understand and begin to wrap your arms around aspects of them. You can begin to see things about them that help you and that interest you without having to go all the way to be the great expert. . . . You can think about and talk about relationships between different domains in the world without having really mastered them.

We have seen that most grantmakers prefer to think of themselves as professionals or workers with other backgrounds and interests who happen to be carrying out a stint in the world of philanthropy. This distance from their current profession may explain the feelings of alienation they often expressed.

As we learned, grantmakers and foundation executives rarely plan to go into foundation work, and while some of them work in the field indefinitely, they do not necessarily plan to stay in the field for their entire professional lives. Philanthropy is not the center of their career; instead, they identify primarily with a previous career, a specific personal mission, or their general analytical abilities, all aspects of professional identity that are not specific to philanthropy.

Why Don't They Identify with Philanthropy?

We have identified several factors that mitigate professional identification with the field of philanthropy. Grantmakers own neither the money they give away nor the work they support with that money. They feel isolated from grantees, the public, and their colleagues. Foundation policies often limit the amount of time they can stay in the field of philanthropy, and the field as a whole lacks a unified set of professional values to anchor and guide them while they are there.

It's Not My Money

Traditionally, philanthropy has been the domain of the wealthy. New philanthropic models, such as donor-advised funds and giving circles, have made organized philanthropy more widely accessible, but still most people making decisions about where to donate organized philanthropic money are connected to the money itself. In capitalist America, philanthropy is built on the fundamental assumption that donors have a right to give away money as they see fit, just as they have a right to accumulate as much wealth as they can. Philanthropic freedom is widely celebrated:

> I think one of the greatest things about philanthropy in the U.S. is the freedom donors have to pursue their own vision, their ideas about how to use their luck and

skill and what benefit it brought to them personally, to help support the hopes and dreams of other people who are still struggling.

Wealthy individuals are free to support public institutions of personal importance. Their philanthropic decisions are respected and rewarded financially through tax benefits. They derive their philanthropic authority from their generosity.

Professional grantmakers break from this philanthropic tradition. They give away other people's money. The right to give it away, however, does not apply as it would were they the donors. They must derive their grantmaking authority from something other than wealth. The legitimacy of professionals in any realm lies in the answer to the following question: Why should society reward them for what they do (Gardner, Csikszentmihalyi, and Damon 2001)? Philanthropic donors are valued for their generosity, but why should society reward grantmakers with money and respect for giving away someone else's money? Philanthropic tradition has not established a clear answer to this question.

Again, the contrast with other domains proves instructive. The traditions of law and medicine provide lawyers and doctors with confidence that their work is of social value; simply by carrying out the work they were trained to do, they legitimately earn the social rewards of money and prestige. Because philanthropic tradition in America is based on the generosity of donors, not on the work of professionals, there is no such confidence among grantmakers, no collective sense that simply carrying out their daily work is enough to earn a respected position in professional society. By centering their identities elsewhere, they reassure themselves of their social value as professionals.

Within the field of philanthropy, grantmakers generally have less power than the donors and board members. Almost all of the grantmakers we interviewed emphasized that they are not giving away their own money. This recognition was not a simple statement of fact but a salient aspect of their work that brings a complicated mix of emotional and interpersonal dynamics. They feel privileged to have the opportunity to spend money that isn't theirs on projects and ideas they deem important. However, the will of the donor and the opinions of board members loom as potential limits on their professional autonomy. In most cases, grantmakers choose to work at foundations that are sympathetic to the specific ideas and causes they want to support, foundations that also offer them the autonomy to make grants they think will make the most difference. However, when their opinions on grantmaking diverge from those more closely connected to the source of the philanthropic money, the whim of a donor or board member can trump the grantmaker's professional expertise. The observations of one grantmaker reflect this tension between wealth and autonomy:

> This is an enormously luxurious circumstance, full of supports. There are financial resources. There is autonomy. There is no ballot box that will vote us out of office. There are no shareholders that will vote us out of office at the next shareholder meeting. . . . So the supports are enormous. Oftentimes we talk about these with some degree of Catholic guilt, I think. . . . [But] just as we are luxurious with all

of those assets, the reality comes to play when you are obviously dependent upon a board to support and acknowledge and ultimately approve the work of the foundation staff.

Another grantmaker framed the involvement of foundation board members in grantmaking as a challenge in her work: "Most foundations in this country still have boards that are actively engaged on the transactional side of grantmaking. And that can be an obstacle."

Adopting a professional orientation rooted in something other than the field of philanthropy gives professional grantmakers a greater sense of legitimacy in their grantmaking decisions. External experience and expertise is a grantmaker's key to professional autonomy.

Dealing with large amounts of wealth can be uncomfortable for grantmakers. Often the grantmakers' progressive political leanings run counter to the capitalist structure that created the foundation's wealth. One participant forcefully highlighted this dynamic.

> Another thing that may be very complicated and complicating is the relationship between the donors and the rich people and the staff of the foundation. If you don't work that out effectively, then it's very hard to make effective grants. . . . Let me just be clear that I think one thing that limits the horizons for foundations is the fact that . . . almost 100% of them have rich people in decision making positions. . . . I think first of all what helps you make a bundle is that you really want to. I think people rarely make a bundle without that being a very core value for them. They get rich because they want to get rich. And they're working in a community where that value is common, widely shared. And it's unquestioned, largely unquestioned. So they're now going to a world where virtually everybody has said we don't want to make a bundle. We're like a professor or community organization or museum director. They're all people who've said we don't want to make a bundle. We have some sense of sufficiency, not maximization. Which makes us kind of strangers in this world.

The grantmakers we interviewed see their access to philanthropic wealth as a potentially powerful corrupting influence. One grantmaker expressed this common fear: "Foundation executives tend to think they're more intelligent simply by their proximity to other people's money." As another grantmaker put it:

> The dark side of philanthropy is that we're treated as though we're wealthy, but we're not. I have a modest little home like every other program officer has a modest little home. We're treated like we're royalty of the nonprofit sector, like we're smarter or our jokes are funnier or we're better looking, and we're not. We have to constantly remind ourselves that the sector looks upon program staff as bags of money moving around. . . . So there is that danger. There is definitely the arrogance danger.

Arrogance is commonly cited as one of the dark sides of philanthropy. In order to avoid the conceit associated with wealth, professional grantmakers distance themselves from philanthropy and root themselves in the fields they support. They would often prefer to be associated with the work of the grantees rather than the wealth of the donors. Many participants emphasized the distinction between grantmakers and philanthropic donors, and nearly all warned against identifying too closely with the philanthropic money.

> I've said over the years that we have a little mantra around here and we ought to say it every morning and that is: it's not our money. It's not our money and that we put on our pants one leg at a time just like everybody else. And we're employees and we draw a paycheck and we ought not to have any confusion about whose money this is. We are a public trust. A lot of folks who work in foundations forget that. And it's easy to forget.

Grantmakers' ambivalence toward wealth is one factor that can dissuade them from centering their professional identity in philanthropy. Grantmakers want to avoid the arrogance stereotypically associated with wealth, but at the same time their distance from the philanthropic money they manage limits their professional autonomy in philanthropy. One participant summed up the connection between grantmakers' ambivalence toward wealth and their lack of identification with philanthropy.

> It's both exhilarating and uncomfortable to have access to this kind of money. I think every grantmaker I know has always felt like this is an incredible privilege. What they do with the emotions that they have tied to that is very different. I think some people can get extremely anxious and other people can get arrogant. Some people kind of despise the source. One of the things I think is really interesting about grantmaking is that it's something that people really love to hate. The money often was acquired in not very honorable ways. It is very much a capitalist tool and I think there is a lot of ambivalence about it. People have ambivalence about wealth anyway. As a result, I think a lot of grantmakers, their orientation is to their grantees and very rarely do they feel an orientation to the field of philanthropy or to their organizations. . . . I think part of it is this ambivalence about not wanting to be seen a) as a philanthropist or b) as being too connected to just the raw money. You want to be connected to the outcome from having this money.

In order to gain professional legitimacy and avoid the arrogance associated with wealth, grantmakers tend to shy away from defining their career as their work in philanthropy.

It's Not My Project

Not only are grantmakers removed from the philanthropic money they manage, they are also one step removed from the social change they support with their grants. While doctors and lawyers can see the results of their work in a cured patient or a desired verdict, grantmakers are inevitably removed from the fruits of their labor. The grantmakers we interviewed acknowledge that they are not directly responsible for the success of the projects that they fund.

> Well, I don't think you can develop a lot of pride out of your philanthropic activities in a big foundation. You are given this extraordinary opportunity to spend

money that isn't your money, and it's just, there isn't anything you can congratulate yourself on except spotting good people.

Another grantmaker presented a similar argument:

> The good foundation recognizes the fact that we operate not center stage, but offstage. The good foundation recognizes that standing alone it really accomplishes nothing. I mean when you really think about it. That it facilitates, that it abets, that it brokers, that it encourages, that it supports, that it celebrates the work of others. . . . You ought not lose sight of the fact that you don't play Brahms, you don't heal the sick, you don't educate the first kid, you don't do anything, okay?

Denying themselves credit for the work of grantees may be in part an exaggerated modesty motivated by a desire to avoid the arrogance that can taint philanthropic work. Indeed, consciously cultivating humility among grantmakers is a wise strategy for good grantmaking. However, their humility also reflects a real underlying challenge for grantmakers—how to claim some sense of professional accomplishment and competence without falsely taking credit for the generosity of some or for the work of others. All of our participants seem to struggle with this dilemma, highlighted clearly by one participant in the following passage:

> I had to learn how to be comfortable being very far behind the scenes, living vicariously through the work of others. . . . I hadn't done it before. I had never been three steps away from the action. And I think it took some time for me to learn. First I was comfortable with it, but then I had to learn how to do it. How do you stay connected to the real work? How do you stay rooted enough in the challenges of that work so you understand it? . . . There's an ongoing need for kind of a reality check about what you can and can't do from philanthropy. Again, part of the potential flaw of arrogance in philanthropy is that you hear from people that work in philanthropy when they say, "We're doing this and we're doing that." We don't do anything. We invest in people who do things.

While grantmakers care deeply about the fields they support, work in philanthropy is not the same as work in those fields and their knowledge about the external field does not translate directly into skills needed for grantmaking. Because of its inherent second-hand nature, philanthropy takes grantmakers away from the groundwork that they want to support.

> The longer you are in a foundation, no matter how hard you try, you get further and further away from what is going on on the ground. . . . I have seen people who have been long disconnected from the field in the sense of actually working in the field who still do wonderful work. But I think it's very hard. It's really hard to do.

The emphasis on staying connected to the outside world as a requirement for good grantmaking and privileging the work of grantees as the "real work" over the daily tasks of a grantmaker makes it especially difficult for grantmakers to root themselves firmly in philanthropy.

Lonely Work

According to many of our participants, grantmaking is a lonely endeavor. Associating with philanthropy can isolate grantmaking professionals from the very people they are trying to serve: the grantees and the public. Many grantmakers also feel alienated from their professional colleagues, both within the foundation and in the broader field.

Isolation from Grantees

The power difference between funders and grantees puts grantmakers in the uncomfortable position of having to evaluate the sincerity of each interaction.

> It's very hard to establish a truly honest relationship in this position and that's very frustrating. . . . I think this is a rather lonely profession because nobody's ever honest with you . . . somebody always wants something from you.

Trusting everything that people say about you as a grantmaker can lead to an overinflated ego. On the other hand, approaching each interaction with skepticism is a lonely way to relate to people with whom you are trying to develop a trusting collaboration, especially when you have to discount any praise you might receive. Identifying with philanthropy makes the power differential more salient. The temptation to try to sidestep this isolating dynamic by identifying with something other than philanthropy is understandable. It may also contribute to grantmakers' reluctance to embrace philanthropy as a professional home.

Isolation from the Public

Not only do grantmakers feel isolated from grantees and potential grantees, they also feel remote from the public at large. The public perception that grantmaking is fun and easy does not match the working reality that grantmakers encounter as they try to navigate the field of philanthropy in pursuit of often-elusive social change. Foundation work can be frustrating for grantmakers with high personal standards, since the success of their work is difficult to measure. As one participant put it,

> This is half in jest, but there's some seriousness to this, when I started to come work here occasionally people said, "Oh, it must be great working at a foundation, just giving away money, that must be lots of fun." And the fact of the matter is it's really hard giving away money and doing it well. You know, so this notion that you're just sitting there in a highfalutin' place giving away money—but that's people's notion of what foundations do. It is so far from the reality of what it is to really try and do this well.

Some grantmakers and executives also cited as a challenge a growing public suspicion about philanthropy. For people who enter the field of philanthropy with the best intentions to help society, public skepticism is a difficult thing to swallow and may deter grantmakers from proclaiming their allegiance to the field of philanthropy.

Isolation within Foundations

Grantmakers often feel disconnected from their foundation colleagues. Most large foundations divide their grantmaking into content areas or fields they support, such as education, the environment, and the arts. Foundations often hire grantmakers because of their experience and expertise in other fields. They place emphasis on the areas they support and expect grantmakers to do the same. This fragmentation of philanthropy can isolate grantmakers from each other.

One participant noticed the type of unanticipated consequence that can arise from the emphasis on specialization.

> Initially we didn't have program areas. . . . We had a cadre of generalists who were working across the full repertoire. . . . As we tried to become more strategic and become more proactive in terms of becoming more focused and more tactical in terms of our work, we started to hire people who were from the field. We said, "Alright, you've done that wonderful work now in X University. Now come and do it in a foundation." And by definition we began to create these areas of specialty. . . . And all the incentives were aligned in such a fashion that the wonderful expert was rewarded and supported for doing her work in that field. . . . How could we incentivize cross-program work? How could we climb up out of our silos, embracing one another and saying, "Let's connect and do our work together"?

Separating grantmakers by content area encourages them to focus on their knowledge of fields other than philanthropy rather than connecting with their professional grantmaking peers across subject area. This policy can have the unwanted effect of isolating grantmakers from each other, even within a given foundation, especially if the foundation's overall mission is vague, a challenge several grantmakers highlighted.

Isolation between Foundations

Just as grantmakers are isolated by subject area within foundations, so they are isolated in the broader field. Collaborative efforts between foundations usually mirror the organization of foundations by grantmaking content areas. While collaborations by funding niche or geographical region are helpful, they rarely focus on best practices for the entire field, preventing a sense of camaraderie and field-wide support. As one participant stated, "Foundations are fiercely independent."

The rare collaborations that do reach across funding areas to address field-wide issues are small and isolated, like the group described by one of our participants in which nine foundation CEOs meet for dinner every six weeks to discuss the ethical dimensions of foundation work. Far-reaching efforts to unite the entire field of professional grantmakers hold little clout. When the Council on Foundations attempted to unite its members with agreed-upon practices for effective grantmaking in the late 1970s, foundations that disagreed with the proposed standards simply withdrew their membership. Because there are few external regulations on the field, there is little incentive for the philanthropic community to band together and regulate itself. Foundations may hold collaboration as an ideal, but they are intensely reluctant to give up their freedom in order to create a philanthropic community.

> That's another problem with foundations. They are still very individualistic. . . .
> It narrows and limits the capacity for good work if each foundation does it all by itself.

Grantmakers rely primarily on foundation culture for professional guidance, but this provides only precarious professional grounding in philanthropy since foundation culture can change dramatically with a simple change in leadership. If the alignment between a grantmaker's goals and the foundation's grantmaking philosophy breaks down, there is little field-wide community to turn to for support.

A focus on content area does not have to preclude a field-wide professional community. To take an example from medicine, cardiologists have their own specialized associations, but they also collaborate with other types of doctors. Similarly, in law, defense attorneys and prosecutors specialize in certain areas but rely on each other to carry out their joint mission of pursuing justice. The fragmented organization of professional philanthropy by content area without substantive field-wide collaboration isolates professional grantmakers in small groups and deprives them of professional associations based on the practice of grantmaking as a whole. It encourages grantmakers to anchor their professional identities elsewhere.

Discussion

Consider the perspective of professional grantmakers first entering the field of philanthropy. The opportunity to help society by channeling philanthropic resources to those who need it sounds promising. They have high personal standards and a strong motivation to help others through their work; philanthropy seems like a good way to use those personal qualities. When the opportunity to work in a foundation arises, they accept the position, eager to learn the craft of grantmaking from the inside and determined to do a good job.

Grantmakers and executives undoubtedly enter philanthropy with the best intentions of helping society and conducting work that is excellent in quality, socially responsible, and personally rewarding, but foundations offer them little support or guidance on how to channel their efforts effectively, thereby wasting precious human and monetary capital. The current structure of the field takes a toll on grantmaking professionals and on the quality of their work.

Because work in the field requires no training, grantmakers are thrown into the deep end, so to speak, when they start foundation work. Theoretically, anyone can become a grantmaker overnight. As one grantmaker put it,

You have to learn it from the ground up because there's no training, there's no apprenticeship. There's just, "Come in, you've got to give away ten million dollars. And make sure you don't make a mistake." There ought to be more intellectual and practical training about [the issue of] What is this business?

In contrast to other professions, professional philanthropy lacks shared norms regarding the purpose and practice of grantmaking. Most grantmakers agree only on "positive social change" as the purpose of philanthropy, a concept so vague it lacks the power of a professional mission. As one grantmaker put it, "You could drive Mack trucks through any of these wonderful philanthropic ideals." More precise philanthropic missions cited by the grantmakers we interviewed, such as supporting grassroots social movements, creating new institutions, or building new fields of knowledge, are idiosyncratic. Grantmakers also lack shared professional standards.[1] What some view as effective grantmaking, others dismiss as bad practice. They disagree on the proper role of board members in grantmaking decisions, the appropriate involvement of program officers with the projects they fund, and the type of experience and training that adequately qualifies an individual to become a grantmaker.

While professional grantmakers often praise such fragmentation as pluralism and diversity and view it as the result of philanthropic freedom, the same individuals often long for more clarity in their roles and more field-wide collaboration. A survey of employees at a large well-known foundation highlighted the dilemma of many grantmakers:

One of the discoveries that we made when we were doing a study of the foundation to understand how people were balancing their work and personal lives was that a lot of people said, "Well, one of the things that's most difficult for us is the stress of not knowing what the job is."

Motivation, clarity of purpose, and satisfaction are difficult to sustain in such a fragmented field. Grantmakers are left to find professional grounding on their own. They pick up what they can from implicit foundation norms. If they are lucky, they may find a good mentor to provide inspiration and trusted guidance on the appropriate role of a grantmaker and model a set of professional qualities and practices to which the grantmaker can aspire. Some foundations have orientations for their new grantmakers in attempt to pass on the grantmaking wisdom accumulated over the foundation's lifetime, but this type of training is inconsistent across foundations and depends largely on the agenda of the foundation's leadership. Many grantmakers rely on their own thoughtful analysis and reflection in order to define their roles, measure their success, and sustain their motivation.

While some grantmakers manage to find lasting satisfaction in their work with the support of good mentorship, personal reflection, enduring stamina, and unusual patience, many other grantmakers eventually burn out. As a result, many potentially good practitioners leave philanthropy, or worse, they stay and let their work suffer.

People do their best work when they enjoy what they do. And they are most likely to experience deep satisfaction and genuine enjoyment in their work—an experience described by Mihaly Csikszentmihalyi as "flow"—when a job provides clear goals, immediate feedback, and a level of challenge that matches their skills (Gardner, Csikszentmihalyi, and Damon 2001; see also Csikszentmihalyi 1990). Along with excellence and ethics, the opportunity for flow experiences may constitute a third element of "good work."

Professional philanthropy provides surprisingly little opportunity for flow. Grantmakers are generally unclear about their roles, and even the most hard-working and well-intentioned grantmakers may not immediately see the direct results of their labor. When a domain limits opportunities for rewarding and enjoyable work experiences, "the risk is that members of the field will become bored and retreat into a rigid orthodoxy in an attempt to protect the relevance of their work" (Gardner, Csikszentmihalyi, and Damon 2001, 32). Professional grantmakers must find a way to stay engaged with their work if they are to fulfill their aspirations to be effective and responsible grantmakers.

Even the exceptional grantmakers who find ways to make their work meaningful and satisfying amid the ill-defined, fragmented field sometimes teeter on the brink of defeat. They have seen others lose energy or lose touch with the social purpose of their work, stop making intelligent grantmaking decisions, isolate themselves, sink into arrogance, or even abuse their power.

> The shadow side of philanthropy may be autonomy run amuck. Power overzealously pursued. Influence thoughtlessly advanced. . . . It's the flip side of having resources to do good.

Many well-respected grantmakers have left the field in order to avoid the disaster that complacency would make of their work.

> For a good year before I was offered [another] job [and left philanthropy], I had real feelings that my situation was too comfortable. I knew all the answers to being a foundation president in New York City. I was able to open practically any door and deal with my problems, and that's not a good sign. I mean, you know that life isn't like that, so if you begin to feel that way, something's closing in on you. You're too familiar with this setting and not faced with the challenge you might be faced with.

Other grantmakers change roles frequently within philanthropy in order to avoid burnout.

> I feel sometimes like I've really lost my edge, myself. It worries me. I think what has kept me fresh in a way is constantly having to reinvent new things within the institution. So I'm always just starting all over again.

Some foundations anticipate the problem of burnout and limit the amount of time a person can work at that foundation in hope of getting people out of the field before they become too complacent or discouraged and do too much social damage. These policies reinforce the mindset that employment in philanthropy is a temporary endeavor that serves as a complement to one's professional activities outside of philanthropy, not a career to be pursued in itself.

When grantmakers consistently encounter systemic obstacles to carrying out good work in philanthropy, it is no wonder that many grantmakers keep the field at arm's length, that they look for professional grounding elsewhere. But does it have to be this way? Could philanthropy be a place to look for professional identity, or is it destined to be a field for amateurs where passion reigns and people leave when they burn out? The field is divided on this question. Neither grantmakers nor foundations want to give up the freedom that the lack of professional structure permits, but they also want more clarity in their own work and more effective and responsible work from the field as a whole.

Perhaps there is a middle ground. Pluralism in philanthropy does not require isolationism. It is clear that individuals in the field of philanthropy—professional grantmakers, board members, donors, and grantees—need to reach beyond their regional, philosophical, and content-based niches. Possibly such discussions, conducted seriously over a period of time, might yield real and perhaps even surprising consensus.

Relying exclusively on exceptional individuals to find their own way in professional grantmaking is not a sustainable strategy for good work in philanthropy. However, there is no need to have a single model of a philanthropic career. Reaching agreement on a few effective trajectories would provide enough guidance to ground professionals in their philanthropic work and provide them with the framework needed to carry out their best work while still respecting the value of multiple philanthropic models.

Notes

We are especially grateful to our colleague Jeff Solomon, whose comments and ideas shaped this analysis. Thanks also to Carrie James, Paula Marshall, Susan Verducci, and William Damon for their helpful feedback on early drafts.

1. See Menon and Verducci (chapter 15) in this volume.

References

Csikszentmihalyi, Mihaly. 1990. *Flow: The Psychology of Optimal Experience.* New York: HarperCollins.

Gardner, Howard, Mihaly Csikszentmihalyi, and William Damon. 2001. *Good Work: When Excellence and Ethics Meet.* New York: Basic Books.

Part Two: Cases of Good Work in Contemporary Philanthropy

Introduction

Susan Verducci

This section presents case studies of contemporary philanthropy conducted as part of a three-university (Stanford, Harvard, and Claremont Graduate University) study of "good work" in today's society (goodworkproject.org). The focus of these studies is the philanthropist's attempt to make sound judgments about whether to support a particular nonprofit organization and, if so, how to support it effectively and responsibly.

We intend these cases to illustrate and detail the obstacles and challenges articulated in Part I. For example, they manifest the various ways that power influences and can corrupt the gift-grant relationship. Specifically, fund-raisers from the religious-based Boston Ten Point Coalition must play "a language game" to garner funding from secular funders. Certain other cases, particularly those of the funding of Teach For America and venture philanthropy, show how a proper relationship itself is fundamental to good work in philanthropy.

Part I argued that donors and grant-makers have not consistently recognized certain inherent features of philanthropy that can divert their good intentions and pose obstacles to effective and responsible grant-making. The following chapters describe such obstacles, including the debilitating amount of human resources sometimes required to raise money for a nonprofit, philanthropy's narrow focus on innovation and systemic change, and the difficulties of trying to measure social impact in the nonprofit sector. The cases also illustrate the pervasive influence of business models in contemporary philanthropy, sometimes for good and sometimes for ill.

There is something missing from Part II that is worth mentioning, because it exemplifies organized philanthropy's lack of transparency, and hence its communicational shortfalls, as discussed in the chapter by Laura Horn and Howard Gardner. In addition to the cases included in this section, the GoodWork Project examined how one established nonprofit known for its high-quality work suddenly failed, to everyone's surprise. After getting by for twenty years on a series of relatively small grants, the organization received a multimillion-dollar project-based grant which required it to expand its operations and shift its focus. Even more money from other funders followed. Then, one year before the end of the large grant, the nonprofit closed its doors. It was unable to absorb the funds that flowed in, and the pressures and demands of its attempt to expand killed it.

We intended the case study of this failure to be published in this book, hoping to provide insight into strategies that could help circumvent the pitfalls that befell these funders. Unfortunately, after they had collected the data needed to analyze this case, the researchers who conducted the project were denied consent to use those data. We were forced to cancel the chapter. As Horn and Gardner write, organized philanthropy too often has a proclivity to keep the details of grant-making (and its failures) opaque to both the American public and other grant-makers, resulting in the lack of a professional community in which failures can be shared and learned from.

In addition to illustrating the obstacles and challenges set out in the first section of this book, the chapters that follow also reveal promising strategies for overcoming them. For example, there is a study of a foundation in the midst of a radical transformation in its strategic orientation. The Edna McConnell Clark Foundation adopted strategies of venture capital on the road to becoming what may be the most promising model to emerge thus far from the social venture movement. Along with the unanticipated obstacles and challenges it faced, the foundation has found evident success in adopting these promising new strategies. Other foundations considering similar strategies (and there are many) should benefit from learning about the Edna McConnell Clark Foundation story.

Beyond venture philanthropy, Part II presents a number of other successful funding strategies that are making a mark in contemporary giving, including e-philanthropy and ideational philanthropy (the funding of innovative ideas for social policy). Such strategies speak directly to the challenge of domain-building discussed in the first part of this book.

In a sense, Part II illustrates and integrates the first and final sections of this book through real-life cases of contemporary philanthropy. It is included as an effort not only to share with members of the field certain obstacles commonly encountered in doing philanthropic work but also to point to ways to circumvent or lessen the harms these obstacles can generate. Thus, the case studies are meant to extend understanding of the way that good intentions in philanthropy can go awry and hint at what can be done to put them back on track.

6 The Role of Relationships in the Funding of Teach For America

Susan Verducci

In 1988, a 21-year-old Princeton student wrote a senior thesis that envisioned a national service corps devoted to tackling the inequities in educational opportunities in this country. Since then, Wendy Kopp and the organization she created, Teach For America (TFA), have gathered tens of millions of dollars in philanthropic support to recruit over 12,000 talented seniors from the best colleges in the nation and place them in the most disadvantaged rural and urban schools across the country. Although the organization is considered "stunningly" successful by the *New York Times* (Wilgoren 2001) and most everyone familiar with it, examination of the funding history of TFA reveals certain patterns and issues that can provide philanthropists and grantmakers with ideas for improving their own work and facilitating the work of the nonprofits they support.

We chose to study TFA as part of the GoodWork Project (GWP) for a number of reasons. It has a long, complex, and somewhat checkered funding history. It also has become a model of a nonprofit successful at fund-raising. For our study, we interviewed seventeen philanthropists and grantmakers and two funders who declined to support TFA. Except for the latter two, all our interviews were with funders who, in the opinion of staff at TFA, had made significant contributions to the organization, financially and through other forms of support. We talked with Kopp and her head of development, Kevin Huffman, numerous times and interviewed four other current and former staff members. Finally, we studied Kopp's chronicle of TFA in her book, *One Day All Children* (2001) and collected and analyzed documents provided by TFA, including grant proposals, final reports, and a key internal fund-raising strategy memo.

We culled from our data patterns and themes pertaining to good work in philanthropy—work that is at the same time high quality and socially responsible. This chapter examines three relational patterns funders had with TFA and discusses themes that emerged across these patterns that were both helpful and harmful to the nonprofit. The chapter concludes with recommendations for doing good work in philanthropy.

Relational Patterns

Throughout TFA's development, funders have been and continue to be a necessary part of its functioning and growth and an intrinsic component of its well-being. They have also been a source of obstacles. Whether funders were supporting the organization in helpful or harmful ways, one thing was clear: relationships with the people in TFA were fundamental to funders' work and to the eventual success of TFA.

TFA bases its approach to fund-raising on cultivating interpersonal relationships. Kopp told us, "I don't view fund-raising as anything other than relationship building." A former TFA staff member said that Kopp is the best fund-raiser the subject has ever met; she has long-term relationships with funders and "cultivates those relationships relentlessly." These interpersonal relationships, for many of the grantors we spoke with, were critical to the continuance of funding and fundamental to the personal meaning they found in their work.

Three relational patterns between TFA and funders emerged from our interviews: *parent, partner,* and *sponsor. Parent* funders were unusually responsive to TFA's needs, consistently accessible to the organization, and fiercely devoted to it in times of trouble. They supported the nonprofit beyond what was typical for them (and the field) and described their relationships in highly personal terms. *Partnering* has become a popular way for donors and grantmakers to establish relations with those they fund since the boom in what is commonly referred to as "high engagement" philanthropy. TFA's partners focused their attention on improving the organizational capacity of the nonprofit, using the strategies of the business sector to do so. Like most venture philanthropists, they fund TFA in order to help it grow, to help it "go to scale." They provide a good deal of technical and operational assistance as well as money.[1] The final pattern we saw, *sponsor,* centered on the principle that philanthropists and grantmakers should pick the best people, fund them, and then give them freedom and autonomy. Sponsors believe that nonprofits are changemakers; they see themselves as middlemen. As an East Coast foundation president put it, "You're facilitating, you're empowering, you're giving the capacity to other people." A West Coast foundation president concurs: "The good foundation . . . facilitates, it abets, it brokers, it encourages, it supports and it celebrates the work of others." The sponsor relationship is based on solid due diligence and trust. Although the people we interviewed primarily exhibited characteristics of one type of relationship or another, we did not find many "pure" relational types—people that remained perfectly consistent across time and circumstance.

Parent

The parental funders we interviewed usually began their funding early in TFA's history. They all showed certain traits in their funding relationships. The first and most important was that they went beyond their usual grantmaking boundaries to help TFA. They funded TFA for longer periods of time, with more grants, with unusually large grants, and with greater patience and flexibility than they did with other grantees. They provided challenge grants when no one else would fund TFA. They leveraged their power and connections and spent their chits to help the organization succeed. These funders went to great lengths to ensure that TFA would flourish. They told us that they behaved in these ways because they believed there was something out of the ordinary about TFA.

Examples of "climbing out on a limb" pervaded interviews with parent funders. During a particularly treacherous financial period for TFA, one program officer helped to meet payroll at the eleventh hour by lending the organization money from her own family foundation. Another parent funder told us, "We rarely do endowments; we like to be alive while the money is being spent and so this was a rare instance when we gave an endowment." He described waiving his usual process of due diligence: "I didn't want to look at [Kopp's] financial statements, which is very rare. I figured they would be bad news. I know that they are bad; what am I going to learn from them? I didn't examine them. I based [the funding] on what she had produced." At one point when TFA was in great need, a program officer successfully lobbied his board to give the organization $100,000 more than the nonprofit had asked for. The foundation wired the money into TFA's account immediately so they could meet payroll the next day. Examples of going above and beyond their usual grantmaking limits were common in our interviews with parent funders.

Further, the relationships between Kopp (the primary fund-raiser) and parent funders were far from antiseptic and bureaucratic, a common nonprofit complaint. They were peppered with the personal, and these funders often talked in these terms about Kopp. One donor told the story of his recovery from major surgery. "When I was sick here, [Kopp] came and visited me with her six-day-old baby and it was such a thrill. I said at the time, and here I am 76, and here is this six-day-old baby, and I really felt this thrill." Still another funder characterized herself as a "mom" to TFA and said she "fell in love" with the organization.

Partner

In his book on venture grantmaking, Paul Firstenberg describes venture grantmaking as "a partnership between grantor and grantee to elevate the capacity and thus the impact of the grantee organization" (2003, 14). In May 2000, a large foundation that works in the venture style approached TFA and offered $8.3 million to bring the nonprofit's work to scale, in effect doubling the amount of teachers it currently placed into classrooms. Since then, the organization has been dedicated to this task. TFA's funding "partners" are tied to this period.

The clearest example of the partnership model can be seen in the following case. Unlike parent funders, the founder of this venture funding organization pursued Kopp. In deciding whether to work together, there was "a lot of discussion and negotiation."

[It was] not at all . . . like any grant process that you've been through [as a grant-seeker] because we were basically saying "Look, do we want a partner or not?" And it wasn't about written documents or applications. . . . It was really about getting to know each other and . . . seeing if there was mutuality. . . . The power dynamic was really balanced. I mean there were many times where we wanted to invest in TFA and TFA wasn't sure they wanted us. So it was a lot of back and forth on that front. It went on for about six months.

When asked why TFA initially refused their offer, the founder said,

I'll make my best guess with that. . . . [Kopp] wasn't convinced initially that our intellectual capital would be of value to her, that she was at the stage to need some of the strategy work that we were providing. So she was just being I think very smart and being very cautious about getting involved in a partnership that would take up too much of her time.

Partners recognized and respected the power of the nonprofit. In the partner model, a power balance was negotiated not only in the decision to work together but in terms of money as well. The organization described above initially offered TFA a significant amount of money. The way the funder tells it is that Kopp came back and essentially said "For the kind of time and energy required by the partnership, I won't do it for [that amount]. I want three [times that amount]." The organization gave twice the amount, plus an additional sum for technical consulting.

Sponsor

The late John Gardner, former president of the Carnegie Corporation of New York, described and endorsed the sponsor relationship in his interviews with us: "You get to take enormous care to study who you're giving money to and then leave them alone. Cut the ties. Don't look over their shoulder. Otherwise you spoil the whole point of creativity out there."

After telling us that he didn't micromanage TFA, a program officer from a large foundation continued,

So, if you have an organization that is very good and you have some confidence in them and you think they are doing a good job, they always have a great need for flexible support. We wanted to give them as much flexibility as possible. So my recollection is that we made it as general support so they can use it for whatever *their* priorities were.

Sponsor funders supported the organization and basically trusted that it would fulfill its mission. The baseline belief of sponsors was that doing good philanthropic work with this particular nonprofit meant performing solid due diligence, conducting periodic evaluations, and providing continued and somewhat flexible funding, but mostly trusting that TFA would do a good job in bringing smart college graduates into the classrooms of underserved populations. One sponsor went so far as to characterize his relationship with TFA as "at arm's length."

Kevin Huffman, TFA's director of development, commented that all these funders—parents, partners, and sponsors—"want us to do well, wish us to do well and are proud when we succeed (even if they wanted us to do things differently)." Their approaches to the grantee-grantor relationship, however, were quite different. Nearly all of the parent funders went beyond the normal limits of grantmaking with TFA and discussed their relationships in highly personal terms. Partner funders engaged in more peer-like relationships. The power differential was well mediated and there was a sense that each partner brought different skills and talents to the table. In contrast, sponsors were more relationally removed than the others. They conceived of their work as different from that of TFA, and after funding the nonprofit they stepped out of its way.

Unlike the sponsor approach, parenting and partnering were primarily correlated with the period of development that TFA was in when individual funding streams were initiated. Parental behavior can be found most often, although not exclusively, in funders who came on board in the organization's early history. Partnering is most prevalent in the current expansion phase of the organization. The sponsor approach was scattered across funders and across the development of TFA.

Themes (and Problems) across Relationships

This tripartite relational model can be useful for what it reveals about the strengths and weaknesses of each pattern and for what the model itself neglects. Three themes appeared across the patterns that are important to explore for their positive and negative implications for good work in philanthropy: the alignment of the personal mission and values of the grantor with those of the grantee, the influence of the philanthropic field's zeitgeist, and the importance of a charismatic nonprofit leader.

Alignment of Personal Mission and Values

Our data revealed that the basis for parent, partner, and sponsor relationships is one that is rarely discussed in the scholarly work on philanthropy: the alignment between the purposes and values of the nonprofit personnel with the *personal* missions and values of individual donors and grantmakers.[2] Kopp herself told us, "I am not going out and convincing people who are not interested in our mission and organization to give us money. . . . I'm finding people who are naturally interested and communicating with them." Her target is people, not foundations. Further, she targets people who are like-minded.

An example of personal mission alignment can be seen in the following action of a parental program officer. TFA's mission was not a perfect fit with his foundation's mission. To get around this incompatibility, he funded the nonprofit out of a pot of money that became available when challenge grants to other organizations were not met. Shared underlying values can also be seen in the example of one wealthy donor who made a point of mentioning TFA's offices to us: "[Kopp] runs [her organization] at a very low cost basis . . . and she pays a low rent and worries about those things. And if you've been to the office, it's very sparse. . . . The last I saw it, it was just like little barriers between desks." Much earlier in our interview he described the way he and his wife live. "[W]e don't have a second home, we never owned a car, we don't drive, and we never thought of, we wouldn't have a chauffeur. . . . So we either take a bus, which we use now with the Metro card a lot, the subway, taxis." These are only two of many examples of the alignment of purposes and values we found in the funders and staff members of TFA we interviewed.

The lack of recognition of the importance of personal alignment in the success of funding relationships presents a number of questions. First, if the role of like-mindedness is fundamental, how does the relative lack of diversity in philanthropists and grantmakers impact the funding of nonprofits across the sector? Who will fund worthy nonprofits run by people whose personal missions and values are different or people who are not savvy in the ways of the upper middle and upper classes?

Second, a related issue pertains to the insularity of the field of philanthropy. In a previous study of traditional organized philanthropy, nearly half of the people we talked with were concerned about funding that focused on personal relationships between funders and fundees, particularly the parent and partner models. A number of these people talked about the dangers of funding the "usual suspects." Not only can funding go to the same people regardless of their effectiveness, but grantmakers tend to rely on themselves and a limited group of their grantees to gather information about the problems in the field they are granting to, thus impacting the way that strategies to ameliorate social ills come to be framed. One person we talked to called this the "echo chamber."

Third, foundations are more likely to support groups that can meet their process requirements rather than "raggedy" nonprofits doing excellent neighborhood work who do not have the staff (or perhaps the skills) to participate in the processes that foundations require. The structures and operations of philanthropy can make funding inaccessible to certain nonprofit populations. All these problems, in part, can derive from the presence of like-mindedness and funding on the basis of relationships.

The Influence of the Field

The relational patterns we perceived in the funding of TFA were also influenced by larger patterns in the field of philanthropy, its zeitgeist. For example, in the field of organized philanthropy high priority is currently placed on funding innovative projects, systemic change, and working with organizations that intend to scale up. One TFA grantmaker captured the emphasis on innovation by saying her foundation tries to be "an incubator, not an oxygen tank." Another essentially summed up the fashion in organized philanthropy: "Our priority is to find great social innovations [and bring them] to scale. . . . We're looking for great innovations that have the opportunity to change the system and I think that we felt that TFA really could have a substantial impact."

This seems well and good, but if we look at this from TFA's point of view, we can see the pressures these aims create. One TFA staff member noted that "just when we began to do what we do better than ever before, funders began to lose interest." We see this pressure clearly during what Kopp called the "dark years" in her book (2001). During the early 1990s, funders had begun to wean TFA from their portfolios because they had been funding them for a while. To regain funders' interest, the nonprofit expanded to include what everyone later came to understand as programs peripheral to the core mission. Eventually, operation of the nonprofit became stretched to its limit and TFA nearly collapsed. Funders had encouraged TFA to start new programs that would satisfy their own organizations' proclivities for innovative projects. Although they remained committed to the health of TFA during these "dark years," funders failed to view (or acknowledge) themselves or their organizations as complicit in shaping the trouble TFA faced.

Another way that the zeitgeist of the field shaped the priorities of TFA pertains to its current expansion endeavors. Helping nonprofits grow so they can have greater or more lasting impact is a primary feature on the current landscape of philanthropy. It was a foundation that approached TFA with the idea and money to begin an expansion phase. Finding the large sums of money needed to successfully complete this phase was relatively easy with this start and the given zeitgeist. Whether TFA would have made this move without the foundation's prodding is an unanswerable question.

Funders in the field never exerted influence by saying to TFA, "This is what I want you to do." And the nonprofit never had the experience of not wanting to do something but having to go ahead anyway in order to receive funding. The field's influences occurred organically; the funders of TFA were not conscious of their influence on the field or the field's influences on them. And unlike many other nonprofits we have spoken to in the course of the GWP, TFA did not perceive the effect of these influences as shifting them from their mission. On the contrary, both funders and the nonprofit were swept along by the priorities of the field, questioning them only when faced, as in the "dark years," with their destabilizing consequences.

Importance of a Charismatic Leader

TFA has a strong, youthful, and loyalty-generating leader in Wendy Kopp. She is not charismatic in a typical way in that she does not possess a personal magnetism that causes heads to turn when she enters a room. On the contrary, she is shy and serious, possessing a quiet and deep belief that her ideas will make the world a better place. These qualities confer on her extraordinary leadership powers. One former program officer told us, "Wendy inspires commitment in a whole army of people." She is the face and the heart of TFA and has been the prime motivator and fund-raiser for much of TFA's life. The relationships the funders we talked with had were with Kopp. As a 21-year-old, she brought naiveté, sensibility, energy, tenacity, and idealism to her pursuit of a national corps of teachers. These characteristics were coupled with a sort of fearlessness about establishing fund-raising relationships and what one interviewee called a "thirst" to learn and grow in this capacity, a willingness to be shaped. It was her deep beliefs, idealism, and efforts that inspired her funders.

Her charisma, however, may have created problems for the organization. One funder who worked closely with TFA said that she would not fund it without Kopp. Another has a clause in the grant stipulating that if "key personnel" left, the funding would be put on hold and the foundation would perform due diligence again. The enormous respect funders have for Kopp may not always carry over to the organization. Their near-unanimous concerns about TFA without her makes it seem likely that even devoted funders are more loyal to Kopp as a leader than they are to TFA as an organization.

The staff at TFA realize that this perception might be a problem. There has been an effort to strengthen the management team, as evidenced by what two of the staff we interviewed mentioned as the increased caliber of the management team. The head of development openly noted at a funders meeting we attended that the organization has recently become less "Wendy-centric." TFA staff seem to recognize the need for funders to become more aware of the competence of other players at the nonprofit. They want to be sure that should Kopp decide to move on, the misperception of Kopp as the organization could be overcome.

Funders' priorities, interests, advice, and types of relationships with Kopp have helped shape the direction and activities of TFA. Certain characteristics of philanthropy—for example, the conception of the work of philanthropy as innovative—have also shaped TFA. Certain missions such as changing systems and bringing programs to scale influenced the organization. Grantmakers acted as a magnet to encourage changes in the organization and its direction, some to the detriment of the stability of the organization. Grantmakers are a force in the lives of nonprofits, for good or for ill. They can certainly add value to the work of nonprofits. However, harm can be done, not just to the stability or viability of the nonprofit and its workers but, by extension, to those in the community who benefit from the nonprofit's work.

Recommendations and Questions

Think about Good Work Developmentally

Given the critical influence that organized philanthropy has on its grantees' ability to realize their missions, funders should pay close attention to the shape of their own work *in relation* to the nonprofit's organizational development. Attention should be paid to the needs of nonprofits in their developmental stages, the shape of the relationships between those funding and the people in the nonprofit, and the influence of philanthropy's zeitgeist. Doing good work may depend upon it. The relationships that worked well for TFA in different phases of development were different. Parenting worked well in its early phases, partnering works well in the growth phase, and sponsorship has worked well across most of its development. What might initially look like a lack of consensus on what constitutes good work in philanthropy may be attributable to the possibility that good work looks different when looked at relationally and across a nonprofit's lifespan.

Develop a Model of a "Mezzanine" Relationship

A common complaint from nonprofit organizations is that there is no "mezzanine" funding available.[3] In the case of TFA, the field seems not only lacking in mezzanine funding, it lacks relational models for this time period. During the "dark years," TFA was not successfully parented, nor was it ready to be the kind of partner that expansion funders were looking for. Sponsorship was not helpful either; at times it was not even possible. What sort of relationship works for the teenage nonprofit? Is the field structurally and systematically unable to relate well during this phase of development? And is this inability connected to the field's narrow interest in innovation, systemic change, and scale?

Consider Both the Benefits and Challenges of Like-Mindedness

Although two-thirds of the subjects in an earlier GWP study of philanthropy mentioned that good work includes fostering good relationships between grantees and grantors, they focused on fostering qualities such as humility, respect, trust, integrity, honesty, and equality. They spoke of negotiating the inherent power differential in the relationships, considering grantees as assets, asking hard questions, being accessible, and being consistent. They did not talk about fostering relationships between like-minded grantees and grantors, those who were motivated by and valued the same things. Like-mindedness worked well for TFA, but as articulated above, will it work well for all organizations? And what are the inadvertent and systematic consequences of funding on this basis?

Recognize and Negotiate the Influence of the Zeitgeist and Charismatic Leaders

The pull of philanthropy's zeitgeist and the attraction funders feel to an individual leader can not only lead to positive benefits for nonprofits and their funders, they can introduce challenges to both. Awareness and sensitivity to the pitfalls of these forces can steer funders from leading a nonprofit away from its primary mission and operations or from leading a nonprofit into a destabilizing situation. Awareness of the effects of charisma can also help funders sort through the "spin" of smooth-talking leaders who may be covering weaknesses in their organizations and, as in the case of TFA, help funders recognize the strength of organizations behind charismatic leaders.

The funding story of Teach For America tells us much about good work in the field of philanthropy. It shows us that the people the nonprofit identified as having been the most helpful to them over the years supported them in different ways, using different relational models. Good relationships depend upon sensitivity to the developing organization, to its mission, and to the influence the field of philanthropy has on both. It also shows us that people are the primary players in funding, not foundations.

TFA's story, however, signals problems that can arise in basing funding on interpersonal relationships. "Relationship" funding may turn out to be a sort of double-edged sword; it can be the basis of both good work and compromised work. It can tell us about the nature of philanthropic work that is high quality and socially responsible and give insight into work that may be well intentioned but is neither of these.

Notes

This chapter was made possible by The William and Flora Hewlett Foundation, The Atlantic Philanthropies, and the open and helpful nature of the people who make up TFA and those who fund it. Special thanks for the comments and clarifications from TFA's president, Wendy Kopp, and head of development, Kevin Huffman. Their participation in this effort to understand good work in philanthropy is itself an example of good work.

1. For a comprehensive view of this relationship pattern, see James and Marshall (chapter 7) and Tierney (chapter 4) in this volume.

2. Usually discussion of philanthropic alignment focuses on aligning the mission of the nonprofit with that of the foundation or alignment of foundation employees with the foundation and/or the alignment of foundation mission with the donor's intent.

3. The term "mezzanine funding" comes from the field of venture capital and refers to the funding of a company that is no longer a start-up and is not yet an IPO.

References

Firstenberg, Paul B. 2003. *Philanthropy's Challenge: Building Nonprofit Capacity through Venture Grantmaking.* New York: The Foundation Center.

Kopp, Wendy. 2001. *One Day, All Children . . . : The Unlikely Triumph of Teach For America and What I Learned Along the Way.* New York: PublicAffairs.

Wilgoren, Jodi. 2001. "Book Briefs: *One Day, All Children . . . : The Unlikely Triumph of Teach For America and What I Learned Along the Way.*" *New York Times,* April 8, 4A:20.

7   Journeys in Venture Philanthropy and Institution Building

Carrie James and Paula Marshall

As our fellow authors in this volume suggest, philanthropy is well intentioned but can be harmful to nonprofit organizations, thus undermining the sector's broader purpose: to create positive social impact. Given these possibilities, we look to new philanthropic approaches in search of promising strategies for creating good without doing harm. New practitioners in venture philanthropy seek to increase the effectiveness of philanthropy and avoid weaknesses and harms in traditional grantmaking.[1] While their ideas have much appeal, a critical assessment of their work is needed to determine whether the reality meets the promise and (and this is important) whether new harms may be wrought. As part of the GoodWork Project (GWP), we studied venture philanthropy in order to understand the goals, challenges, and strategies of these would-be changemakers.

Venture Philanthropy: A "New" Philanthropic Approach?

In this chapter, we explore the work of venture philanthropists—practitioners who seek to marry best principles and practices from business with promising social change efforts in the nonprofit sector. Venture philanthropy (VP) has been controversial since the concept and practice was hyped in the late 1990s. While its most visible practitioners heralded VP as a "new" and more effective model of philanthropy, critics questioned whether there was anything new about it (Eisenberg 1990). To be sure, many of the practices venture philanthropists promote have been used for decades in some traditional foundations. However, what *is* arguably new is that VP folds these practices into a systematic framework that mimics the vaunted for-profit venture capital model. In short, venture philanthropists aspire to build the capacity of nonprofit organizations, which they often refer to as "investees" or "investment partners."[2] To achieve this objective, they provide long-term (multiyear) monetary and management assistance through high-engagement relationships, in which funders advise grantees about the operation of their organizations. In some cases, nonprofit executive directors can end up feeling disempowered in these relationships. Whether they agree with the funders' advice or not, they may experience it as a mandate to take certain steps. Moreover, advising about organizational matters can cross the line to recommending major programmatic changes, which may distort the original mission of the organization and further disempower its leader. Investees are accountable for results, and from the beginning of the funding relationship, the funder's exit strategy and the nonprofit's ideal future state are central concerns of strategy and planning.

Although VP currently occupies a relatively small niche in philanthropy,[3] the field is quite diverse—a range of individuals and organizations practice VP in some fashion. And while they ideologically embrace the framework described above, not all practitioners are equally committed to every principle or practice in the prototypical approach. Rather, in practice, some focus on donor engagement or writing business plans for nonprofits. VP is also practiced in different organizational contexts, including private foundations established by a single donor, giving circles, nonprofit consulting firms, and community foundations.

This diversity in the field of VP is partly a reflection of the background of its practitioners. True to the media's depiction of VP as an outgrowth of the technology boom, many participants are businesspeople who are relatively new to philanthropy. However, some come to the approach from traditional foundation and nonprofit sector experience. The most well-known example of the latter is the Edna McConnell Clark Foundation (EMCF), once a family foundation and more recently a traditional foundation that has shifted its grantmaking to an "institution building" approach.

Drawing on twenty-eight interviews with founders, leaders, staff, board members, and consultant organizations using a venture model, we explore the journeys of VP's practitioners. We draw on the accounts of those who had established careers, work experience, or education in business and now have careers in VP. We also include the perspectives of veterans of philanthropy and the nonprofit sector who have adopted a VP-inspired approach in a more traditional grantmaking context: individuals who are part of the change effort at the EMCF. Each path to this model (business and traditional grantmaking) introduces distinct strengths and challenges. The diversity in the field ultimately benefits the model, especially when practitioners engage in dialogue about the work. In other words, VP's success hinges on the presence of and knowledge-sharing among individuals who have had exposure to both sectors.

To highlight the promise and perils of the path from business to philanthropy, we first describe the inspirational vision and missteps of early advocates. These pioneers either began their careers in the for-profit world or otherwise came to embrace the concept of using business principles in philanthropy. We argue that a business mindset is to some extent culpable for practitioners' missteps, but it is also responsible for their successes and (and this is important) for their capacities to improve the model. We then turn to a discussion of the efforts of the EMCF to increase the effectiveness of its grantmaking by shifting to a VP-inspired institution-building model. We note how the EMCF's history as a traditional foundation was both helpful and a hindrance in implementing this new approach. Taking stock of the lessons learned by both newcomers from business and philanthropy's veterans at the EMCF, we conclude by delineating promising VP strategies for good work.

From Business to Philanthropy: Journeys of Venture Philanthropists

The publication of "Virtuous Capital: What Foundations Can Learn from Venture Capitalists" in *Harvard Business Review* (Letts, Ryan, and Grossman 1997) was heralded as the starting point of the venture philanthropy movement. Indeed, this work was the first written articulation of the defining principles of the model. VP became an exciting concept during a unique historical moment—one in which significant new wealth was being created, notably among young people working in technology. Wealth coupled with the "can do" spirit and the exuberance of the new economy led many successful entrepreneurs to believe that they could use their business know-how and newly acquired wealth to create positive social impact. One interviewee aptly described this attitude: "Well, we created this great technological innovation so of course, poverty—boom—give me six months." While this depiction of venture philanthropists is arguably a stereotype, it was one that was frequently presented in the media hype.

Many practitioners with whom we spoke began their work well before the Letts article and the buzz created by the new economy had called attention to the approach. Business entrepreneurs who were early advocates of VP believed that philanthropic grants frequently harmed rather than helped nonprofit organizations. How did they come to this critique of traditional philanthropy? Seeking to do good but also committed to using a rigorous approach to their giving, some VP pioneers first did due diligence on the field of philanthropy, talking to experienced donors and grantees. These conversations affirmed their suspicions that philanthropic dollars often reaped little in terms of concrete, demonstrable results. The nature of funding relationships was perceived as largely to blame; they were described as superficial and lacking true accountability for dollars granted.

Other interviewees arrived at similar beliefs through direct experience in the nonprofit world. The background of a young founding director of a VP organization is illustrative. Driven by her compassion for the homeless, this interviewee volunteered for nonprofits in her teen years, made homelessness and urban poverty her academic focus in college, worked for a large nonprofit, and even co-founded a volunteer service organization. Though passionate about the work, she was continually frustrated by the inefficiencies and poor management practices of many nonprofits. Having also spent two years in the business world, she knew what a well-run enterprise looked like. First-hand knowledge of problems in the sector coupled with exposure to the business world suggested to her that nonprofits could thrive if guided by the expertise and tools that build strong for-profit enterprises. This belief inspired her decision to pursue an MBA and then return to the nonprofit sector: "I wanted to . . . be somebody who had both the passion and the skills and could bring both to the nonprofit sector to help the poor and the homeless."

VP's forerunners rightly pointed out that some traditional grantmakers pay insufficient attention to results—the social return on investment (SROI). Moreover, they asserted that traditional funding relationships were problematic in a number of ways: their duration was too short, they ignored general operating or management needs of grantees, and funder-grantee interactions were often "dances of deceit" in which nonprofits distorted their missions to fit into funders' guidelines (Tuan 2004). Perhaps most centrally, there was inadequate concern and certainty about the end of the funding relationship—the exit—and (this is important) grantees' futures beyond it. By contrast, VP was an intriguing alternative that promised to confront these weaknesses. As one subject described it, VP sought "to quality engineer a much higher reward on the dollars invested" through multiyear high-engagement investments. Many practitioners came to this work with essential skills and capacities for meeting this agenda, including conducting due diligence, writing business plans, scaling organizations, and using outcome measurement tools to track progress. As we will show, these skills and the business mindset that often accompanied them both helped and hindered their work, setting them up for missteps but also helping them navigate them.

Early Missteps

While venture philanthropists' concerns about traditional philanthropy were well grounded and their agenda was certainly compelling, their entry into the field was somewhat ungraceful. Interviewees were candid about the well-intentioned mistakes they made early on in their attitudes, assumptions, and conduct with grantees. More specifically, they cited: 1) overly dismissive attitudes toward experienced grantmakers; 2) a failure to define in advance how to execute the model; 3) difficulty selecting appropriate grantees; 4) missteps in high-engagement relationships with grantees; and 5) unrealistic expectations about scaling nonprofits and the exit strategy.

First, the early attitudes of some pioneers, which ranged from arrogance to naiveté, and their bold claims—such as the claim that VP would revolutionize charitable giving—were understandably off-putting to experienced grantmakers. The brash "we can do it better" rhetoric of some high-profile practitioners created unnecessary antagonism with people from whom these newcomers had much to learn. Many of our interviewees lamented these beginnings, pointing to the media's coverage of the worst stereotype of venture philanthropists—young, naive dotcom millionaires—as the problem. Others conceded that they too were culprits and years into the practice of VP were humbled and deeply regretted these careless first steps. One founder of a VP organization commented,

When we started, we created our own resistance. That was our stupidity. . . . For some reason . . . we felt that we had to present this as a better approach. And that was really a mistake. There was no need to cast this against traditional philanthropy as we did. There was just no need to do that. . . . It's like in my business life, with our sales force, I always encouraged our sales force to sell our solutions and not sell negatively by criticizing their competition. And here we were doing the same thing. So to a certain degree, we created some of the resistance by our attitudes.

Divisive attitudes detracted from what was of value in the VP agenda, and antagonism with experienced grantmakers precluded a constructive dialogue about philanthropic practices. Such a dialogue could have been mutually beneficial and might have prevented other missteps that were ultimately made.

Second, venture philanthropists noted difficulties with translating the concept of VP into practice. One pioneer regretted his failure to lay out a clear plan before making funding commitments:

I think the biggest single challenge was execution. . . . The big mistake I made is that I wasn't clear enough. We had this very lofty view and premise. To me, it was just so natural, this stuff. I assumed far too much . . . the lack of clarity about what we laid out for this concept, what it really meant in execution. We left too much open to play . . . and therefore did not set people up to succeed.

Because the premise of venture philanthropy felt natural to this successful business entrepreneur, he underestimated the complexity of putting it into practice.

Third, many venture funders spoke about missteps in grantee selection. In general, the model itself makes selection more difficult, as one subject noted: "The hard thing about the model is to find the fit. . . . And when I say fit, that means the trust stuff and the structure for the relationship and all that stuff put together." Extensive due diligence was promoted by venture practitioners to facilitate a good fit. Nevertheless, well into a funding commitment, some discovered that their investees were unprepared or in too early a stage of development to reap the benefits of the approach. In some cases, this miscalculation led to early termination of funding.

Some investees were enthusiastic about the significant funding and assistance venture grants promised, yet the realities of a high-engagement grant proved more difficult than they had envisioned. When encouraged to make changes to strengthen and grow their organizations, some nonprofit executive directors were reluctant to take needed steps. An interviewee recalled her experience with one investee: "As we worked more closely together it became clear that in terms of wanting to be committed to continuous improvement, of making hard decisions in the short run that would benefit you in the long run, he wasn't interested or willing to do those things." The unanticipated challenge of latent resistance by nonprofit staff led to termination of funding in some cases. VP's pioneers were aware of the complex and insincere dynamics that often characterize funder-grantee relationships, yet their stories suggested that they may have been underprepared for managing them. Although the fit problem is not unique to this model, VP's high-engagement approach may result in greater harm to a nonprofit if funding ends prematurely.

Fourth, as suggested above, interviewees perceived a number of perils associated with the high-engagement aspect of VP. Engagement is the hands-on work (e.g., writing business plans, developing financial systems, leadership coaching) venture philanthropists provide to help strengthen and grow their investees. Because organizational change is inherently difficult, distinguishing inevitable strains from engagement missteps can also be difficult. One pioneer commented:

> The danger with venture philanthropy is the engagement model. . . . I think a lot of harm can come. . . . One of your premises is: do no harm. And that's a tough statement to live up to because the reality is that something is going to break in there. But you want the breakage to occur by the organization themselves, not by us.

Some practitioners conceded that their early style of engagement created tensions with investees. After asking for feedback about the relationship between funder and grantee, one venture philanthropist was surprised to hear nonprofit staff express deep dissatisfaction.

> While I thought we had had great communication back, that was not the case. . . . I had this vision about what it was that we were going to do, and goddamn it, we were going to do it. And because of the nature of the dances of deception between nonprofit foundations, even though they thought they were being honest with me in terms of feedback, they really weren't being honest. And even though I thought I was being open to receiving feedback, I really wasn't listening to what they were saying.

This funder admitted that in his drive to carry out his vision, he failed to listen well enough to investees and reflect on his own communication style. Although venture philanthropists had critiqued traditional grantmakers for arm's-length, insincere interactions with grantees, many came to see that honest, transparent interactions were far more difficult to achieve than they had imagined. Moving beyond the typical "dance of deceit" between funder and grantee to build trusting and transparent relationships was the most significant challenge of doing VP, according to our subjects. Nonprofits must be able to trust that if something goes wrong, they won't be penalized by their funders. Most practitioners conceded that it took at least a year of work with a nonprofit—far longer than they expected—to develop enough trust to communicate openly.

Finally, many venture philanthropists admitted that they held unrealistic expectations about nonprofits' growth capabilities and their own exit strategies. The scope of change—going to scale, expanding to provide services to more recipients—that is a primary goal of VP requires major changes in investees' organizations—changes that can be far more difficult to effect than some funders anticipated. Growing a nonprofit is not only difficult, it also creates the possibility of harm. As the director of a venture fund reflected, "Venture philanthropy is often going to the nonprofits saying, 'Can I help you grow?' And the mentality doesn't really understand the downside of that, really. In the gut, they don't understand that. I think it can be a danger." Organizations that scale up require greater resources to sustain themselves over the long term. Growth can also create distance between a nonprofit and the community from and for whom it was originally established, thus undermining its original mission.

Lessons Learned

What did venture practitioners learn about philanthropy, the nonprofit world, and the efficacy of the venture model by implementing it? While at the outset most venture philanthropists knew that funding nonprofits would be different from incubating start-up companies, their missteps proved to be critical learning experiences that brought stark differences to light.

Describing them as "different worlds," interviewees learned that the nonprofit and for-profit sectors have distinct languages, values, norms, and types of goals. These cultural differences were frequently cited as barriers to building trust with nonprofits. For example, the use of terminology such as SROI and "the bottom line" by VP funders and staff was sometimes confusing or offensive to nonprofit staff who were not accustomed to defining their work in such terms. According to our interviewees, language differences reflected deeper differences in values and norms across the sectors. One participant noted: "The nonprofit culture has been one where a lot of times, things are given away or shared." This director of an early literacy fund found that her bookbag program violated this norm. Interested nonprofit directors were often puzzled when they learned that the bookbag was a trademarked product available only for purchase. While selling the bookbags gave the early literacy fund the revenue it needed to sustain itself, it also blurred the line between for-profit and nonprofit, thus confusing and even offending staff members of nonprofits who were the fund's target customers.

Venture funders also learned how the goals of nonprofit organizations are qualitatively different—they are often bigger, vaguer, and broader in scope—from business objectives. Several interviewees spoke to this point:

> Amazing amounts of things happen in businesses because they're driven by profit. I don't mean that in a bad way, but it's just an enormously clear goal. And in a way, it shakes out a lot of problems; it shakes out a lot of issues because at the end of the day the company is either making money, they're profitable, or they're not. And in this [nonprofit] sector, it's the whole thing about fuzzy outcomes and not having black and white goals, and it's true.

Nonprofit organizations often strive toward broad, "fuzzy," and ambitious goals, such as ameliorating poverty and homelessness. And while there are smaller, more measurable objectives, such as increasing high school graduation rates, their relationship with the big-picture goals is not always clear-cut. Reaching consensus on what the goals are can be difficult, as one subject learned:

> In business . . . on the for-profit side, it's very clear what you're shooting for: it's the bottom line, it's . . . how much money do you make. Whereas a nonprofit, that's not the case, and it's much harder I think to get consensus in a way on what's the most important thing.

The goals in the nonprofit world are not merely different, they also affect how individuals relate to one another and the overall pace of work. Venture practitioners who spent years in business learned to focus on results above all. In their work with nonprofits, they saw that good relationships are a priority and a prerequisite to results. As one interviewee put it, in the nonprofit sector, "out of relationships come results. The reverse is true in business." Some interviewees reported early frustrations with the normative practice of consensus-building that often precedes action in the nonprofit sector. Accustomed to a faster pace in business, they were impatient with the slow pace of goal-setting, decision making, and outcomes. However, years into their mission, practitioners came to see that relationship-building was time well spent. Experience demonstrated that a trusting relationship between funder and investee is the linchpin of success in VP. One interviewee felt that this fact was an important limitation of the business metaphor: "This is why the analogy of venture capital is so bad. Because in venture, you've got to shoot people really fast." Venture philanthropists learned that social investments are qualitatively different from financial ones, requiring longer time frames—and therefore greater patience—to achieve results.

Nonprofits have ambitious goals, yet unpredictable funding often prevents their realization. Operating with constrained budgets in a survival mode, some nonprofit directors feel pressured to restrict their visions and avoid taking risks. This plight contrasts with the entrepreneurial business mindset which—helped by more-abundant resources and the promise of great profit—embraces risks, as one interviewee pointed out:

> The investors . . . they're all Silicon Valley . . . and they made their money by going to scale, by taking for-profit ideas and ramping them up. And bigger is better. Bigger is more money coming in. In the nonprofit world . . . bigger is harder to sustain, bigger is harder to find the money, it's the reverse.

VP gives nonprofits the resources to help them achieve bold social goals. The ideal outcome of a VP funding relationship is a stronger nonprofit organization that has expanded its reach and touched more lives. In reality, however, it is extremely difficult for most nonprofits to sustain themselves when a venture funder walks away. Among other important lessons learned, venture funders found that crafting a successful exit strategy in the nonprofit sector is at the very least a difficult feat.

VP's pioneers came to philanthropy with a fresh perspective and essential skills garnered from their experiences in the business world. Yet our research suggests that their backgrounds failed to prepare them for the complex dynamics of funding relationships. Practitioners discovered that the norms and goals of the nonprofit sector were not an easy fit with a more aggressive, fast-paced entrepreneurial mindset that is common in business. Given the differences between the sectors, it is clear that the business model, when carelessly applied, has the potential to be harmful to nonprofits. While the skills and tools that venture philanthropists use are not harmful in and of themselves, the manner in which they are implemented can produce harm.

Fortunately, business training also provided many VP practitioners with a work ethic—of continuous assessment and improvement—which helped them weather their missteps. Our interviews suggest that serious practitioners of VP reflected on their mistakes, considered lessons learned about the uniqueness of the nonprofit world, and are dedicated to improving their approach.

The Edna McConnell Clark Foundation: The Journey

We now focus on what happens when a traditional philanthropic foundation elects to transform itself into a hybrid VP model. What helped this transformation, what hindered it, and what are the implications for the philanthropic sector?

History

The Edna McConnell Clark Foundation, a traditional family foundation, opened its doors in 1969. In the early days, the EMCF focused on methodological and systemic innovations. In the late 1990s, it risked its reputation and programs to transform itself into a high-engagement, institution-building enterprise using the kinds of strategies that dominated the VP movement. Similar to early VP practitioners, according to one subject, the EMCF's board "saw big systems-reform movements eating up money without having any evidence to show the good that was wrought." In February 1996, in its eagerness to help the EMCF evolve, the board hired Michael Bailin as the foundation's executive director. Previously, Bailin had been the founder, former president, and chief executive officer of Public/Private Ventures, a nonprofit organization dedicated to improving opportunities for young people in poor communities. He had also worked as a consultant with the Ford Foundation to advise many nonprofit organizations. Bailin had experience in both the foundation and nonprofit worlds, and his methodical and conscientious leadership steered the EMCF into unknown territory.

The VP model that appealed to Bailin asserted that philanthropic foundations should be investing in the success of the nonprofit organizations by providing deeper investments, creating and fostering clearer long-term plans, and offering needed nonfinancial assistance. Bailin's theory of change asserted that the EMCF would fund successful nonprofit organizations within the Northeast and help them grow to scale. He remarked:

> We don't decide what is the right thing to do and then have other people [grantees] carry out those right things. We're looking for only one thing in a program: Is it effective and working well for kids? . . . Show us evidence of what's working. The whole idea is, let's help good people who are running good organizations that we know are helping kids and position them to help more kids. . . . My whole approach here is [that] the expertise is out there.

While it is still too early to confirm the success of the transformation, the EMCF stands out in its willingness to risk its reputation, in its commitment to serving the needs of grantees with respect and transparency, and in its preparedness to be accountable by opening its doors to outside commentary and the critical thinking of others. At the same time, it is worth reflecting on both the competencies that helped the EMCF with this change and on the struggles the foundation faced.

Stages of Change

Unlike some venture philanthropists who came to philanthropy with little knowledge of the sector, Bailin's experience with nonprofits helped him understand the potential harms of different types of funding. He recognized the importance of building a foundation staff that would be respectful of the nonprofits they were serving and sensitive to the challenges they faced. The EMCF had advantages, but even those did not alleviate the growing pains it was to experience.

Changing a Foundation Is Never Easy

Despite Bailin's conscientious and methodical approach, the transformation from traditional foundation to capacity-building foundation was not easily accomplished. The EMCF had some long-term board members who were comfortable with the status quo by which specific projects were funded and championed by project directors who held their grantees to a loose set of outcomes. While the trustees were eager to help the EMCF evolve, they were not always in sync with each other on how that could best be accomplished. The original EMCF staff had strong ties to the board, so much so that the foundation president had become a secondary figure in the process of funding programs. Moreover, Bailin had to contend with a single board member who found it difficult to relinquish authority over the staff and the foundation. As a result, the early moves of the new foundation management were slower than anticipated.

Convincing the EMCF's project directors to accept Bailin's theory of change was also not easy. He realized that in the move toward capacity-building of nonprofit organizations, the foundation would require less youth development expertise from the staff and more organizational and management skills. The venture approach also required a collaborative effort among senior managers to change the foundation's program structures from the silo model, in which each project director was the leader and defender of his/her project, to a management group responsible for all youth development projects. This required the EMCF to build an entirely new staffing structure. The project directors had one choice: to participate as active and supportive change agents or to leave the foundation. Ultimately, this led to the resignation of all but one project director.

Finding the Right Grantees

The EMCF soon learned that although there were many organizations working in youth development, surprisingly few were financially stable, organizationally strong, and prepared to expand or ready for the funding approach the EMCF offered. As a result, it had to extend its reach beyond the Northeast. This meant hiring individuals to research potential youth development organizations across the country. It also meant considering less "mature" organizations for funding and helping them build their infrastructures by teaching them how to develop and use business plans.

Although the EMCF has provided smaller grants to small organizations to help them establish a stronger management infrastructure, the foundation's main focus has been on providing megagrants to large successful nonprofits such as the Boys and Girls Clubs of America. Smaller innovative nonprofits that are providing quality services and meeting the needs of fewer young people, albeit in novel ways, are often not eligible for the EMCF's institution-building grants.

Balancing Power with Transparency

The dynamics between the executive director of a nonprofit and a funder are complicated. Funding relationships breed different expectations. How these differences are resolved determines the level of trust between the two enterprises. Two major issues make it difficult for grantees and grantmakers to build trust: the power imbalance and a lack of transparency between funder and nonprofit. Under Bailin's leadership, the EMCF was as committed to the ideal of foundation transparency and accountability to the grantee as it was to ensuring that grantees met their obligations to the foundation. This was meant to ensure that all parties understood the commitments that they were making. To reinforce the foundation's commitment to transparency, Bailin met with every nonprofit's board prior to funding and reviewed with them and the executive director the contract of agreement: what the EMCF expected from the nonprofit and what the nonprofit could expect from the foundation. The EMCF and its grantees understood that trust was co-constructed by individuals over a period of time and would be built, in part, through transparency and honesty in word and deed. As in any relationship, disagreements and discussions are inevitable, but it is the ability to resolve those conflicts to the satisfaction of both parties that allows trust to develop.

Introducing Nonprofits to the Business of Social Change

Although a daunting task, drafting a business plan was required of all nonprofits and proved to be the scaffolding that would define expectations, establish a formal strategy for feedback, and encourage dialogue between both sides. The EMCF's commitment to the success of its grantees was reflected in its efforts to apply business processes and indicators to the nonprofits' specific needs and development. Most important, nonprofits working for social change had the responsibility to represent their efforts and perspectives accurately. This included pushing back when the EMCF's expectations were not in line with the nonprofit's mission and goals, enabling the grantees to maintain their vision, focus, and direction.

Supporting Evaluation as a Tool for Success

As with many VP organizations and some traditional foundations, the EMCF was committed to a thorough evaluation of the impact and success of grantees' program efforts. To that end, the EMCF provided significant monetary and technical support. As one EMCF grantee reported, quantifying the impact of a program was valuable because it helped the nonprofit organize its efforts and manage the effective expansion of its programs.

For some nonprofits, however, the foundation's advice seemed overly cautious. Assessing impact often meant something different to a nonprofit seeking long-term social changes than it did to the EMCF's leaders, who looked for short-term changes that would eventually lead to long-term reform. For example, one nonprofit director stated that the EMCF preferred to measure students' math skills because it was easier. However, the mission of the nonprofit was to instill leadership and writing skills, which, while more difficult to measure, were more indicative of the program's priorities. Using the foundation's yardstick for effectiveness seemed short-sighted to the nonprofit. Although the EMCF was focused on long-term social change as well, gauging effectiveness by relatively simple metrics was not fully honoring the nonprofit's mission to effect *long-term* social change. However, the nonprofit felt safe enough to disagree with the EMCF, which led to a compromise that addressed both concerns.

In another instance with the same nonprofit, the EMCF wanted to assess how many students stayed in school as opposed to how many students showed leadership and writing skills and went on to college. This was a point of disagreement between the EMCF and the nonprofit. Again, communication, respect, and trust—the backbone of successful relationships—can easily be threatened if manipulation and capitulation dominate funder-grantee interactions. In response, the EMCF worked with the grantee and agreed to a compromise that supported the grantee's perspective. Equally important is the recognition that effectiveness is not always an assessment of quality. For example, the number of students who attend classes may increase, but the increase may not be indicative of improved literacy. The EMCF appreciated and acknowledged this difference. However, in the field and across the philanthropic sector, the concern for impact and success can be oversimplified.

Exiting the Old to Develop the New

Given the complex challenges of changing the old foundation while simultaneously trying to establish a new foundation, in 2000, the board gave Bailin the go-ahead to exit all existing programs. Bailin found new funding sources and "homes" for many of the old projects, honorably exiting them. While the EMCF is forthright about providing the end date of a grant to its new grantees, exit strategies remain a conundrum for the foundation. The EMCF has used multiple strategies to that end. They have built grantees' development capabilities by hiring and training development specialists as a component of the grant and by seeking funding partners for nonprofits' development needs. These strategies have not yet survived the test of time, but the EMCF is hopeful. Another strategy suggested by an EMCF interviewee was that foundations or venture philanthropists fund the nonprofit until the social problem has been eradicated or solved. He laughingly (albeit seriously) reiterated what he had often heard others say:

> Do we really have to have [an exit strategy]? Don't we just exit when what we're trying to accomplish is finished, and we work at it until it's done, or until we all agree that it's not possible to accomplish? I think this exit strategy business is, in many ways, an artifact of these big foundations that are preoccupied with the fact that they have to have an initiative, and it has to prove something, and then they have to get out and do something else. I think that's just another example of a fundamentally disrespectful attitude toward what they're trying to accomplish because if they're really serious about their goal, then they'll work at it, and they'll keep working at it. And their exit will happen either when it's accomplished or when they admit failure.

Unfortunately, funding a nonprofit in perpetuity is not a strategy used by the EMCF and is rare among other foundations or VP funders, although some provide considerable endowments to keep nonprofits solvent. The exit strategy continues to beleaguer the entire philanthropic sector, not just the EMCF.

In summary, the transformation of the EMCF required that the foundation 1) gain consensus among the foundation staff and board for the ensuing changes; 2) hire new staff for the new priorities; 3) shift from four program areas to the single area of youth development; 4) provide larger grants to fewer nonprofits with a focus on capacity-building rather than project development; 5) find successful grantees ready for capacity-building; 6) focus on the impact of services provided by the nonprofit; 7) create partnerships between nonprofits and the foundation staff based on openness and trust; 8) establish rigorous business plans appropriate for nonprofit contexts; and 9) develop viable exit strategies that would diminish the financial burden of the grantee's increased budget.

The EMCF has accomplished what few foundations have been willing to do: it has risked its reputation, its endowment, and its standing in the community and made itself accountable and transparent to those it serves. Still, in spite of the EMCF's track record, we suggest that the conceptual issues around the VP model raise some concerns for the philanthropic sector. What happens to nonprofits that require greater fund-raising skills and resources to survive the process of growing to scale? What happens to small innovative organizations that do not qualify for large capacity-building grants? What is lost when social change is reduced to metrics? When the trends within the philanthropic sector are building capacity and quantifying results, who will fund the research and development projects that fuel innovations and broad conceptual ideas?

Conclusion: Strategies for Good Work in Venture Philanthropy

In philanthropy, in helping people, it's going to be a journey. . . . If anyone really wants to get out and help somebody . . . you're going to have failures. You're going to have periods where you feel like you're not making progress. Poverty is such a huge and overwhelming enemy, you're going to have times when you wonder, Why am I doing this? And you've just got to, at the end of the day, have the faith that you are making a difference.

When VP emerged as a trend, critics (Eisenberg 1999; Kramer 1999; Sievers 1997) sounded alarm bells about the approach. And indeed, our study finds that venture philanthropists did not fully anticipate the complexity and potential harm of transferring venture capital investment practices to the funding of nonprofits. Their missteps, while unintentional, highlight the perils of VP. The leadership of the EMCF also faced difficulties and risks in implementing an institution-building approach, suggesting that traditional grantmaking experience does not make one immune to the challenges of using this philanthropic model. However, there is much to be hopeful about. The most dedicated of VP's pioneers learned valuable lessons and are committed to evolving the approach. By the same token, the EMCF's leaders drew on their deep experience in traditional grantmaking and the nonprofit sector in their efforts to fulfill the promise of this philanthropic model.

Successful Strategies

The journeys of both venture philanthropists and the EMCF suggest promising lessons and strategies for doing good work—work that is effective and not harmful. First and foremost, creating partnerships based on trust and deep respect for the expertise of the nonprofit, though difficult, is essential. As the EMCF knew and venture philanthropists discovered, trust takes time and you can never be certain you have it. However, it is the linchpin of the model—a necessary (though not sufficient) condition for success in engaged philanthropy. Honest communication between funder and nonprofit is a critical indicator of a successful relationship. To achieve this, funders must have a high level of awareness of the power differential between them and their investees. Some interviewees describe an effective strategy as a balance between listening and asserting or (as another chapter in this volume describes) between being a "partner" and "parent."

Good funder-grantee relationships acknowledge the boundary where the funder's knowledge ends and the grantee's expertise begins. The foundation must serve the nonprofit and not vice versa. This helps define the appropriate level of engagement with each investee. Some nonprofits require far more hands-on assistance than others. Deeper engagement can be tremendously valuable but also poses greater risks. Some VP organizations now take conscious steps to prepare their staff and volunteers for responsible, sensitive engagement. In some cases, this means a more respectful, careful way of working with grantees; in other cases, it means less direct engagement.

Second, our interviews testify to the importance of crafting an ideal future state collaboratively with nonprofits. While the exit strategy is still an unresolved piece of VP (and of philanthropy as a whole), the mindset of long-term planning with nonprofits is invaluable. Doing this well means recognizing that scaling up is not appropriate or desirable for all nonprofits; indeed, it can be destructive. As the EMCF's due diligence process found, fewer nonprofits were prepared to grow, much less go to scale, than anticipated. As the leadership there decided, good work can also be done by strengthening organizations through business planning with the hope that they might be equipped to grow at some future point. Recognizing the potential and limitations of individual nonprofits is therefore critical. At the very least, exits should be custom-developed for each grantee. Even then, any exit leaves some nonprofits with an uncertain future. Our research also suggests that collaboration among funders to support successful nonprofits may be a promising exit strategy.

Third, our interviewees reveal that certain qualities in a practitioner can facilitate good work. As one important example, venture practitioners and EMCF leaders share the quality of being self-reflective grantmakers. They invite constructive feedback through comprehensive evaluations of grantees' experiences and perceptions of them, often by third-party consultants. Practitioners use this input as a basis for continuous improvement. Accordingly, one interviewee describes his VP organization as "a learning organization." They also share their war stories and missteps publicly with their peers. This commitment to transparency with the field is impressive. Their public dialogue contributes to the evolution of the approach and sets an example for the larger field of philanthropy —creating a model for knowledge-sharing that others would be wise to follow.

Finally, to create transformative impact, venture philanthropists need an articulated theory of change beyond the benchmarks they set out for their small portfolios of grantees. VP contributes a methodology or a strategy for social investing. However, as President Paul Brest of The William and Flora Hewlett Foundation notes, "A strategy comprises the unromantic, nitty-gritty working out of the *means* to accomplish one's goals. It is never an end in itself, but only a tool to aid an organization in achieving its mission" (Brest 2004). Unlike other foundations that are known for the social problems they hope to mend, venture philanthropists lead with their methodology. As one practitioner stated: "I guess I feel that venture philanthropy is a way to work. It's not issue specific, so I don't worry about which issue."

Implemented carefully, VP can help build nonprofits' capacities for creating positive impact. However, as with any movement for change, it raises questions. Beyond promoting greater effectiveness and the scaling of successful nonprofits, do venture philanthropists have a larger vision for social change that guides their funding decisions and collaborations? Do venture philanthropists aspire to make philanthropy more effective and, if so, to what end? If they hold a larger vision of their work, is that vision transparent to their grantees, fellow philanthropists, and the public? Ideally, good philanthropy should not only strengthen a portfolio of nonprofit organizations to help them grow and be more effective change agents; it should also be part of a larger vision of the good society. Because funders are powerful agents with large sums of money, it is important that they articulate the social change agendas their philanthropy pursues.

Notes

We are grateful for the support of The Atlantic Philanthropies and The William and Flora Hewlett Foundation. We are thankful to Bill Damon, Wendy Fischman, Howard Gardner, Laura Horn, Jenni Menon, and Susan Verducci for helpful comments.

1. Such efforts are variously described as "venture philanthropy," "high-engagement philanthropy," "capacity-building," or "institution-building." In this chapter, we generally use the term "venture philanthropy," or VP, to describe this funding model, except when discussing the "institution-building" approach used by the Edna McConnell Clark Foundation.

2. Venture philanthropy organizations generally use the term "investee" to refer to nonprofits in which they invest. This language highlights venture philanthropists' roots in venture capital. The EMCF continues to use "grantee," the term used in traditional philanthropy.

3. According to *Venture Philanthropy 2002: Advancing Nonprofit Performance through High-Engagement Grantmaking*, venture philanthropy grants totaled $50 million in 2001, making up only 0.2 percent of all foundation grants (Venture Philanthropy Partners 2002).

References

Brest, Paul. 2004. "In Defense of Strategic Philanthropy." Menlo Park, Calif.: Hewlett Foundation. Available online at http://www.aps-pub.com/proceedings/1492/490202.pdf.

Eisenberg, Pablo. 1999. "The 'New Philanthropy' Isn't New—or Better." *The Chronicle of Philanthropy,* January 28.

Kramer, Mark R. 1999. "Venture Capital and Philanthropy: A Bad Fit." *The Chronicle of Philanthropy,* April 22.

Letts, Christine, William P. Ryan, and Allen S. Grossman. 1997. "Virtuous Capital: What Foundations Can Learn from Venture Capitalists." *Harvard Business Review* 75, no. 2: 36–44.

Sievers, Bruce. 1997. "If Pigs Had Wings." *Foundation News & Commentary* 38, no. 6: 44–46.

Tuan, Melinda. 2004. "The Dance of Deceit: A Power Imbalance Undermines the Social Sector." *Stanford Social Innovation Review* 2, no. 1: 75–76.

Venture Philanthropy Partners. 2002. *Venture Philanthropy 2002: Advancing Nonprofit Performance through High-Engagement Grantmaking.* Washington, D.C.: Venture Philanthropy Partners.

8   Ideational Philanthropy: The Impact of Funding Social Ideas

Liza Hayes Percer

In the period following the social turbulence of the 1960s, the large foundations that had long dominated American philanthropy became increasingly focused on grassroots applications of accepted approaches rather than on the development of new ones. As a result, much of mainstream philanthropy lost interest in exploration and debate about the causes of and solutions to social problems and turned rather to supporting purely practical work. The Ford Foundation, for example, became concerned with funding "action-oriented rather than research-oriented" programs meant to "test the outer edges of advocacy and citizen participation" (MacDonald 1996). The nonprofits supported by these large mainstream foundations worked on solutions to social problems that liberal thinking of a prior generation had identified, such as efforts to promote diversity, equality, and the civic and economic prospects of minorities and marginalized populations.

In the mid-1970s, a few conservative foundations with modest resources took philanthropy in a radically different direction, investing in the development of new ideas and approaches to social problems. With this determinedly intellectual strategy, these small foundations managed to transform public policy in the United States in a major and lasting way. While large foundations were spending huge sums on practice-based projects that were prone to disappear without a trace once the funding ended, ideational efforts supported by these small conservative foundations were being leveraged many times over in their impact on social and political policy.

This ideational strategy was not accidental; it was consciously adopted by foundation officials who became convinced of the power of supporting new ideas. With the appearance of a series of articles by Irving Kristol in the *Wall Street Journal* (1973a, 1973b, 1975) and the publication of William Simon's book, *A Time for Truth* (1978), a call went out to fund ideas that promoted a stronger private sector. Kristol suggested that conservative donors consider philanthropic giving as a way to shape public policy, promote free enterprise, and limit government (Piereson 2004). As a result, key conservative donors set out to support those individuals, institutions, and publications that could best forward these ideals. Drawing upon significantly less financial resources than their liberal counterparts, these conservative foundations focused their philanthropic efforts on supporting the few that could influence the many.

Few could have anticipated the impact they achieved. A recent report from the National Committee for Responsive Philanthropy compared the $252 million conservative foundations donated from 1999 to 2001 and the $30.5 billion grant-makers across the nation donated in 2001 alone and found that by concentrating on operational support and funding those with the potential for great political leverage, the conservative foundations enjoyed a great deal more effectiveness as a result of their philanthropic donations (Wilhelm 2004). In higher education alone, ideational philanthropy was responsible for the creation of the John M. Olin Institute for Strategic Studies at Harvard University and the promotion of the Law & Economics movement, and was enormously influential in the school choice and welfare reform movements (Miller 2003).

Yet despite such publicity, most of what has been written about this philanthropic revolution focuses primarily on the simple fact that it occurred, rather than on providing any in-depth analysis into understanding how others might be able to learn from its successes.[1] In the interest of furthering good work in philanthropy, the project's research team set out to understand what these foundations did right and how future practitioners might learn from them. The team attempts to understand this movement in a manner somewhat removed from the politics associated with it. This approach reflects current interests within the field of philanthropy in seeing the funding of ideas as a potential and actual strategy for philanthropists from a variety of political stances. In this vein, those involved in this research have come to consider the phenomenon that arose out of the conservative efforts to fund ideas in the 1970s as ideational philanthropy rather than simply the work of conservative foundations. For the purposes of our research, we have come to define ideational philanthropy as philanthropic work that focuses primarily on the funding and dissemination of ideas that influence public policy. In this chapter, which is based on interview data collected from several key figures from the ideational philanthropy movement, I bring attention to elements they perceive as contributing most to their unprecedented success and consider whether these elements are applicable to philanthropists from all political arenas.

Mission and Goals

In order to understand the success of ideational philanthropy, it is first important to get a better sense of the missions and goals that were the inspiration behind this movement. These can best be understood in two ways: the desire to shape public policy and promote free enterprise and the conviction that powerful and successfully promoted ideas have tremendous potential to impact American society. In keeping with the calls to action made by Bill Simon and Irving Kristol, John M. Olin, with the help of his associate Frank O'Connell, refocused his foundation's energies in the 1970s on the support of "scholars and think tanks that favor limited government, individual responsibility, and a free society" (Miller 2003, 10). Several years later, The Bradley Foundation began to pursue its desire to become "Olin West." It was "committed to preserving and defending the tradition of free representative government and private enterprise which has enabled the American nation and, in a larger sense, the entire Western world to flourish intellectually and economically'" (37). Both of these foundations, in the company of others such as the Sarah Mellon Scaife Foundation and the Smith Richardson Foundation, believed firmly that funding ideas would be the way to achieve their ideological goals. They made up for their marginalized ideas and small numbers with drive, determination, and a somewhat revolutionary employment of strategic tactics to achieve their philanthropic missions and goals. Many ideational philanthropists have pointed to this mission-oriented drive and these tactics as the reason for their unusual success.

Strategies for the Funding of Ideas

The ideational philanthropists that we spoke to, despite the differences in their views of their work and its success, had in common several perceptions of how and why ideational philanthropy has been so successful. These perceptions can best be understood as a series of unique strategies that conservative philanthropists used to overcome common philanthropic obstacles and a series of standards they used in response to harms that are commonly encountered in the world of philanthropy. Specifically, these veteran ideational practitioners disclosed the use of three particular strategies and the avoidance of two particular harms as key elements of the ideational approach. This approach may be the reason why the ideational philanthropists were at once different from and more successful than many of their colleagues. What follows is a description and analysis of these particular strategies and harms.

The Ideational Approach:
Informality and Flexibility in Successful Giving

One way ideational philanthropists see their approach to philanthropy as differing from and as more effective than the approach of their counterparts has to do with the ways they monitor and manage their grantees. Across the board, philanthropists agree that it is extremely difficult to measure success in philanthropy. "The fundamental structural problem of foundations," one of our subjects told us,

> is that we haven't got a good enough model yet. If you're in business, you get feedback from your customer. . . . It's not as if you can tell how many widgets are selling [in philanthropy]. It's not as if you can tell how many votes you're getting at the ballot box or how many contributions come to the plate after your Sunday sermon.

In other words, it is difficult to know if larger political and/or societal aims have been achieved because of money that has been given to a particular organization. Perhaps because many conservative foundations emerged out of informal beginnings and are staffed by small numbers of closely knit individuals, many of the ideational philanthropists tackled this obstacle by maintaining an informal and flexible relationship with their grantees. Rather than attempting to develop formal means by which to hold their grantees accountable for the funds that were given to them, these foundations worked against the desire to produce clean-cut measurements of immeasurable activities. Instead, they seemed to embrace the informality the situation called for and sought to develop flexible, trusting relationships with their grantees.

Indeed, some even saw the inability to measure success as an opportunity to foster greater creativity and encourage risk. With the minimization of formal accountability, organizations funded by ideational philanthropists could have the opportunity to take risks and try new ideas without fearing that funds might be pulled if a foundation disagreed with how they were used. This is not to say that these foundations gave money away to whomever came asking for it; they took care to get a sense of potential, dedication, trustworthiness, and mission, but once an agreement to fund had been made they did their best to let the organization use the money as it saw fit.

Along these lines, rather than using any formal method of assessing due diligence, ideational donors worked toward strengthening relationships with their donees and relied on communicating openly and maintaining common goals and approaches to the monitoring of their grantees. As one individual told us, "You can't interfere. You can advise, you can suggest, you can put them in touch with other people who might be able to support them, but the most effective way of doing philanthropy involves not second-guessing the people whose job it is." Another claimed that he "hire[s] people precisely because they can run their own show. . . . We try to be flexible and adaptable and reasonable and non-bureaucratic." A third, from the John M. Olin Foundation, reported that "Olin is kind of well-known for being hands-off with its grant-making in the sense that it tries to identify worthy recipients and gives them money with understandings about how that money will be spent but without pestering them or without micro-managing them." It may seem naive or extraordinarily risky to operate so informally, but these foundations capitalized on what others may have perceived to be an obstacle to successful philanthropy. They worked to strengthen relationships, creativity, and risk-taking among their grantees.

The Ideational Approach: Persistence and Long-Term Support

In the same spirit of remaining flexible and informal in their approach to monitoring the use of funds, many of the ideational philanthropists spoke of confronting the obstacle of impatience in philanthropy by cultivating their own persistence. One individual commented on the challenge impatience can present:

> I think the times that we erred, it was impatience. Patience is the hard part of all of this. And I think the enthusiasm of many of the professionals in philanthropy makes patience awfully hard to consider. We get the big meeting together to collaborate . . . and by God, we're going to go out there and solve the problem of teenage [pregnancy] and we're going to do it with a lot of money and we want quick results.

Many of the ideational philanthropists we spoke to felt that one of the most problematic manifestations of impatience is the temptation to fund organizations only when they are doing well. "One of my pet peeves with the funding community," one subject told us, "is how when an organization is in trouble they cut and run instead of sticking with them and seeing it through." The approach of many individuals who spearheaded the funding of ideas was to invest time and money in organizations over the long haul, again focusing on the bigger picture of an organization's health and potential for success rather than responding in any conclusive fashion to particular moments of distress. "Of course we care deeply if it succeeds but we're not going to withdraw funds if it doesn't," we were told.

> There's such an emphasis in philanthropy on hands-on work and direct results and so forth. What I've learned from the Olin and Bradley experiences is that sometimes you need to invest in ideas and be patient and stick with them for twenty years. The result you see later on will be enormously important, but it takes a lot of patience and time and resources and dedication and understanding.

In this vein, many of the ideational philanthropists built long-term relationships with particular organizations, offering them yearly grants for periods of twenty years or more (Krehely, House, and Kernan 2004). These foundations embraced long-term investments and sought to cultivate them rather than just accommodate them out of necessity. In the face of both of these obstacles, the ideational philanthropists saw and developed opportunities.

The Ideational Approach: Matching Good Intentions with Strategic Thinking

The final common obstacle in response to which the ideational philanthropists developed unconventional strategies can be understood as a paucity of purposeful thinking within the philanthropic community. Many of the philanthropists we spoke with felt that it is all too easy to believe that good intentions and money are the primary means by which successful philanthropy can be done.

Many of the ideational philanthropists felt that the way to achieve their goals (which were, as stated before, to affect public policy and strengthen free enterprise) they would need to involve a great deal of leverage. They knew that given their comparatively limited financial resources, one of the only ways they had a chance to get their word out would be to identify the most promising thinkers and market their ideas in the most effective manner possible. As one subject succinctly stated, "I think we wanted to fund people that would be influential. Either they had influential students or they had a platform or position that would make their ideas and their work influential." The ideational philanthropists ended up adopting a strategy that enabled them to get the most "bang for their buck." In addition to funding promising individuals, they funded otherwise neglected or marginal academic initiatives that had excellent reputations. "Seventy percent of our dollars go to create institutions or to start projects that would not otherwise be funded by anyone else," a subject told us, "and that's one of our most important tasks." One philanthropist elaborated on his particular take on the funding of ideas, drawing upon the example of the Mothers Against Drunk Driving organization:

> This is the power of one. One woman whose child was killed by a drunk driver brought that to fruition. Changed the law. To me that is the best example. So the guy who is talking to us as philanthropists said don't throw your money into doing, boosting what we do. You're a drop in the bucket no matter how much money you have; the government spends trillions of dollars. Even your five hundred million dollars like Annenberg is a drop in the bucket. Fund things that we don't do. Fund stuff that we can't do.

In this vein, many ideational philanthropists were as committed to funding the dissemination of ideas as they were to funding the thinkers themselves. If they funded an academic, they were sure that she had the potential to write a book that could be distributed to the larger public. If they saw that there was an exciting gathering of academics at a reputable institution, they encouraged them in their efforts to develop an organization or start a journal. Indeed, some even saw the difference between charity and philanthropy to be the difference between giving money and giving money that promises to effect change. As one individual put it:

> You hit those places that are going to make a difference for the picture as a whole. You don't do charity, you do philanthropy. You do stuff that is aimed at changing the system. Systemic change. It's the only thing that's going to work in this field.

The ideational philanthropists knew that in order for their funding to be successful, they would need to have strong beliefs and equally strong practical considerations about how those beliefs could be received and disseminated. Much of their success had to do not only with the decision to fund ideas but also with the recognition of the need to get those ideas into public consciousness.

Advantages of Long-Term Giving and Leverage

It makes sense that these foundations, which focused on investing their money in the development and dissemination of ideas that affect public policy, would have strategies that respect and take into account the benefit of support-ing activities that do not yield immediate or ready results. Ideas, particularly as they are developed in academia, take time to mature and become fruitful and may undergo a great deal of revision and change before they do so. By contrast, foundations that are interested in action-oriented, hands-on approaches may be less likely to focus on the benefits of investing in strategies that may or may not result in a goal being met or strategies that may require a great deal of time and resource investment before any positive results can be met. It seems that in de-ciding to invest in ideas, ideational philanthropists uncovered, almost inciden-tally, a whole new set of strategies from which the entire philanthropic commu-nity may benefit. These strategies take into account the positive side of taking the time to invest in what is not immediately beneficial. They demonstrate the ways a less controlled approach may be not just useful but also necessary for success to be achieved.

Standards and Harms in the Funding of Ideas

In any field, a keen sense of the harms that can be caused by poor work and an awareness of the standards that must be employed to offset these harms will play a critical role in the level of success that can be reached. Many of those who played key roles in the ideational philanthropy movement did not just ac-knowledge that philanthropic work can cause harm but also spoke passionately about the importance of understanding the harms that philanthropic work may cause and the need to be constantly vigilant in one's awareness of and avoidance of these harms. These key players identified two harms that philanthropists in general are particularly susceptible to and outlined for us the specific ways they have sought to overcome them.

The Ideational Approach: Perspective and Humility

Among many of the subjects interviewed regarding good work in phi-lanthropy, including those not associated with the ideational philanthropy move-ment, there was an almost universal awareness of the dangers that egotism pre-sents to those who wish to do good work in philanthropy. This egotism takes the form of a tendency to succumb to flattery that may be disingenuous, the temptation to act as if the money you are donating is yours, and an overall in-flated sense of the importance of one's ideas and perspectives in the face of expertise from other operators in the world of philanthropy.

Many of the ideational philanthropists counteract these harms by working toward maintaining a certain level of humility in considering the value of their contributions and the wisdom of other contributors. This is done by honoring and respecting the expertise and insights of those to whom the money is given. One subject goes so far as to seek to work only with those whose egos also ap-pear to be in check. Another tackles this challenge by seeking to maintain anonymity for her foundation's activities. Others work on listening carefully to their grantees, seeking advice and expertise from multiple sources regarding the area in which they wish to provide funding, remaining open to new ideas, and constantly reminding themselves that the money is not theirs. Finally, many donors realize that they must work toward challenging themselves, recognizing that the challenge may not come from those who are seeking funds. "The best you can do is try to be hardnosed yourself about assessing whether projects you're funding actually had any impact or made any difference. And then also to not rest on your laurels, so that even if something did [make a difference], you become the driver for making it do more."

The Ideational Approach: Precautionary Thinking

It can be easy to assume that good intentions and plentiful funds will result in philanthropic success. Despite the flexible approach ideational philanthropists took toward giving and their donors, they took great care to assess the implications of how their funding would be used. Unfortunately, according to the ideational philanthropists that we spoke with, if philanthropists do not take the time to consider the potentially harmful consequences of their work in addition to the potential benefits, they can end up creating harms where none were intended. We were told, quite simply, that "most people, when they get into this, they just think they're going to do good. Or they think that it's their intentions that are the critical thing. And they don't really see much beyond that. I think you need to see that some things can happen that you never anticipated."

In response to this possible harm, many of the ideational philanthropists have imposed on themselves a standard of carefully considering the potentially harmful consequences of their plans as they are put into effect and otherwise executed. They impose this standard on themselves and their grantees: "I force you to reason in a practical way through a long chain of consequences." In fact, The Philanthropy Roundtable, many of whose members were or are a part of the ideational philanthropy movement, has set as one of its primary goals helping philanthropists clarify their visions and how they might be realized. This is done by studying those who have enjoyed, over some period of time, repeated positive impact in their philanthropic endeavors. Toward this end, it organizes meetings and offers counsel to individuals who wish to be in touch with those who have done similar work before them and those who seek advice about how to align their goals with best practices.

Conclusion

It is not atypical to speak of ideational philanthropy as a war of ideas, with conservatives on one side and liberals on the other. Despite this rhetoric, after speaking with many dynamic individuals who have been or are involved in ideational philanthropy, it appears that their focus is not driven by belligerence but by a genuine dedication to successful philanthropic practice. To characterize ideational philanthropy as important because it advanced the conservative movement is to ignore what is perhaps most significant about it: that it was able, with small funds and few members, to generate ideas powerful enough to reframe national debate and shape public policy for at least a generation. It is important, therefore, to study ideational philanthropy as a model by which philanthropists from multiple perspectives may learn how to better achieve their goals.

Along these lines, despite its enormous success, there is much concern within the philanthropic world that the funding of ideas is in danger of dying out with the sunsetting of key foundations, such as the John M. Olin Foundation, and the retirement of the key founding individuals. In order for ideational philanthropy to continue, it needs an infusion of new support in the form of individuals and foundations to replace the natural losses that will occur as the first generation of ideational philanthropists fade. As James Piereson has written, "There are few final victories in the contest of ideas. The ground gained . . . in recent decades can be quickly lost if those ideas are not renewed and persistently articulated in public forums. This requires talent, energy—and money" (Piereson 2004). It is worth considering, therefore, that one possibility for retaining the valuable lessons of ideational philanthropy for future good work is to regard its strategies and approach as one that is applicable across the philanthropic world rather than specific to a select few with particular visions. Ideational philanthropy should be viewed as a philanthropic tool that is ready for many future successes rather than a unique phenomenon destined to retire with the achievement of the specific political goals that inspired it.

Notes

1. John J. Miller's monograph (2003) is a notable exception to this rule.

References

Krehely, Jeff, Meaghan House, and Emily Kernan. 2004. *Axis of Ideology: Conservative Foundations and Public Policy Executive Summary*. Washington, D.C.: National Committee for Responsive Philanthropy.

Kristol, Irving. 1973a. "The Misgivings of a Philanthropist." *The Wall Street Journal*, March 14.

———. 1973b. "Social Reform: Gains and Losses." *The Wall Street Journal*, April 16.

———. 1975. "On Conservatism and Capitalism." *The Wall Street Journal*, September 11.

MacDonald, Heather. 1996. "The Billions of Dollars That Made Things Worse." *City Journal* 6, no. 4. Available online at http://www.city-journal.org/html/6_4_a1.html.

Miller, J. J. 2003. *Strategic Investment in Ideas: How Two Foundations Reshaped America.* Washington, D.C.: Philanthropy Roundtable.

Piereson, James. 2004. "You Get What You Pay For." *Wall Street Journal,* July 21.

Simon, William E. 1978. *A Time for Truth.* Chicago: McGraw-Hill.

Wilhelm, Ian. 2004. "Conservative Foundations Promote Ideas More Effectively, Report Says." *The Chronicle of Philanthropy* 16, no. 11.

9   Funding on Faith:
Boston Ten Point Coalition

Laura Horn

Can a nonprofit organization operate effectively without being able to freely discuss an important source of its effectiveness? A well-known faith-based organization in Boston highlights the importance of this question to the philanthropic world. In its effort to stay afloat financially, the Boston Ten Point Coalition (BTPC) has found itself looking to foundations and corporations to fund its church-based social service programs. The world of organized philanthropy, however, tends to view social service as a secular rather than a religious activity and may shy away from discussing issues of faith and religion. In addition to the fund-raising challenges most grassroots nonprofit organizations encounter, BTPC faces an added challenge: communicating with traditionally secular funders about the role faith plays in its work without alienating the funders or compromising its Christian identity.

As part of a case study of BTPC, we asked the organization's leaders as well as its funders to describe the role of faith in the organization, and we sometimes received very different answers. Consider the following two descriptions.

A staff member told us, "It is in the mission that this is a Christian organization. . . . All of our programming is done through church-based volunteers. . . . [Faith] is the reason that we are here. That is the motivation from which we do everything we do. . . . We have a daily time of prayer, we open and close our meetings with prayer, and all of us share the same spiritual motivation. And it's very clear and very much in common."

In contrast, one of BTPC's funders told us, "The marketing materials don't necessarily suggest that the Ten Point Coalition is primarily a faith-based organization. . . . The only way I knew that it was faith-based was doing a site visit. It is part of a church school. But that's going into the building. Once you go into the building itself, I would still defy you to say that it's associated with any type of quote unquote church. Because corporate headquarters is in a building that houses a school."

The sharp contrast between these two descriptions of the organization raises an important question: How do traditionally secular funding organizations and faith-based organizations communicate with each other about the role of faith in social service? This question is especially important at a time when faith-based organizations are receiving national attention.

In order to survive in a competitive funding environment without compromising its core identity, BTPC's leaders must play a language game. They repackage the description of their organization depending on the perceived attitude of the foundation, corporation, or individual program officer to whom they are speaking.

As the (now former) development director described, whether the leaders of BTPC discuss faith with a funder and how they frame it if they discuss it at all "depends on the funder."

> With United Way Faith and Action, we talk about it until we're blue in the face, because they want to see it. They want to know how it works. With a secular funder who's not particularly interested in the faith component . . . I'll put that whole spiritual transformation process—I could put totally Christian words on this—but I'll mention that it's got a spiritual foundation and connect that with the funder's desire to see a change in the person's behavior, which we want too. You know? For us to say it's a legitimate spiritual transformation, we need to see the fruit of that. So you're not compromising who you are. You're putting it out there, but you're choosing language that is within their cultural set of words and not choosing offensive words to them.

As one funder told us, the hurdle for BTPC "is that they've got to make the belief system that they're operating in understandable to secular funders." BTPC has to translate its mission and process into a faith-neutral language and logic, but it is not alone in the translation. In order to help faith-based organizations such as BTPC compete for more funding in the secular funding world, a handful of individuals in local foundations help the leaders of BTPC translate the language of faith into the language of secular philanthropy.

In what follows, I focus on the role program officers who fund BTPC play in this translation. I briefly describe BTPC and its funders and then outline three ways in which BTPC's program officers describe the organization using the language of secular philanthropy: they emphasize measurable results, they frame religious institutions as valuable community resources, and they focus on the administrative capacity of the organization instead of the faith-based programs. I discuss the benefits and potential costs of these translations. Describing a faith-based organization in secular philanthropic language is a strategy to secure more funding without lying about the organization or compromising the organization's core identity, but it may also obscure the real strength of the organization. Instead of making BTPC's belief system understandable to secular funders, the translation may render it invisible. If funders do not understand how faith-based organizations are using faith, they may not be fully able to assess the results of the organization. They may lose an opportunity to increase social impact or they may unknowingly support an evangelical agenda. Such lack of understanding can limit the range of funding strategies they can use to engage with these organizations. I highlight the possibility of a more nuanced and productive discussion about faith and social service, using the conversation surrounding the creation of the United Way of Massachusetts Bay (UWMB) Faith and Action Initiative.

The Boston Ten Point Coalition

The Boston Ten Point Coalition is a nonprofit organization that works with community churches, local police, and government officials to keep at-risk youth from criminal activity. In 1992, four ministers began to organize the local Black church community to address escalating youth violence in Boston. The ministers' efforts started as an informal street outreach conducted primarily by the founders themselves. BTPC has since evolved into a well-known nonprofit organization with a handful of paid staff and fifty-two member churches that run various outreach programs and provide a large network of volunteers.

Although it is a Christian organization, BTPC's goals are not specifically religious. Its programs offer faith as one tool for life change, but BTPC does not require the people it serves to adopt religious beliefs or participate in religious activities. The primary purpose of the organization is to help churches connect with at-risk youth. Its member churches run a wide variety of programs that range from explicitly religious Bible study to mentoring programs that resemble their secular counterparts. One of BTPC's greatest successes has been the creation of a bridge between the secular and religious communities so they can work together on issues that concern them both. Reducing youth violence is both a secular and sacred goal, and BTPC has partnered with local corporations, law enforcement, and government agencies to address a wide range of problems that affect primarily African American youth. The Coalition's efforts were widely credited by the media with influencing the city's reduced homicide rates in the 1990s, a period known as the Boston Miracle. Numerous people see great potential in this organization to gain a large and stable funding base. However, in spite of its credited success and future promise, after thirteen years, it continues to operate on a very limited budget.

The Funders

BTPC receives donations from churches and individuals, most of which it collects at its annual fund-raising dinner. Too often, however, the money raised at the annual dinner barely pays for the cost of the event itself. The organization's financial survival is largely determined by its ability to secure grants from traditionally secular funding organizations, including foundations, corporations, and the federal government. Currently, BTPC receives grants ranging in size from roughly $5,000 to $100,000 from a small group of local foundations and corporations. The organization also receives a small amount of federal money that is regranted through the Boston Police Department. Early in the organization's development, it received two grants from a large national foundation, but since then it has not been able to access funds from such prominent sources.

For this case study, we interviewed three of the organization's founders, the executive director, the development director, four development consultants, and a board member. We interviewed thirteen of the organization's current and former funders who were recommended by BTPC's leaders as representative of their best funding relationships. Our sample included five program officers from local foundations, two from a large national foundation, three from local corporate foundations, one from a religious foundation, one from a church, and one from a government agency. (Although these individuals hold various positions, for the sake of simplicity, I will refer to the funders we interviewed as program officers.) We also interviewed two individuals from organizations that chose not to fund BTPC.

As Black Christians, several key individuals within the foundations and corporations that support BTPC share a cultural background with BTPC's leaders. Although we did not ask about the specifics of the program officers' religious affiliations, it was surprising how often this information emerged during the interviews. Two of the program officers volunteered that they are members of Reverend Hammond's church, and one mentioned that the gang-related shooting incident that catalyzed the formation of BTPC happened in the church that he attends. Two of the program officers with whom we spoke are trained as ministers themselves and several spoke more generally about their personal experience with the Black church.

BTPC is most successful in securing funding from traditionally secular corporations and foundations when it connects with individuals within those organizations who have some personal familiarity with the Black church. Many of BTPC's program officers who fund BTPC can articulate the role of faith in social service in both secular and religious terms. Direct personal experience with the Black church helps them understand the role of faith at Boston Ten Point Coalition and the potential impact of the Black church on important social issues. On a deeply personal level, the program officers for BTPC believe in the importance of the Black church to the communities they want to serve as funders. At the same time, their experience in the funding world helps them articulate the value of faith-based social service organizations in secular terms.

The program officers work with BTPC to facilitate communication between secular funders and faith-based organizations. One program officer who has helped turn the attention of local foundations to faith-based social service organizations described how her personal experience has influenced the role she plays in helping philanthropic and faith-based organizations understand each other:

> Once I got inside this industry [philanthropy] and understood more about their intentions and what we are striving to do in terms of supporting good work in the community, and understanding also, having been a product of the Black church

and understanding the value of the work that the church does in the Black community, I felt like our goals were aligned in a lot of ways. But there was misunderstanding on both parts. . . . A part of what I saw my role was to bring these groups together so that they can talk about what their fears, concerns, questions were in each of their respective areas, and try to figure out did they have common goals or could they work together. As it turned out, they did.

BTPC has attracted a solid core of supporters in the local philanthropic world who share a cultural background and strongly believe in the organization's social value and potential to help those who need it most. Privately, the organization has been able to discuss faith honestly and openly with many of its program officers. However, personal alignment with the organization's mission and culture is not enough to secure foundation funding for the organization. Program officers have to communicate their funding decisions to their board and to the broader philanthropic community, and faith is a delicate topic for many people in the organized funding world. Because faith is such a personal and emotionally charged topic, it is not easy to communicate about the use of faith in a social service organization to those who do not already share the same understanding of faith. While BTPC has connected with a small group of program officers who personally understand the importance of the Black church, most people in organized philanthropy are unfamiliar with Black church culture. Although they share many of the same social goals, they may not share an understanding of the role faith can play in an individual's life, an organization, or a community, especially a Black community.

The Translation

In order to secure funding for BTPC from their foundations or corporations and, more generally, help faith-based organizations such as BTPC compete for funding in the secular funding world, program officers sympathetic to BTPC's use of faith must find ways to articulate the strength of the organization —a strength they understand on a personal level—to their philanthropic colleagues in a way that deemphasizes faith and makes sense in the secular funding world. One of the funders spoke directly about the translation a program officer must do to secure funding for a faith-based organization:

> A number of us had to have lots of discussions about how we packaged a submission of a recommendation. . . . Though it was consistent with the funding priorities as far as we could determine, we knew that the nature of what we were funding might be difficult in terms of the sort of public image or the culture of the institution. And so it wasn't just around faith-based work, although that was clearly one area that was a pretty sticky wicket. There were always lots of discussions about how do you sell this to the [foundation]. You've been given a portfolio, you've been given guidelines and boundaries, you have something that you think fits within those, but you also know that people may be uncomfortable with it, so how do you sell it?

BTPC's program officers have used three main strategies to "sell" faith-based organizations to their colleagues and to the broader philanthropic world: focusing on results, framing the Black church as a community asset, and funding the secular administrative work of the organization rather than the faith-based programming.

Focusing on Results

When asked explicitly about the role of faith in their decision to fund BTPC, some funders repeatedly redirected the conversation to results. For example, one corporate funder emphasized the supreme importance of measurable results in his funding decision:

> I need data. I need hard data on the difference that my shareholder dollars have made in terms of [a] child's life. . . . So my rationale for Ten Point, regardless of the fact that Reverend Hammond is a minister, I did not think about the Ten Point Coalition as a faith-based organization. I thought about the Ten Point Coalition as an organization that had credibility in the community, that had identified a niche and that had professionals in the organization that would work with a Fortune 50 company like [name of company] to give me information and develop impact standards that would allow me to go to my board of directors and say "Here's how hard [name of company] dollars are working in the community."

When it comes to funding, this funder insists that faith is irrelevant. He focuses on measurable results. Another corporate funder, when asked whether faith was an essential part of BTPC, answered, "I think that's a difficult question for me to answer. Again, I'm trying to just look at the results."

As one church funder said to us,

> I think a lot of people, because they disagree with the faith, they don't look at the results. My feeling is that the results of what they are doing are effective and beneficial to society whether you agree with their faith motivation or not and that people need to be able to separate those two and look at the results.

Black Church as a Community Resource

Another common rationale Ten Point's funders used to describe their decision to fund BTPC and faith-based organizations in general is that the Black church is an important but underutilized community resource. Although the program officers' belief in the power of the Black church was informed by their understanding of faith, they were able to appeal to philanthropy's values of community and diversity to frame a more secular argument.

One funder presented this logic clearly throughout the interview.

> It was people of faith who were willing to take on this task that everybody else was pretty much afraid of. . . . They were the only ones there willing to tackle the problems, motivated by faith, by a call to be concerned about those who were oppressed. . . . And what gave rise to the Boston Ten Point Coalition is that

a church trying to minister to a gang member's family ended up having the church shot up in the midst of a funeral. There weren't a lot of people willing to hang around for that kind of madness, but the churches were there. They stayed, for the most part. . . . So we had to work with who was there twelve years ago, and faith-based organizations were in many cases the only real institution left.

Another funder presented similar logic.

It seems to me, and I think studies have proven, that in the lower economic communities in the greater Boston area, and I'm talking specifically Roxbury, Mattapan and Dorchester, and Jamaica Plain to some extent, the only leadership left is faith-based. . . . Frankly, that's part of the reason that Ten Point got going in the first place. The ministers said, "Hey look, if we don't step up and do something here, nobody is." And they were right. So still to this day, to my knowledge, I haven't seen any other leadership group emerge that is as strong and has such a loyal following among the citizenry as the faith-based leaders; that is, the ministers, principally.

We spoke with a program officer at a corporate foundation that has a policy of not funding religious activities. When we asked her about her funding relationship with BTPC, she said,

What we try to do is not focus on organizations that are solely involved with faith. What we recognize, and we struggle too, is that particularly in the Black community, so many social services, civil rights organizations have come out of the church, and we realize the galvanizer that the church is.

Presenting religious institutions as a community resource, as these funders do, includes faith-based organizations in philanthropic strategy without directly engaging the issue of faith.

Secular Operating Support

A resourceful way to sidestep discussion about faith with people who might misunderstand its role is to focus instead on the administrative aspects of the work. One of BTPC's early supporters was personally interested in supporting the work of faith-based organizations addressing issues affecting young African American men.

The faith-based element, the manner in which they were modeling faith in the public square with restraint and respect for choice and free will was in fact part of what I wanted to encourage and highlight . . . and so it was the faith, and it was the kind of faith exhibited that was attractive and I wanted the Foundation to know more about that.

He worked in a large national foundation that was "a little out in front with respect to taking note of what clergy and congregations were doing in communities." However, he understood that faith was still a delicate topic in a traditionally secular foundation. He found a way to support the organization without offending the foundation's secular tradition by funding BTPC's first full-time executive director.

> I thought that it would be an easy sell within [the foundation], to make a strategic grant for infrastructural organizational development that we could watch and get some fairly short-term results on whether it was making a difference.

While this grant filled a real need for BTPC, it was easier to pass through the foundation's vetting process as a capacity-building grant that supported administrative work than a grant to support specific faith-based programming would have been.

Boston funders were focused on faith-based organizations well before President George W. Bush took office. The president's current faith-based initiative, however, has reinforced the focus on building the administrative capacity of faith-based organizations rather than explicitly supporting the use of faith in their social service programs. Because of the separation of church and state, federal money granted to faith-based organizations cannot be used for any religious programming. As a result, federal social service grants supporting faith-based organizations separate secular administrative work from the faith-based work of such organizations. In partnership with the UWMB, the Black Ministerial Alliance, and the Emmanuel Gospel Center, Boston Ten Point Coalition received a $2 million grant from President Bush's Compassion Capital Fund. While a small amount of this money supports the administrative costs of these four organizations, most of the money is distributed among both secular and faith-based nonprofits in the form of technical support and training in order to "[make] them more competitive out there in the secular funding world."

Risks

Emphasizing results, framing the church as valuable community resource, and focusing on the administrative work of the organization all serve as bridges between the secular funding world and faith-based organizations. These strategies have helped faith-based organizations gain the attention of the philanthropic community; they also serve as noncontroversial ways to describe and present faith-based organizations to the secular funding world, avoiding some of the sensitive issues that might arise if the role of faith in social service was discussed more directly. However, I believe that the difficult issues cannot be avoided indefinitely without consequence.

Viewing faith-based organizations through the existing lens of secular philanthropy poses certain risks. When direct discussions about the role of faith are avoided because of their difficult emotional content and potential to offend, a crucial, defining, and *unique* element of the individual organization gets lost in the translation to secular language. Not all faith-based organizations use faith in the same way. At a certain point, if they are to engage with the issue of faith and social service, funders have to disaggregate the term "faith-based organizations" and examine the role faith plays in each individual organization, neither avoiding faith nor supporting it blindly. Framing faith-based organizations in secular terms using the three strategies outlined in this chapter obscures the more direct and nuanced discussion about faith that happens on a personal level between BTPC and its program officers. A more public discussion about faith should not replace the foundations' consideration of results, community resources, and administrative capacity; it could enhance these conversations.

Foundations should look not only at the results of individual faith-based organizations but also at the way each organization uses faith as a tool for social change. Adding an open discussion about faith to the current discussion about results will help funders assess a faith-based organization and interpret the results they attribute to the organization's work. Some of BTPC's funders spoke of measuring results as an objective way to compare individual organizations and a promising way to level the field between faith-based and secular organization. However, measuring an organization's impact on society remains an abstract ideal, not a concrete reality. In truth, foundations assess the quality of an organization based on many factors, including mission, organizational structure, leadership, financial stability, and reputation, not just on abstract impact measures. In the case of faith-based organizations, the assessment should involve a direct conversation about the role of faith in transforming lives. Also, as foundations work to develop more tools to measure social change, faith is an important variable to consider. Considering faith as an independent variable may inform the types of measurement tools that are used and may help interpret the results of the outcome tests. Funders will not know what role faith plays in an organization's effectiveness without openly examining the specific role it plays in the organization. The funder will miss an opportunity to understand and potentially extend those results.

The discussion of faith-based organizations as important community resources is valid but vague. It skirts the question of where foundations should draw the line between supporting the community and supporting a religion. Foundations should discuss what they consider to be an appropriate use of faith in social service and what, specifically, they would consider inappropriate. If foundations fund faith-based organizations without regard for the specific use of faith, adopting a "don't ask, don't tell" mentality, they might fund an organization that crosses the line between using faith in the service of the broader public interest and using faith in the service of a more narrow religious interest. On the other hand, if they avoid all faith-based organizations, they lose a potentially powerful model for social change and an opportunity to increase social impact.

Discussing faith candidly may open a wider range of funding strategies for foundations that currently fund only the administrative capacity of faith-based organizations as a way to avoid supporting religion. This strategy or the strategy of funding only secular research on religious organizations rather than funding the direct service programs that use faith may support the process requirements of philanthropy more than they support social change. While measuring outcomes and building administrative capacity are legitimate ways to foster an organization's effectiveness, focusing on these tasks to the exclusion of supporting the direct faith-based programs can unintentionally detract from the organization's ability to respond to the most pressing community needs. If the organization's funders are focused on measuring outcomes and building administrative capacity as a means of justifying their funding decisions, the organization will be pressured to spend time on these bureaucratic tasks rather than on vital community concerns, such as responding to incidents of gang violence. Even if the funding strategy remains focused on administrative capacity and research, these strategies should be developed based on an honest assessment of the organization's and the community's needs and an open discussion of faith rather than a reliance on guidelines aimed at avoiding an uncomfortable discussion about faith.

A Different Dialogue

Skillful engagement with faith-based organizations requires foundations to have a more nuanced discussion about the role of faith in social service. Such a discussion challenges some of the underlying assumptions that lead many foundations to separate the secular from the religious. BTPC and its program officers have started to create such a dialogue. The UWMB's Faith and Action Program serves as a model of the type of discussion a traditionally secular foundation can have that moves beyond the current dialogue. One recent case study (Lundberg 2004) describes the process by which this traditionally secular funding organization developed its Faith and Action Initiative. This subdivision of the foundation distributes roughly $300,000 of the foundation's money each year to programs serving inner-city youth that specifically encourage religious or spiritual belief.

Influenced in part by the success of BTPC, the UWMB began to view faith-based organizations as valuable resources for effecting social change in underserved communities. Like many foundations, UWMB had previously supported the secular activities of some faith-based organizations while avoiding potential controversy by insisting that faith be kept separate from the programs they funded. But in 1997, UWMB took its analysis and involvement to another level. If faith-based programs are indeed important and effective community resources, the leaders asked, don't they deserve the possibility of more direct philanthropic support? Together with a group of local philanthropic and religious leaders (including several people associated with BTPC and its funders), UWMB went beyond the "safe" discussion topics framed in this chapter. It courageously confronted the difficult questions that had to be explored in order to define a new relationship between the foundation and local religious organizations.

Leaders of the UWMB initiative openly discussed the process of spiritual transformation and the power of faith to positively influence lives. They wanted to fund quality programs that would intentionally introduce children to faith but that wouldn't exclude anyone for religious or other reasons. The leaders talked about the difficulty of distinguishing between proselytizing and using faith as a tool for social change. They also discussed the importance and the challenge of measuring the results of such programs. They wanted to ensure that they continued to fund effective organizations, since increasing the foundation's community impact was the ultimate aim of the program. They considered possible consequences of funding individual churches and their programs. For example, what if a funded church took a position on homosexuality that contradicted the foundation's political philosophy? These vital issues cannot be addressed unless the conversation moves beyond the usual subjects of results and administrative capacity to a more open discussion of faith.

In order to have this type of conversation, UWMB had to overcome two obstacles: institutional tradition and the personal beliefs of foundation leaders. These two barriers to open and honest communication arose throughout our interviews with BTPC's staff and program officers. Many philanthropic institutions and individuals within those institutions operate according to the principle that secular and religious activities are separate and that organized philanthropy belongs in the secular domain. While BTPC was able to connect with philanthropic leaders who had a personal understanding of the Black church and its role in communities of color, the majority of staff in organized philanthropy come from white secular intellectual populations. They may be uncomfortable with the idea of religion playing a role in addressing what they view as secular human service issues.

These underlying institutional and personal assumptions must be directly acknowledged if faith-based organizations and philanthropic organizations are to have more productive discussions about the use of faith in social service. The separation between religious and secular activities need not be abandoned, but it should at least be reexamined to open the potential of forming new partnerships with the common mission of increasing community impact.

Conclusion

BTPC and its program officers bridge two disparate worlds: the secular funding world and the Black church. One might even say that they speak two different languages. Together, they have found ways to describe BTPC using the language of secular philanthropy in an attempt to secure more funding. However, this translation obscures an important element of the organization: its use of faith. Having to describe the organization in the language of secular philanthropy in order to ensure the organization's survival can undermine trust between the organization and potential funders. One of BTPC's founders described a concern some of the church-based programs have when interacting with funders: "Can I be genuinely and authentically who I am or do I have to surrender that at the door?" At the same time, funders also have valid concerns, such as unwittingly supporting proselytization, an issue that can't be addressed without discussing faith. If funders do not understand how a specific organization uses faith, they cannot fully assess the organization's results. They risk either supporting an agenda of proselytization or dismissing an opportunity to support a powerful tool for social change and they may unnecessarily limit their range of funding strategies for creating social impact.

BTPC and its program officers have been successful in initiating communication between secular and religious leaders. The dialogue they have started, exemplified in the case study of UWMB, demonstrates the possibility of a new language for discussing faith-based organizations that privileges neither religious nor philanthropic language. Rather than translating faith-based organizations into secular terms, the dialogue between philanthropic and religious leaders could combine both secular and religious understandings and invite all parties to speak authentically. If the broader funding world engaged in this type of dialogue, organizations such as BTPC could operate more openly and effectively. Such conversations would also create opportunities to discover new ways of working together to address the shared social concerns of religious and philanthropic communities.

Note

I am grateful to the Boston Ten Point Coalition and its leaders and the funders who agreed to participate in this research. Thanks to Paula Marshall for her work conducting interviews in the initial phase of the case study. I am also grateful for the helpful feedback and comments of William Damon, Carrie James, Howard Gardner, Seth Wax, and Susan Verducci. This research was funded by The Atlantic Philanthropies and The William and Flora Hewlett Foundation.

References

Lundberg, Kirsten. 2004. *United Way Mass Bay and the Faith & Action Initiative (A): Should Faith Be Funded?* Case number C16-04-1759.0. Cambridge, Mass.: Kennedy School of Government Case Program.

10 Network for Good: Helping the Helpers

Tanya Rose and Sarah Miles

The Internet has not only changed the way we do commercial business but also the way we do philanthropy. James Austin, a professor at Harvard Business School, explains:

> As the Internet exploded, it made its way into every segment of the for-profit world. The nonprofit sector was the Internet's last frontier. Since the late 1990s, we have seen the creation of a new Internet industry, populated mostly by dot-coms but also by dot-orgs devoted to serving nonprofits. (Austin and Kind 2002, 39)

Today, with the proliferation of this electronic tool, hundreds of thousands of nonprofit organizations have taken their place in cyberspace, modifying to a certain extent the field of philanthropy. The Internet has shifted the philanthropic climate by making giving more accessible and facilitating communication between nonprofits and the donors they seek. Anyone with Internet access now has the world at his or her fingertips as what were once geographic barriers are stripped away and replaced by web pages and e-mail addresses. One interview subject identifies this as the "democratization of the nonprofit sector."

As with any big change, the introduction of the Internet to the nonprofit world brought some problems. One of these problems was finding a way to help donors navigate the increasingly crowded online nonprofit landscape. Potential donors were looking for a "more efficient, networked marketplace where [they could] find information about giving opportunities, compare potential recipients along various criteria, and make gifts online" as opposed to "what [was] an opaque and scattered philanthropic marketplace, especially for individual giving" (Blau 2002). For those who want to do this as efficiently and effectively as possible, the Internet can seem the perfect medium. However, along with its power and expansiveness, it can often be overwhelming, even paralyzing; it can often offer too much with too little guidance.

For many nonprofits, another problem with going online was that they did not have the technological and financial resources to have a high-quality, efficient, and effective web site. As a GoodWork Project subject told us, having an Internet presence can create a change in dynamics of how [nonprofit] business gets done, and the impact that technology can have on that can . . . inhibit it because the [nonprofit] organizations can't tap into those networks because they don't [understand] the technology or they don't have [it].

As the Internet grew and more and more nonprofits created web sites and began doing business online, both these organizations and donors needed help navigating this new landscape.

In traditional philanthropy, intermediary organizations have often served as the bridge between corporations and foundations and the nonprofits they fund. A primary role of traditional intermediaries has been as an informed distributor of funds; foundations or other donors distribute money to the intermediary that then researches and doles out the funds to appropriate nonprofits. Other functions have included capacity-building for the foundations or donors and acting as a consultant of sorts for further grantmaking (Szanton 2003). Overall, intermediaries have not only influenced who was funded but have fully decided the flow of funds. They have taken over duties that were traditionally performed by foundations in efforts to produce more effective grantmaking.

Internet intermediaries are different; they respond directly to the needs of donors and nonprofits that come to their site. On a single web site, they connect the public with information about nonprofits and opportunities to give and provide nonprofits with access to donors. They "foster the informed use of the Internet for civic participation and philanthropy" and "work to advance nonprofit adoption of the Internet as a tool for fundraising, volunteer recruitment and community engagement" (Network for Good 2005).

This chapter focuses on one such intermediary organization, Network for Good (NFG). Drawn from seventeen interviews conducted for this study, it examines challenges that this Internet intermediary and its corporate funders have faced as they seek to satisfy the demand for easier and more efficient philanthropic giving and some of the strategies they have used to meet these challenges. It looks at how other Internet intermediaries can learn from the examples, both good and bad, NFG has provided. Finally, we present some further ideas about ways to meet these challenges.

Network for Good

In November 2001, NFG was started by three pioneers in the Internet economy: AOL, Yahoo!, and Cisco Systems. A new configuration of an earlier model (Helping.org), NFG was designed as a portal through which both individuals and groups such as other nonprofits could more easily access one another for donating, volunteering, and citizen advocacy. Individuals use the site to find information about particular nonprofits, make donations, find and accept volunteer opportunities, or speak out on issues through such methods as online petitions. It also includes information from the expansive database of charities offered through GuideStar, thousands of volunteer opportunities from

VolunteerMatch, the contact information of elected officials and media contacts, links to web sites of other philanthropic resources, and how-to materials. For groups such as other nonprofit organizations, it provides tools, training, education and resources "to expand their reach and develop their Internet strategies" (Austin 2001, 12). Information and resources for raising funds online, recruiting online, and advocacy are also included as was a library of articles, a Q&A series, and links to other nonprofit resource web sites that focus on using technology in fund-raising. Ultimately, in providing resources to both individuals and groups, NFG represents the united goal of its founders of, as one subject told us, "growing the percent of philanthropic giving online."

Since its inception, NFG has proven its ability to reach a large scope of donors and address global concerns through its response to disaster relief efforts. One such occasion was the response to the December 2004 tsunami disaster. NFG launched a dedicated home page that provided not only a comprehensive list of the charities and organizations acting for the relief effort (along with brief descriptions of their roles in that effort) but also resources to learn more about earthquakes and tsunamis, find pictures of the disaster, and learn more about how to research the charities and organizations listed on the page. A December 29, 2004, press release described the power of the site: "Tsunami Relief Distributed through Network for Good: Americans Give $1M in One Day through Network for Good toward Tsunami Relief."

The Business of NFG

Network for Good is a mixture of people, values, ideas, and structures from both the commercial and nonprofit sectors. As one subject said, "This was a venture brought together by Cisco, Yahoo!, AOL. You need to understand those kinds of companies; you need to understand that environment. . . . Network for Good is not your typical nonprofit. . . . It's got to be structured and run more like a business." Its staff is composed primarily of individuals from the business world or those with business backgrounds. Many subjects spoke about wanting to use their experiences in the business world to create greater effectiveness and efficiency in the nonprofit world. And many were drawn to the Internet because they saw the opportunity to find a way to achieve that goal. Network for Good is operated in a fast-paced manner in response to the Internet's fast-paced demands and, more like commercial companies, it has a business model. But NFG is a nonprofit; its mission is to facilitate the use of the Internet for nonprofits and help individuals find appropriate nonprofits.

Network for Good is treading upon new ground; as one former staff member said, "There is no real road map for this kind of organization. You are constantly walking that tightrope." It has brought together corporations, nonprofits, and individuals in a way that does not happen off-line. With this innovation, however, come challenges not only to the effectiveness of the organization but also to its potential to maintain good work in the field.

Challenge: Serving Multiple Masters and Performing Tasks

One of NFG's early challenges included building trust and cooperation among its corporate founders, AOL, Yahoo!, and Cisco. Dynamics among the funders had to be managed by executives at NFG, and each of these companies brought its own agenda to the table, often pulling NFG in different directions. While each company was ultimately involved in NFG for the greater social good, they were each also invested in the strategic funding of NFG, making sure that their involvement also benefited their individual corporations.

In addition to challenges it faced with its funders, NFG was not easily accepted into the nonprofit community. Primarily because of its association with these technology companies, the community was suspicious of NFG. Nonprofits often steered clear of dealing with large corporations due to what they perceived as a dramatic clash of interests and a threat to the pursuits of their individual missions. Early in its development, NFG struggled to find a place that did not fuel the suspicion of the nonprofits yet maintained its relationships with its corporate funders.

Finally, NFG had to think about the individual donors coming to the site. NFG was created to answer a need David Eisner voiced in a Harvard report on NFG: "Consumers . . . want to know not just where to give money and where to volunteer, but also what are the issues and what can they do about it" (Austin and Kind 2002, 8). NFG had to find a way to effectively answer those needs. It faced the challenge of serving individuals, organizations, and corporations, each in different capacities.

Challenge: The PipeVine Debacle

Another challenge that created an immediate impact upon the growth and development of NFG occurred in the summer of 2003. At that time, Pipe-Vine, a San Francisco–based company that handled all of NFG's credit card donations, abruptly closed due to mishandled funds, leaving millions of dollars of donations unallocated. The PipeVine shutdown left NFG $3 million poorer, which was the amount NFG had to pay out to charities whose donations had been lost during this crisis.[1] Fortunately the staff at NFG had read the signs it was being given of impending distress and cut off PipeVine before more serious damage could be done. In addition, NFG took it upon itself to not only contact organizations about the situation but also to make sure the lost money was reimbursed out of its own pocket.

In return, NFG gained "ownership" over many of the things it had relied upon PipeVine to handle. Its frankness with its nonprofits in this matter won NFG stronger, less adversarial relationships with them, and because NFG was now handling all aspects of its exchanges with nonprofits and donors it experienced a strengthened connection to its mission. It also became more efficient as it became more directly accountable for its day-to-day processes. An insider at the time noted that NFG didn't really know its customers until the PipeVine crisis but that "that experience has sort of changed us. . . . It made us realize, let's focus on value, keep it simple, come up with the right tools and have that line of communication open with them."

Challenge: Remaining Viable/The Double Bottom Line

One challenge unique to NFG and other Internet intermediaries is finding a sustainable model. As mentioned before, these organizations are treading new ground, creating new spaces, and in so doing must find their own identities in order to remain viable in the philanthropy as well as the Internet landscapes. They struggle with finding a balance in their quest for the double bottom line; that is, in an effort to maintain their presence online, they must find a feasible model for producing both the financial return necessary to remain operational and the social return necessary to remain functional. The double bottom line is the tightrope they tread, with the nonprofit world in one hand and the commercial world in the other, both mentalities threatening to knock the intermediary off balance.

Challenge: Staying Current and in Touch with What Is Needed in an Increasingly Saturated Market

As a result of NFG's stated mission and external conditions within the field of philanthropy and society in general, it is necessary for NFG to always be current and relevant; that is, NFG must be fast paced to keep up with the immediate needs of those it serves and stay on top of crisis-relief efforts. This challenge is complicated by the fact that it serves hundreds of thousands of nonprofits and the millions of individuals who might donate to them. As a result, it must keep current on all causes, not just one. As one subject said, "There is not one continuum of events that are going on related to a certain project; there are multiple [events]."

One subject deeply involved with another Internet intermediary voiced a similar concern:

I think the landscape of philanthropy is changing in that there's saturated messaging, just like there is with for-profits. I think we're going to have to stay on top of trends and things that are meaningful for the user in the end, and I think we're going to have to stay true to what our mission is and communicate that mission effectively.

In order to keep the organization's head above water, it is necessary to stand out, find a niche, and constantly respond to the ever-changing climate of the Internet. This challenge is extremely demanding in that it requires the staff to stay aware of trends and users' needs and requires people with the expertise to develop and implement responses to these trends and demands.

As Internet use continues to grow and as more and more nonprofits and donors come to the Web, intermediaries will be more and more necessary to facilitate productive and effective philanthropy. NFG has helped forge a path for other Internet intermediaries through its experiences, challenges, and actions within the e-philanthropy space. NFG's history and its experiences as an Internet intermediary offer similar organizations a model for more effective philanthropic practices online. But in order to ensure continued effectiveness of the organizations as well as growth on and through the Internet, certain aspects of online engagement and operation must be considered and require further attention.

Meeting the Challenges: Cooperate and Coordinate

The Internet requires a broader breadth of skills and knowledge than is generally required for success off-line. This need for more expansive skill sets necessitates collaboration among companies on and associated with the Internet. Such collaboration is particularly necessary for intermediaries on the Internet for several reasons.

First, due to the nature and mission of intermediaries, they must be able to answer a host of problems and challenges donors and nonprofits bring to them. In order to effectively serve that purpose, they must rely on the expertise that has been garnered and built by others with more immediate exposure to and experience with those problems and challenges.

Next, the Internet remains an intimidating landscape for many users (both donors and nonprofits). Through cooperation with outside organizations, NFG promotes a mutual environment of trust and empowerment. This cooperation works to its own benefit, and it also helps make the Internet more manageable for its users by enabling them to more effectively and efficiently use its resources.

Finally, as more and more nonprofits and donors come to the Internet, the pool of users of Internet intermediaries will inevitably grow as well. In order to more effectively keep up with that demand, collaboration will become increasingly important. By coordinating efforts across the Internet, more users can be reached and served.

Meeting the Challenges: Retain the Spirit of the Nonprofit While Using the Practices of Business

While the Internet has made it necessary to adopt certain business practices in order to "keep up," it is vital for Internet intermediaries to remember the unique position they hold not only in the philanthropic space but in the business space as well. They must find a balance, using the business practices and adopting businesslike characteristics when necessary but all the time keeping the ultimate mission in mind, one that is primarily nonprofit in nature. NFG is a nonprofit operating in a business landscape.

Meeting the Challenges: The Speed of the Internet

Nonprofits and corporations operate at different paces set by their respective fields. Internet intermediaries must operate at an even faster speed: that of technology, which requires organizations to change, act, react, and adapt quickly to remain viable and relevant. Maintaining this rate of speed can often be difficult, but an organization must do so to remain current and useful to users. Intermediaries must constantly find ways to help the nonprofit world adapt to this demanding environment while keeping themselves abreast of the trends and issues.

Meeting the Challenges: Creating and Maintaining a New Level of Nontraditional Giving

In her interview, a former executive of NFG offered her take on the organization:

I would say that NFG, as an intermediary, plays a serious role in the sector. . . .
And I think it's an important role to bringing non-traditional giving to its next level. . . . Here is an organization that represents transparency, that represents self-direction, that represents empowerment and tries to do it in an environment that's accepting, confident, and objective.

The Internet represents any number of opportunities to "[reorient] our expectations" of philanthropy and giving. NFG has positioned itself on the threshold of e-philanthropy, helping to create a useful tool that presents a different approach to giving which, in turn, helps attract new donors and present new opportunities to nonprofits. In addition, NFG has the opportunity to strengthen its position as a leader in this nontraditional mode of giving. It must take advantage of the uniqueness of its position, however, in order to take full advantage of that opportunity. Its uniqueness provides the opportunity to not only establish a firm hold in the world of philanthropy but also to launch a new direction in philanthropy. In so doing, it has the chance to create new relationships between donors and nonprofits and between the business and nonprofit worlds.

Conclusions

The Internet has continued to become a more and more viable option for fund-raising. While 53 percent of nonprofits still did not use the Internet in their fund-raising efforts in 2003, that number was down from 66 percent in 2002. In addition, among those organizations who did use online solicitations, 61 percent raised more funds in 2003 than in the preceding year (AFP 2004). These numbers indicate a clear increase in Internet fund-raising. E-philanthropy as a whole and Internet intermediaries represent a great potential to provide more efficient ways to give through providing online access and an expanded potential for good work through increased accessibility and transparency.

In its years of operation, NFG has distributed over $45 million to thousands of nonprofits and matched tens of thousands of volunteers with nonprofit organizations nationwide (AFP 2004). It has also rebounded from potential disaster, as in the PipeVine crisis, demonstrating some resilience that may serve as a model for other organizations that enter the realm of the Internet as intermediaries.

But in order to maintain the forward momentum NFG seems to have gained since its inception, it must continue to adapt and transform. It is important for intermediary organizations to focus on collaboration with other Internet professionals, to maintain a balance between nonprofit and business practices, to keep up the pace necessary for success on the Internet, and to constantly build the strength of e-philanthropy as a nontraditional form of giving. As the Internet continues to become more of an influence in all sectors, it will become especially important for the philanthropic intermediaries operating in cyberspace to offer the strongest guidance and connection possible to their users— donors, nonprofits, and corporations alike.

Notes

This chapter draws on interviews with seventeen individuals involved in e- philanthropy. These included four NFG staff members, one NFG board member, and two funders as well as six individuals from other e-philanthropy intermediary organizations and four e-philanthropy consultants.

1. This shutdown affected hundreds of other companies and thousands of charities that had relied upon PipeVine to process incoming credit card donations.

References

AFP (Association of Fundraising Professionals). 2004. *State of Fundraising 2003 Report.* July 12. Available online at http://www.afpnet.org/content_documents/AFP_State_of_Fundraising_2003_7-9-04.pdf.
Austin, James. 2001. "The E-Philanthropy Revolution Is Here to Stay." *The Chronicle of Philanthropy,* March 8.
———, and Elizabeth Kind. 2002. *AOL, Cisco, Yahoo!: Building the Internet Commons.* Harvard Business School Case No. 9-302-088. Boston: Harvard Business School.
Blau, Andrew. 2002. "Plenary Presentation: How the Internet Is Changing Philanthropy and Civic Life." Available online at http://www.northpark.edu/axelson/pdfs/AndrewBlau.pdf.

Network for Good. 2005. Network for Good web site. Available online at www.networkforgood.org.

Szanton, Peter. 2003. Toward More Effective Use of Intermediaries. *Practice Matters: The Improving Philanthropy Project.* New York: The Foundation Center. Available online at http://fdncenter.org/for_grantmakers/practice_matters/practicematters_01_paper.pdf.

11 Power and Mission in the Funding of Social Entrepreneurs

Lynn Barendsen

Throughout history, innovative leaders have tackled social dilemmas. But the classification and recognition of these individuals as "social entrepreneurs" is relatively recent. In 1980, William Drayton founded Ashoka: Innovators for the Public. Ashoka was one of the first organizations to use the term "social entrepreneurs." Broadly conceived, social entrepreneurs are individuals who use business knowledge and an entrepreneurial approach to directly tackle social problems.

This chapter, drawn from a study of seventeen social entrepreneurs and supported by interviews of several venture philanthropists and a few leading funders of social entrepreneurs, begins with background on the emergence of social entrepreneurship as a field. It then examines some of the features, problems, and potential strategies in funding social entrepreneurs.

According to the Schwab Foundation for Social Entrepreneurship, social entrepreneurship is "an approach to a social issue." It cuts across disciplines and "cannot be learned in academia" (www.schwabfound.org). The word "entrepreneur" is often associated with monetary success, and this terminology has led to some confusion. J. Gregory Dees stresses that social entrepreneurship is about "innovation and impact" and not about generating income. The organizations formed by social entrepreneurs are usually not profit-oriented (though there are some interesting exceptions and some compelling arguments against this norm, to be discussed below). Social entrepreneurs are entrepreneurial because they have "pioneered creative ways of addressing social problems and marshaled the resources to support their work" (Dees 2003).

French economists first used the term "entrepreneur" in the seventeenth and eighteenth centuries. In French, the word means "undertaking." In its earliest uses, entrepreneurship involved the discovery or invention of something new and the creation of value. Austrian economist Joseph A. Schumpeter expands on this understanding: "the function of entrepreneurs is to reform or revolutionize the pattern of production by exploiting an invention or an untried technological possibility" (Schumpeter 1942, 132). Schumpeter's emphasis on pattern change is a theme we heard reiterated during our interviews. Social entrepreneurs are interested not only in the revolutionary idea or the timely invention but also in the establishment of a replicable model for change.

Entrepreneurship and entrepreneurs themselves continue to be of interest to economists, psychologists, and professors of business. The most influential thinker on the subject in this century is Peter Drucker, business philosopher and the father of modern management. Drucker's definition of entrepreneurship focuses on change:

> Entrepreneurs see change as the norm and as healthy. Usually, they do not bring about the change themselves. But—and this defines entrepreneur and entrepreneurship—the entrepreneur always searches for change, responds to it, and exploits it as an opportunity. (Drucker 1985, 27–28)

Social entrepreneurs are set apart from the entrepreneurs described in Drucker's definition by their relationship to change. They regularly bring about change, unlike the varied professionals who would fit Schumpeter's rubric. In fact, a desire for change is usually the impetus for the creation of their organizations. Although business entrepreneurs may bring about change (the services they develop may alter an industry or the innovative products they create may change our way of life), this is not always the *reason* they start their businesses. Social entrepreneurs typically form organizations because they want to make change happen.

Individuals who combine a desire to ameliorate society's ills with a business background are often reluctant participants in the fund-raising methods nonprofits have traditionally used. They dislike these methods and resent the amount of time they take in the day-to-day operations of nonprofits. Many prefer to cultivate long-term relationships built on trust and a collaborative process, often with venture philanthropists. Social entrepreneurs often mention feeling isolated or not "fitting in" at various times in their lives. This sense that they are outsiders may help clarify why social entrepreneurs are motivated by a particular cause or movement. Once a social entrepreneur founds an organization and work starts, this sense of isolation may become more pronounced. Because the work social entrepreneurs attempt is original, few people understand the challenges of what they do, and there are few peers with whom to consult. Because they are innovators, social entrepreneurs must spend a great deal of time explaining their work to potential funders. Because of financial pressures, some social entrepreneurs "spin the truth" or are dishonest with their funders. When the ends (helping the homeless, combating violence, improving education) are noble, they may feel that questionable means are justified. I point to strategies social entrepreneurs have used to successfully and honestly negotiate tensions in the past: reframing challenges so that they might become opportunities and drawing strength from their convictions.

Social entrepreneurs are intimately connected with their organizations. As a social entrepreneur and his or her organization starts to mature, it is important that he or she consider the survival of the organization after they are gone.

Sometimes organizations need someone more managerial than visionary, and sometimes the entrepreneur is ready to move on to his or her next challenge. The organization and the vision must be strong enough to stand alone without the charismatic leader. One of the primary concerns in planning an exit strategy is ensuring that an organization's mission will remain strong and consistent throughout the process of transition. But this process is not always a smooth one, and a mission may be lost along the way or be put at risk because of financial pressure.

Background

Since the 1980s, several social entrepreneurs such as Drayton and Sara Horowitz have garnered international attention by receiving the MacArthur Prize Fellowship Award. Sara Horowitz is the executive director of Working Today, a national nonprofit organization that represents the concerns of America's independent workforce, including freelancers, consultants, independent contractors, temps, part-timers, and the self-employed. In 1998, the Schwab Foundation, in conjunction with the World Economic Forum, established the Schwab Foundation for Social Entrepreneurship. Each year, the foundation selects between ten and fifteen "Outstanding Social Entrepreneurs." These individuals receive three years of financial and technical support and attend one of Schwab's Social Entrepreneur Summits and a meeting of the World Economic Forum.[1]

Currently, several new initiatives, organizations, and foundations are helping to expand the field of social entrepreneurship. Venture philanthropy organizations such as New Profit Inc. have partnered with promising social enterprises to provide financial and other support. Jeff Skoll, the first president of eBay, has started the Skoll Foundation, which invests in social entrepreneurs around the world. Several other organizations offer financial and other support to social entrepreneurs, including Echoing Green, the Edna McConnell Clark Foundation, the Peninsula Community Foundation, REDF, the Social Venture Network, and Venture Philanthropy Partners.

Entrepreneurial Leadership

Social entrepreneurs typically identify with business entrepreneurs, not with leaders of other nonprofits. In fact, social entrepreneurs define their organizations against more traditional nonprofits as a way to demonstrate what they are *not*. Although this view may be stereotypical, social entrepreneurs regularly characterize standard nonprofits as disorganized. For example, one social entrepreneur suggests that nonprofits are inefficient because they fail to hire businesslike, efficient employees:

> You see a lot of inefficiency and low quality and things that don't quite work. Now why that's a case, I don't know, but I think putting into play the discipline, putting

into place a process is inherently not a skill that a lot of folks in the sector just grow up with. . . . They don't value the person who is boring, anal, get it done right a hundred times. . . . They are attracted by idealistic [people] so they suffer from hiring people who are too like-minded as well.

Another social entrepreneur points to other problems with the typical nonprofit organization:

Nonprofits are generally not that good at carrying out a broader mission or goal. They're better at projects. They have often not been strategic enough to [understand] how are we going to effect change that really is going to affect that ultimate goal. But there are exceptions to that. I think nonprofits don't pay well and that's part of the reason why they don't attract and keep enough of the kind of talent we need to really make the nonprofit sector thrive.

Social entrepreneurs point to detailed business plans that, in their minds, help them differentiate their work from that of traditional nonprofits.

Though the vast majority of social entrepreneurs run nonprofit organizations, there are some notable exceptions to this norm. A few social entrepreneurs fund themselves by running for-profit businesses. The for-profit social entrepreneurs with whom we spoke were adamant in their reasoning about why their work must be profit-driven. One subject we spoke with is the founder and CEO of an Internet services company dedicated to creating economic opportunities for urban communities. He explains:

I view us as a business. And what I think is radical or powerful about what we're trying to do is that we're legitimizing the talent and the potential of an unrecognized—group of people is too strong a word—but people who come from areas, neighborhoods, and so forth that are not associated with technology. We will have been successful at doing that when no one says "inner-city kids" anymore. And when people can actually—when it's not a surprise that somebody coming from Harlem has a job in technology.

According to this subject, it is vital that this company is understood as an Internet-services provider, not as an organization working for the economically disadvantaged. His organization is working to change preconceptions about urban populations, and this will be possible only if his company is able to compete with the larger, more established institutions. Preconceptions will begin to change when his business is able to win clients, maintain high-quality work, *and* employ a large number of individuals from inner-city neighborhoods.

Venture philanthropists are often themselves entrepreneurs, and some assert that as a result of this mindset they are able to understand social entrepreneurs at a fundamental level. One venture philanthropist describes his organization as particularly suited to funding social entrepreneurs because entrepreneurs are typically quite comfortable with risk:

So for me this whole idea of portfolio has real meaning in that you look at a series of investments, some of which are high risk and some of which are not, and the portfolio evens itself out just like an investment portfolio would. But the ones that have high risk also have potential of high return, in a social context, social value. That you've got a dynamic leader out there that has significant organizational issues that need to be addressed in building an organization or building a board or building systems, whatever, but this guy, or woman, really has a great idea and seems to have the energy and ability to carry it out and are you willing to invest in that individual?

And . . . we've said that we are willing to do that in a certain parameter, knowing full well that it's a risky investment and that that's part of our role as private funders. Certainly government, and most corporate foundations, are not going to be willing to fund that kind of work. In fact, they're not going to touch it with a ten-foot pole. So if there's a role for organized private philanthropy it needs to address this issue of risk-taking.

Taking a risk, investing in a dynamic individual: this is entrepreneurial language used to describe a potential funding relationship. Some venture philanthropists and social entrepreneurs seem to understand one another quite well. Certainly even these relationships have issues, but for the most part, social entrepreneurs seem to have more in common with venture philanthropists than they do with traditional nonprofits.

Losing Valuable Time

As businesspeople, social entrepreneurs are particularly frustrated by the amount of time they feel is "wasted" in pursuit of financial support. Because they are atypical participants in the nonprofit sector, social entrepreneurs do not fit neatly into a traditional funding structure. In fact, Bill Drayton believes that what traditional foundations and government offer and what social entrepreneurs need are completely at odds with one another:

> Most foundations and governments have very little sense of who the entrepreneur is or why they've got to invest for ten years in the entrepreneur and help him or her through this long cycle. The time frame is also completely wrong. And the entrepreneur needs a large sum of money, not little dribs and drabs, in other words. There is a complete misfit between what the entrepreneur needs and what these institutions provide.

Drayton asserts that investment in the social entrepreneur ought to be a long-term proposition. This is certainly at odds with the more standard forms of foundation support, which typically involves smaller sums of money over a few years.

Social entrepreneurs all agree that fund-raising takes a tremendous amount of time. And as one subject describes it, positive results are never guaranteed:

> I have just watched so many nonprofits that spend a huge amount of their energy trying to raise money and I feel like it almost doesn't matter how good of an idea you have or how well you frame it or anything like that. It is all about or largely about who you know and timing—all about solid connections and timing and that feels pretty fundamentally unfair.

When this time might otherwise be used to work with a community in need in a more direct way, lost time becomes even more frustrating.

Establishing Effective Funding Relationships

The fact is that the funding process takes time. Because so much time is devoted to fund-raising, it is important to use that time as wisely as possible. When funders and grantees are working together with a shared sense of purpose, social entrepreneurs are less likely to feel that the time they spend with funders is "wasted." The process of funding social entrepreneurs is described, by grantees and funders alike, as establishing and maintaining a relationship. Particular elements make this relationship healthy: mutual understanding, maintenance, trust, and clear assessment.

Drayton argues that social entrepreneurs need funders who understand them:

> So the social entrepreneur needs someone who will invest in an idea that's new, different, crosscutting. They need people who will invest in them as a person. Foundations and governments . . . they're just personally not the right people to make judgments about these people. It takes one to know one. A very serious point. They're basically coming from the academic end of the spectrum, where expressing an idea rigorously and clearly is the goal. They don't get the institutional "how-to" dimension of the entrepreneur's vision. They don't want to invest, because they don't get it. Nor do they want to invest in the institution. They call it overhead. And so they usually give small, short-term grants for a portion of a project. And so the entrepreneurs in this sector spend 70 percent of their time— way too much—running around to get little drips and drabs. It's a terrible waste of a most valuable resource.

Drayton is not alone is his belief that social entrepreneurs lose valuable time engaging in fund-raising. Parties on all sides recognize that forming and maintaining funding relationships is time-consuming work.

One subject describes the "work" of the organization as a product that individuals may invest in. Investment is inspired (or not) by the entrepreneur, who is responsible for generating interest:

> We're selling the opportunity to get connected to the work that we're doing changing lives. It's what we have and if you pay us money for it you can feel like you're connected to it basically. There is a value transfer there. People have to believe like—they have to believe you're going to do what you say. And I stand up and say look we've grown ten times and we've got the best assessment results ever, and I can talk their language in a way that fills them with confidence, and they get a sense that they like me.

Grantees say that once a positive relationship is established, they need to maintain it. Relationships with venture philanthropists are involved and long-term. They involve regular contact and a high level of engagement. But relationships with traditional foundations or relationships with private individuals also require support. One social entrepreneur refers to this process as "donor stewardship":

> And often [funders] are investing in a nonprofit because they believe in the leader. And it is a big responsibility for the leader. And it just emphasizes why it's so important that I pick up the phone and call funders even when I don't have a specific agenda item, that I make sure we visit each other in person just so they get to know me and vice versa. And they talk about something called donor stewardship, which is really taking care of your donors: you thank them a lot and keep them updated, you don't only talk to them when you want money, you keep them in the loop, keep them invested. And it's a key part of fund-raising.

When the relationship is between venture philanthropist and social entrepreneur, the dynamics become more intricate. It is interesting that venture philanthropists also talk about forming relationships with their grantees, but they structure the discussion in terms of establishing trust. This is one way venture philanthropists differentiate themselves from more traditional foundations; by establishing trust with a grantee, they build collaborative relationships:

> We really need to respect what our grantees bring to the table as well. That's not always true, I would say, in some traditional funding organizations, and as a result, there is a lot of collaboration [that] has happened I guess by definition; engaged philanthropy relies on collaboration and real shared decision making. . . . It depends a lot on trust, and trust takes time, so we make long-term investments that allow for the engagement to grow organically over the time that we're working with a particular group. I don't think you can do engaged philanthropy well if you just make a one-time grant.

The process of establishing trust in these relationships is not straightforward, however. As one venture philanthropist describes, there is a fundamental imbalance in terms of power in these relationships. Time is necessary to form and sustain positive relationships, and the process is not an easy one:

> But doing five-year relationships kind of engaged, sustained in an intense way with a nonprofit, that's really hard to do. So the challenges are it starts with trust, how do you build trust with them? We're the funder, they want the money, so you've got this power imbalance. How do you lower the power imbalance? How do you get honesty in there?

But another venture philanthropist sees this dynamic slightly differently. She believes that the venture philanthropist has the most to lose:

> First of all, venture philanthropy is about a triangle, and . . . the people who have the most at stake [are] the venture philanthropist[s]. . . . Because we have the most at stake, we have the most to lose. They could walk from us and probably find another funder. Our investors could walk from us and find another grantee. [We] can only survive with both. . . . We have the most at stake; and therefore, we are deeply connected to trying to understand and listen to the problems our nonprofits are facing, the problems our investors are facing and integrating those in ways that, I think, ultimately call both the investors and the social entrepreneurs to a higher order because they know that we do care, we have a lot at stake, and we're still chal-

lenging them on this point, or we're still asking tough questions, or encouraging them in positive ways.

Venture philanthropists often discuss the issue of exit strategy. All parties are concerned with the issues of how the funding will end, when it will end, and what, if any, might be the continued relationship. As I'll describe later, social entrepreneurs also have concerns about exit strategies.

Working in Isolation

Several social entrepreneurs specifically mentioned feeling alone or not "fitting in" at various times in their lives. This feeling is not about being ostracized in school; in fact, most of them were well liked and were often leaders in school. They describe a sense of solitude because of the work and the marginalized groups or unusual issues that compel them. Some social entrepreneurs still feel isolated. One describes the challenges he has faced since graduating from college and founding his organization. He recognizes that isolation is a consistent issue in his life: "That is a pretty consistent theme of not feeling like I had a peer group. High school and college were similar in that I had a lot of people who respected me but didn't understand me." Some social entrepreneurs feel solitary because the work they do is so innovative. The organizations they start are typically charting new territory.

For many social entrepreneurs, feeling like an outsider starts early and provides the connection to a specific cause. One subject, the victim of violence at an early age, runs an organization to combat the use of violence by elementary school-aged children. She does not describe her sense of isolation as a problem but rather as the source of her beliefs:

> I was ten and had really decided that life just wasn't so great. So I was sitting there contemplating not living anymore, and I remember sitting there and thinking that life is like this big equation and that for everything bad that happens on this side, something good is going to happen on this other side, and I wasn't going to check out until I got to the other side of the equation. . . . This really strong feeling, not of entitlement because I didn't feel . . . like someone else owed me something, but it really turned into the sense of righteous anger that this isn't okay, that this is not my fault, and that things have to be different because it is wrong.

Once the organization is founded and work starts, isolation may become more pronounced. Because the work being attempted is innovative, few people understand the work and its challenges and there are few peers with whom to consult. Social entrepreneurs do not always describe isolation as a problem; some see it as a predictable outcome of doing innovative work. In fact, some social entrepreneurs are empowered by the solitude of their path. Because they are doing work no one has done before, they know they are filling a niche.

Isolation becomes a problem when innovative individuals seek funding. It is interesting that a few venture philanthropists also talk about feeling isolated in their work; these issues typically involve finding support for their work. As one venture philanthropist explains:

> So we really don't have any, there are reference points to . . . some of the tactical things we do, but there are really almost no reference points to what we're doing strategically and model-wise. I don't really have anywhere else to go to, to say, well, what are all the lessons learned about how you take high potential professional people and philanthropists and engage them in long-term strategic work with nonprofits to help them build their capacity? I don't know. It doesn't exist. . . . So that's probably the biggest challenge, is there's nothing else to rely on.

Venture philanthropists are able to recognize that traditional foundations often misunderstand social entrepreneurs, and, as mavericks themselves, they understand the difficulties involved in innovation. Social entrepreneurs have to spend an unusual amount of time explaining their work to potential funders. Their sense of isolation becomes particularly frustrating with respect to financial concerns.

Spinning the Truth

In the worst-case scenario, these pressures can result in less-than-honest practice. One social entrepreneur reports "spinning" the truth in a way that funders might find attractive: "I'm a salesman. I'm taking the information and lining it up in a way that I know you will like." Other subjects describe the tension between service to the community they serve and the preservation of the organization. One social entrepreneur openly admits lying to funders:

> It's a strategy. You can't show that you have too much money, but then you can't show that you need too much. . . . And sometimes I'll lie. . . . Numbers basically stayed flat because some other investments that we expected didn't come through. So what am I going to do? Sit there and say, "By the way, we didn't use your money the way you said, but would you give us another $75,000 so we could do it next year?" I could, but I don't do that.

Another social entrepreneur describes the pressure when time is short and funds are low:

> We needed to raise some money fairly fast. I talked with a woman about doing a challenge grant. We sent in the proposal, but she never said yes. Then she went [away] for a couple of weeks. So I started fund-raising, and [the challenge grant] helped us raise probably $20,000 we would not have raised otherwise. [Then she called us and said that] she is not doing a challenge grant. Do I go back and tell those folks that she changed her mind? I probably should. I am not going to. I just don't have the time, and it's not worth the energy, and it's hard. So there are a lot of things like that that govern my day-to-day work.

Some social entrepreneurs see these moral difficulties as challenges to confront. They struggle with their personal standards and make decisions that are more in keeping with the beliefs and values they espouse. For example, some social entrepreneurs say no to money because they refuse to cross certain lines. One founder describes how he passes along his beliefs to one of his employees:

> It was so important for me and for this person to make it really explicit that this was a line that we will not cross for me as an individual, for this person as an individual, for us as an organization that no marginal gain of a small amount of money was worth the compromise of integrity as an organization and as individuals. It's just clear-cut.

Another social entrepreneur decided not to take money because she predicted that it would entail a difficult relationship with a funder: "No matter how good your mission is, if you are going to have to spend all of your time working with some horrible person, it's just not worth it." In addition to standing on principle, this social entrepreneur acted pragmatically and rejected what might have become a time-consuming, draining relationship.

Reframing Challenges and Drawing on Conviction

Effective funding relationships address a number of concerns of social entrepreneurs regarding funding. A positive funding relationship, for example, may alleviate some of the pressures that cause some individuals to spin the truth. But in the absence of these types of relationships, other solutions must be sought. The social entrepreneurs we interviewed have developed strategies to negotiate the various tensions they encounter. A particular kind of drive seems to carry some through regardless of current conditions.

Many of the social entrepreneurs we spoke with have faced trauma or describe deeply transformative experiences in their lives. Some social entrepreneurs have the capacity to recognize that potential good, such as a commitment to change or to working on behalf of less fortunate others, can result from tragic circumstances. Those who have faced tragedy show an ability to reframe these difficulties into possibility and change. Some social entrepreneurs face challenges in the workplace in a similar manner and reframe difficult situations to view them as opportunities. For example, one social entrepreneur describes how challenge inspires her and keeps her going. Her organization works to encourage entrepreneurship in foreign countries. In spite of what seems like an intuitive connection between entrepreneurial success and a country's economic climate her organization succeeds even under the most difficult of circumstances:

> I think that most though, the intuitive obstacles I see as opportunities; the fact that [foreign] economies are collapsing, [our organization] couldn't be stronger. . . . Ironically, in the most difficult periods, I think is when we thrive and it's when my juices are flowing. So, to me, one of the obstacles was actually this boom period when it was harder to make our mission, the development angle, really clear.

Social entrepreneurs also express a strong sense of obligation to their work and the people it affects. They feel responsible to the communities or causes they serve, to investors, and employees. Sometimes this responsibility is a source of strength. When times are difficult, subjects think of the good they do and feel empowered and rejuvenated. In some cases, however, these varied obligations lead to a feeling that they have no choice but to push forward. They continue, despite difficulties, because they believe they have no alternative. The founder of an organization dedicated to the financial empowerment of low-income inner-city residents explains:

> As a founder, you feel so invested that it is not a job that you can just quit. I really couldn't just quit and walk away and say, "Well, I did my best, and whatever happens, happens." I don't have that luxury, and there are probably many days where if I did, I would have. But it's a situation where you've got an extraordinary burden on your shoulders that you just can't turn away from under any circumstances.

Social entrepreneurs describe their work in absolute terms, insisting they have "no choice" but to stay involved. This, of course, is not true: they choose to remain committed under the most difficult of circumstances. Deep convictions make them *willing* to answer to their obligations.

Deep Ties between Founder and Organization

We have already seen that social entrepreneurs are entrepreneurs first. Like their counterparts in business, they are able to transform an idea into a functioning organization. Their vision inspires the program, their charisma attracts funders and employees, and their drive keeps the organization going when conflicts arise. But particular issues emerge when an organization is so connected to its leader. As organizations start to mature, it is important that they consider their survival beyond the tenure of the charismatic social entrepreneur. Some venture philanthropists who fund social entrepreneurs work to make goals explicit so the organization can go beyond the individual. The transition period can be difficult because both investors and employees are inspired by the founder.

The entrepreneurs are aware of this issue:

> My first dream is to have [my organization] be successful. And I want [this organization] to be way bigger than me. It's very associated with me as the entrepreneur and the founder, which is awful for me because of the pressure and also people need to not think that way anymore for us to get past the start of this.

A successful organization moves beyond this initial stage and then confronts new issues. Employees are hired and the work is then shared by others who may not be as personally involved as the founder. As another social entrepreneur explains:

> I think there's nothing like the leader of an organization sitting in front of someone and saying here's what we're doing, please support it. And I think the people respond. And one of my biggest fears is: when we grow and we hire fund-raising people, are they going to be able to do that? They could be more capable and better

than me, but it's how they're perceived. And I really wonder if someone else is going to be able to come in and do that.

"Can someone else do this as well as I can?" As the founder, as the individual whose vision inspired the formation of this organization, it makes sense that this leader would wonder whether someone else might be able to raise money as successfully as he has. But he also recognizes that this is part of the growth process and is an issue he must eventually confront.

Other social entrepreneurs approach this question from another angle: "Can someone else do this work *better* than I can?"

> And whatever it takes to do that; so to make [this organization] work I'm going to have to stay, and I want to stay CEO . . . for a while. It'll have to be at least five years, I think, probably longer than that even after. If I ever leave the CEO role, it'll be because there will be a point where somebody can do it as well or better than I can and I'll move to the board and still play an active board role.

From the funder's perspective, some nonprofits are not meant to last forever precisely *because* they are so connected to a single leader. In speaking about one organization that worked with a very difficult population, one venture philanthropist said that the executive director eventually got "burned out." She was passionate and young, but eventually the pressures of the work simply got to her. And it became impossible to find someone who could replace her:

> But when she decided to leave it was just impossible to find somebody who would come in at $45,000 dollars a year, or even $60,000 dollars a year, and do the work that she was doing and be as effective as she was. And there was no succession planning even though we were trying and trying. . . . It was just such a unique population and unique organization and culture that even if we were to change the pay scales completely that would have just changed the organization overall. . . . I'm just so sad that [this organization] doesn't exist. And yet at the same time, nonprofits aren't meant to exist forever.

As another venture philanthropist describes it, deciding when entrepreneurs should move on is critically important. She believes that input regarding this critical decision is part of the function of a highly engaged funder:

> We just have entrepreneurs who have innovative ideas, but they can't scale them. And we take out the entrepreneur too soon, and then the idea is sort of scaled, but the magic is gone. . . . And what we're trying to do is keep the entrepreneur in and scale them. And then at a certain point, I do think that all of these organizations will have to be independent of their entrepreneur. But they'll have built the culture of being an entrepreneurial organization.

The social entrepreneurs we spoke with were all under forty-five, and for many of them the prospect of leaving was still something to consider in the future. There are many reasons why an organization's founder may move on. Not the least of these is the fact that, like business entrepreneurs, social entrepreneurs enjoy the process of seeing an idea grow. Once the organization is successful, some move on to begin another. Aaron Lieberman was the co-founder of Jumpstart, a national nonprofit educational program. After establishing this highly successful organization, Lieberman handed over Jumpstart to current CEO and president, Robert Waldron. Lieberman is now founder and CEO of Acelero Learning, another education-centered organization.

Whatever the immediate impetus, change may be facilitated by a healthy relationship with a funder. According to one venture philanthropist, the relationship between funder and grantee can help see an organization through an awkward transition or help phase in changes when leadership shifts:

> I think, yes again, we're not just connected by one thread; there's a whole fabric of connections that works together to strengthen the relationship. And then you know, that way, if there is turnover . . . it's not all based on one person, and the relationship can survive difficulties or turnovers. It's interesting [that], in some cases, we are the institutional memory for some of these organizations because we've been there in some cases for you know seven, eight years, maybe longer, a couple, and sadly, turnover is often a lot higher than that, and so there have been cases where a business might say, "Hey, we were thinking about starting a new business around blank." And then we could say, "Hmm, actually, you thought of that five years ago, and here is what you decided, and here is why."

Losing Track of the Mission

One of the primary concerns in planning an exit strategy is ensuring that an organization's mission will remain strong and consistent through the process of transition. The organization's mission may also be lost or at risk at other times because of financial pressure. One subject describes this process as "mission creep":

> And the reason why mission creep happens is usually because of money. You start off in a sector and suddenly you realize all the funders are funding this, and you're over here, and so you're like, "Hmm, let's move this way, and we can get more money." But then you're not starting from conviction, right? You are starting from, "I just want to run an organization that can get money so I can pay my staff."

But the line between conviction and need is not always easy to observe. Many of the social entrepreneurs we spoke with discussed this issue, with varied but never straightforward answers. One social entrepreneur explains this tension and determines that to a slight degree, a shift in goal might not be all bad:

> So ideally, in my opinion, there is no question it's better to have a real conviction on what the organization does and go out and find the people who believe in that mission. In practice, though, it's very difficult to be puritanical about that because so many funders have, if not an agenda certainly preconceived ideas about what they want their money to be used for [that are] not entirely unrealistic or unreasonable. And so it's hard, it's very hard to avoid committing to tweaking your programs to meet a specific funding application, particularly if there is big money involved.
>
> An organization like us: a $100,000 grant is dangled in front of us, boy, it's hard not to do a little bit of tweaking with your program to meet with that. And at the

end of the day, I think executive directors and boards . . . as long as they make the judgments, . . . I think that it's reasonable to . . . attempt to meet funders' needs to a small degree. But it can be very dangerous if done in excess.

Funders also recognize this pressure. One venture philanthropist describes the potential for mission creep from the funder's perspective:

Funders can come in and be heavy handed. Funders can give only restricted grants and suggest that a nonprofit start a new program that isn't really aligned with what they want to do. It happens all the time, and sadly, you know, [we often hear], "Oh, but if you only just served, you know, high school youth instead of elementary school youth, then we could give you lots of money."

A colleague in venture philanthropy acknowledges this power differential but at the same time asserts that a bit of pressure might result in positive impact:

It's hard to turn down money. That gives you a position of power and you have to be very sensitive to that power and at the same time you have a responsibility for your own values and experiences in giving. Because sometimes the nonprofit needs to be pushed a little bit.

Funders and grantees agree that keeping track of the organization's mission can be particularly difficult through periods of transition and financial pressure. And in the social entrepreneurial world, organizations are almost always experiencing one or the other.

Establishing Long-Term Measures

Many businesses and organizations have assessment measures. But because social entrepreneurs are so uniquely connected to their organizations and because staying true to their missions is a concern, it is important that these organizations establish measures that can evaluate success beyond the founder's tenure.

Because social entrepreneurs are typically building a movement (in addition to building an organization), measuring success is difficult. Many social entrepreneurs speak about difficulties in assessment. They talk about judging themselves by "impact" yet admit that impact is difficult to measure. Some social entrepreneurs manage to set measures for themselves that are very similar to business models with detailed standards that guide them as they evaluate progress, products, and mission fulfillment. Some subjects assert that they will have achieved success when their organization can exist without their leadership, and one says he will have reached his goal when his organization becomes obsolete or unnecessary. Others concede that they will never feel satisfied but will always push farther. The for-profit social entrepreneurs with whom we spoke argued that one of the benefits of answering to a bottom line is that it provides a clean and easily measurable method by which achievement can be judged.

According to one social entrepreneur, performance does not guarantee access to capital, but it should:

I'm perpetually frustrated by the disconnect between performance and access to capital in our little slice of the nonprofit world. . . . There's a set of things we do to raise money and we've raised $25 million. I mean, we raise a lot of it. And there's a set of things we do to make sure we have a great program and they're tangentially connected largely by us promoting all the great things happening in the program. But it's not like if we get really great assessment results more money pours in. We get really good assessment results and then we have to go raise more money to do this in more places.

He also argues, like many social entrepreneurs, that success should be measured, at least in part, by growth:

We have a set of metrics that we measure the success of the organization by, how many kids are we serving, and what [do] our assessment results tell us on the quality of the progress each kid makes. It's pretty transparent. Implicit in that is growth. We're growing 8 to 10 new programs a year, because impact is a function of the quality of what you're doing times the number of people who are doing the work.

Venture philanthropists also recognize problems in assessing what they do. They attempt to measure three levels of impact: their own work as funders, the work of the grantee, and the impact or social change achieved. One venture philanthropist discusses the many layers involved in attempting to measure success in funding social entrepreneurs and their organizations:

One thing that we're thinking a lot about these days is how to measure the impact of our work on the organization. We've done obviously a lot of measurement about the impact on the individuals who are served by the organization, so, you know, do they stay in their jobs . . . are they in more stable housing, are they moving out of poverty by a number of measures. We have done anecdotal and some qualitative assessments of how the organizations have grown and thrived or not, you know, within the relationship that we have. But I would love, we're trying to find a way to do a third-party study, to really assess that, and I think it's hard to assess and attribute changes in an organization's capacity . . . to a particular relationship, a particular funder, a particular anything.

One venture philanthropist describes long-term measures his organization uses to assess success. He describes how some alumni of Wendy Kopp's organization Teach For America have been deeply motivated by their experience in working in the organization. This kind of impact goes beyond current measures, but he argues that it must be considered when attributing value to the work accomplished:

They're doing great work in the schools they work in. And I don't know how she would answer this. I'm not sure she thinks [that] that's the greatest outcome or [that she thinks that] the greatest outcome is . . . teachers that are in this thing for two years and what they [can] do later. . . . You'll see someone that's . . . the assistant superintendent of schools and you read their bio, and then in there somewhere . . . they did Teach for America. . . . It's the same thing, to me the measure of success. The other measure of success is long term. In twenty years are the people that came through [subject's organization], are they five mayors and whatever?

According to one venture philanthropist, a major goal involves impact not only on the nonprofits with whom they work but also on their investors: "My aspiration is to transform the investors as much as we transform the nonprofit." At least one venture philanthropist determines level of success, in part, by the nonprofit's level of satisfaction with the venture philanthropists' work.

Conclusion

This chapter draws a quick sketch of the social entrepreneur, describes some of the potential problems in his or her funding, and offers some suggestions about how these issues might be avoided. Social entrepreneurs are problem-solvers at a most basic level. They approach social problems with entrepreneurial spirit and business know-how. Colleagues in the nonprofit sector follow more traditional paths to do their work and operate within existing structures to help others. But like business entrepreneurs who see a void, a need for a gadget, or the potential of a new product line, social entrepreneurs see problems and present solutions. Ideally they will be able to apply this creativity to some of the problems in the field so that time is well spent, questionable means are no longer considered, and missions remain steady.

Notes

My thanks to Howard Gardner, who has provided guidance during both the research and analysis phases of my work on social entrepreneurs. I am grateful to Kim Barberich for her thoughtful initial inquiry into the financial challenges the social entrepreneurs in our sample faced. Major funding support for this research was provided by The Atlantic Philanthropies, The William and Flora Hewlett Foundation, and the Christian A. Johnson Endeavor Foundation. Timely additional support was provided by the John Templeton Foundation and the Louise and Claude Rosenberg Jr. Family Foundation.

1. The World Economic Forum (weforum.org) is an international organization that brings together world leaders to work to improve the world's diverse economic and social climates. The Schwab Foundation's Social Entrepreneur Summits typically bring together 500 social entrepreneurs and other leaders.

References

Colby, A. and W. Damon. 1992. *Some Do Care: Contemporary Lives of Moral Commitment.* New York: Free Press.

Dees, J. Gregory. 2003. "Social Entrepreneurship Is about Innovation and Impact, Not Income." Retrieved September 21, 2003, from http://skoll.socialedge.org/?293@202 .dJJHaMBQaB0.2@1ad86d9e.

Drucker, Peter F. 1985. *Innovation and Entrepreneurship: Practice and Principles.* New York: Harper and Row.

Schumpeter, Joseph A. 1942. *Capitalism, Socialism, and Democracy.* New York: Harper and Row.

Schwab Foundation. N.d. "What Is Social Entrepreneurship?" Retrieved September 21, 2003 from http:www.schwabfound.org/definition.htm.

Part Three: Further Strategies
                for a Domain of
               Responsible Giving

12 Philanthropy's Janus-Faced Potential: The Dialectic of Care and Negligence Donors Face

Paul G. Schervish

There is an ever-present potential in every philanthropic approach to help or hinder charities and their beneficiaries. Philanthropy, the voluntary social relation of care by which donors respond directly to others in need (Schervish 1998), possesses an especially potent capacity to affect the prospects of others. Wealth-holders are capable of both extraordinary care and extraordinary carelessness in carrying out their philanthropy. This Janus-faced potential of philanthropy is what I refer to as the dialectic of care and impairment, negligence, or dominion. This chapter explores this dialectic, drawing on intensive interviews with wealth-holders about their lives and philanthropy I have carried out over the past two decades.

I begin with a cautionary tale that illustrates the dialectic of care and carelessness that hovers around all well-intentioned good work. In the second section, I discuss the notions of care and friendship to highlight just what is at stake when philanthropy succeeds or falters. In the third section, I explain the affective basis and need for practical wisdom in the exercise of philanthropic care. In the fourth, I describe how the dialectic of care and dominion gets played out in business-oriented philanthropy and in anonymous giving. I conclude by recommending that a process of critical self-reflection can aid wealth-holders who wish to be wise rather than injurious in their philanthropy.

The Philanthropic Dervish: The Potential Discrepancy between Intent and Effect

Good intentions do not alone generate good work. Philanthropy is about care, and care is about meeting the true needs of others. That it is the effect, and not just the intention that matters is shown in the story of the philanthropic dervish. H. B. M. Dervish (1982, 30) recounts a tale told by Idries Shah about how a dervish (a novice holy man) set out to help a poor family who refused all ordinary charity. Looking for a way to help the family, the well-meaning dervish pretended to be a carpet merchant and offered the family 100 gold pieces for a worn rug in their home. The wife said she needed to check with her husband about the sale when he returned home. Upon hearing the offer, the husband grew suspicious and had the rug appraised. He learned that the rug was in fact worth ten times what the dervish had offered. When the dervish returned the next day, he was arrested for an attempt to take advantage of the poor. In the end, the dervish's philanthropy was ineffective. Despite its purported goal, the scheme produced negative unintended consequences, or dysfunctions, for the family and, equally important, for the dervish.

The notion of "dysfunction" was introduced over fifty years ago by Robert K. Merton (1949/1968) precisely to emphasize the fact that the consequences intended by actors do not necessarily ensue from purposeful action. Merton points out that motives and purposes are "often and erroneously merged with the related, but different concepts of objective consequences of attitude, belief and behavior" (104). This disjunction between motive and purpose as intent and actual effect points to the importance of discerning whether and in which ways the objective consequences actors seek actually come to fruition. While "functions" are observed consequences that allow for organizational accomplishment of a purpose, "dysfunctions" contradict or undercut the accomplishment of a purpose (105).

Although we leave the story of the dervish unclear about whether in due course the dervish extricates himself by explaining his honest mistake, it is clear that the initial intervention turned out to be dysfunctional. While the dervish's intentions were unassailable, his actions did not fulfill the needs of the family; indeed, they initially caused more harm than good. He crossed the sometimes evident and sometimes subtle line from care to negligence. Such is the difference between benevolence, or wanting to do good work, and beneficence, or actually doing good work.

Care and Friendship: The True Ends of Philanthropy

As Merton suggests, the notions of function and dysfunction apply only in the context of an intended purpose. Accordingly, it makes sense to speak of philanthropic activities as functional or dysfunctional only if we can identify a central purpose of philanthropy. We need to identify the purpose that makes philanthropy distinctively valuable when it is served and distinctively injurious when it is forsaken. I believe that this purpose revolves around the social relationships of care (Schervish and Havens 2002; Schervish 2005) and friendship. With Toner (1968), I see care as the implemental or instrumental aspect of unconditional affective regard for another, or love. The cardinal characteristic of care is that it is an activity directed toward treating other people as unconditional ends by meeting their true needs. Defining the purpose of philanthropy as meeting the true needs of others begs the question, of course, of just what in any particular setting the true needs are. However, it is the correct question. It locates philanthropy in the context of love and it insists on an intelligent practical implementation of love that advances rather than diminishes the welfare of others.

We can view the purpose of philanthropy from a second complementary direction that heretofore has not been stressed in philanthropic studies, namely that of friendship. The word philanthropy derives from the Greek *phileo* and *anthropos*. The two terms in combination are almost always translated simply as love of humankind. No special attention is given to the particular kind of relational love connoted by *phileo*, however, which is most accurately understood as the love of friendship, or simply friendship. *Philia* (the noun), or friendship love is the starting point for Aristotle in Book 8 of the *Nicomachean Ethics*, where he speaks about the concentric circles of love extending from family outward to the species. In the *Ethics*, says Provencal (2001), the family "is precisely a society of self-relations" in which the members love each other as other selves (§ 37). From such mutual friendship in the family, *philautia* extends outward to the friendship love of the species as other selves. Aristotle tells us that a "friend is another self" when speaking of the kind of friendship that brings individuals together for mutual benefit (1998, IX:9).

Friendship love is the noble purpose of philanthropy when exercised with care. And friendship love is what is violated when philanthropy is exercised with negligence. In philanthropy, the same conditions that offer the occasion for friendship also offer the opportunity for one soul, under the auspices of good intentions, to impair the other soul.

The Affective Base and Need for Practical Wisdom in Philanthropy

For philanthropy to exist, let alone be creative, targeted, and effective, the sentiments of a donor must be stirred and activated toward unmet needs. This is different from what happens in business and politics. In commercial and political relationships, those who supply resources do so by responding to the medium (of dollars or votes) through which the needs are expressed. This is what economists call a relation mobilized by *effective* demand. This means that those with a demand can discipline those who supply the goods and services that meet those needs. Commercial and political consumers are able to withhold their dollars and votes from those who fail to deliver on those needs. In contrast, the donor is not materially disciplined by those in need. Another way of saying this is that philanthropy is led by supply rather than by demand. A transaction between donors and recipients occurs only when donors freely recognize and respond to the needs of the recipients. And the *quality* of that transaction depends, at least in its initial phase, on how well the donor organizes and administers the gift so that it actually addresses the true needs of the intended recipients.

If commercial and political relations are mobilized by effective demand, philanthropic relations are mobilized by what I call *affective* demand. It is the person in need rather than the medium through which the need is expressed that motivates donors to supply resources. Different from the firms and elected officials that constitute the supply side in commercial and political relations, donors that constitute the supply side in philanthropic relations are under no material pressure to meet a demand or to do so appropriately. In contrast to business and politics, philanthropy entails no financially "coercive" downside for those on the supply side should they choose not to allocate their resources to offer the appropriate quantity and quality of goods and services to meet the demand of need. Even though there are occasional commercial shortages or political stalemates, the demand side inevitably exerts its will through the punitive system of consumer sovereignty.

Philanthropy comes to fruition only to the extent that donors recognize and respond to what is materially unenforceable by those in need, namely the humanity that is to be advanced by philanthropy. Philanthropy advances caring consequences and deters negligent ones to the extent that donors are affectively engaged and employ practical wisdom about the consequences of their giving. Philanthropy requires that donors recognize a call to caring friendship that derives from the worth of the person or cause in need. Such a relationship is vulnerable from the outset to not being established, and once it is established, it is vulnerable to being inadequate, distorted, or coming to an end. None of this denies donors the authority to set the directions, conditions, and standards of their gifts. But in the absence of the countervailing market relations that are present in commercial and political relations, donors need to be especially vigilant about the subtle responsibilities of the friendships they enter.

Evaluative Strategy to Distinguish Care and Negligence

Over the past two decades, my colleagues and I have interviewed close to 300 donors about how they tie together capacity, character, and wisdom in their philanthropy. Virtually all tell their story as a moral tale, emphasizing how they have in one way or another exercised virtue to make a moral life from the hand that fortune dealt them. We learned about the regrets they harbor about their philanthropic failures and the steps they have taken or are now taking to remedy them. Even from these narratives, we seldom learn enough to form an independent evaluation of whether their philanthropic activities are ultimately caring or debilitating. So how can we appraise the functions and dysfunctions of philanthropy without indulging in off-the-cuff judgments about how well a philanthropic endeavor meets the criteria of care and strategic friendship?

The inability to calculate a balance sheet of functions and dysfunctions from narratives about philanthropic endeavors need not exclude the possibility of setting out criteria to formulate evaluative judgments. The evaluative approach I suggest derives from a framework of strategies for giving wealth-holders use that has come out of my research (see Schervish and Herman 1988).[1] Evaluation criteria can be based on determining the distinctive aspects of each approach and elaborating the ways in which those characteristic elements can lead to both positive functions and negative dysfunctions.

A strategy of philanthropy is a way of acting, thinking, and feeling in an effort to meet one's own needs and the needs of others simultaneously. In a word, a strategy of philanthropy is a distinctive mode of engagement of a donor with a charity or beneficiary. Although donors may tend to emphasize a specific strategy in all or most of their giving, most often they pursue an array of different strategies depending on what they are doing and how they wish to be engaged. For instance, when carrying out a contributory philanthropic strategy, donors tend to simply write checks to support a cause and do not otherwise participate in activities in and around their gift. In contrast, when following an entrepreneurial strategy, donors contribute investment capital as well as their own skills, ideas, and time to the creation of a self-directed philanthropic enterprise.

For each strategy, distinctive attributes of donor engagement offer an opportunity for that strategy to be more or less caring. I find that what is potentially most caring and potentially most debilitating or manipulative about any particular strategy derives from the same source. For instance, in contributory philanthropy, limiting involvement to making a contribution can be especially caring for an organization that is well-directed and neither needs nor asks for any greater personal involvement. It can be a trusting and generous act for a donor to give resources and allow the charity to carry out its mission unhindered. At the same time, in other circumstances, simply making a contribution may express a donor's desire to be unengaged even though the charity may welcome and need greater engagement. Similarly, as we will see, in entrepreneurial philanthropy the personal funding and hands-on direction of a new philanthropic venture or a new direction in an existing charitable organization can result in a breakthrough in meeting people's needs or a heavy-handed intrusion of business logic into an arena not suited or actually hindered by it.

In what follows, I review the elements of three business-related strategies and the general orientation of anonymous giving, which in some form can accompany any philanthropic strategy, and chart the particularly salient opportunities and obstacles for care inherent in each of these four approaches. The business analysis is based on interviews from our 2001 High Tech Donor Study (Schervish, O'Herlihy, and Havens 2001). The analysis of anonymous philanthropy is based on interviews from a 1988 Study on Wealth and Philanthropy (Schervish and Herman 1998).

The Dialectic of Care and Negligence in
Three Business-Oriented Strategies

Strictly speaking, "venture capital," the term that spawned the analogous "venture philanthropy," denotes the more or less active dedication of an investor's money and expertise to propel the entrepreneurial activity of someone else. But as the term has come to be associated with philanthropy, it refers to a range of approaches that are in fact more widespread and multifaceted than what is strictly parallel to venture capital in the business world. Much of what is regularly included within the category of venture philanthropy is more accurately a set of three (and perhaps more) distinctive strategies that fall under the rubric of business-oriented philanthropy. The three forms of business philanthropy include *managerial* philanthropy, *entrepreneurial* philanthropy, and *venture* or *investment* philanthropy. Each is a specific way that donors carry out what is essentially self- or agent-animated philanthropy. Donors who use these strategies contribute to the direction of the charity in addition to contributing their financial resources.

Managerial philanthropy is the mode of engagement in which an individual's central contribution to a charity is the gift of organizational expertise without the contribution of financial resources. "What I felt was my greatest strength is the managerial side," explains Edward Morrison, a former software entrepreneur-turned-philanthropist.[2] "I can manage people, I understand how people work, I don't try to categorize them all the same and I understand the differences." He is working with a nonprofit whose head is what he calls a "pure entrepreneur." She is like her counterparts in the business world who "are typically pretty horrible managers because they want everything to happen in five seconds." He is sympathetic to this demon because he too was once one of those entrepreneurs. The key to his managerial contribution is that he knows from experience "that there's a brake . . . and I know when to use it."

In contrast to the *managerial* strategy, an *entrepreneurial* strategy of philanthropy engages both the human and financial capital of a donor in order to inaugurate either a new charitable enterprise or a new component within an existing charity. For instance, Robert Shorette, founder of Digital Hardware, expends most of his philanthropic dollars and time overseeing the start-up of his own educational charity. What differentiates commercial from social entrepreneurship, says self-described social entrepreneur Eugene Willey, is not the lack of measurement of return on investment. The difference is that the return on investment focuses on a "social return, which is measured in community capital or human capital or social capital."

The third business-orientated strategy is that of *investment* or *venture* philanthropy. Venture philanthropy is that "middle" form that infuses managerial advice and financial resources into a philanthropic effort but does not interject the hands-on daily direction that is the hallmark of an entrepreneur. For instance, Boston software entrepreneur Brian Taylor started his own family foundation, which he now uses as the base from which to contribute both his money and skills. His objective is to help others get charities off the ground by assisting them with goal definition, planning, and advice about how to leverage funding. He is not directly running a new charity but is combining, in a middle way, pieces of both managerial and entrepreneurial strategies.

The leading characteristic of today's popular business-oriented philanthropists is that they are agent-animated and shape direction. Even when simply making contributions to established organizations, these donors view themselves as actively appraising the effectiveness of the organizations to which they contribute. Taken together, this view and its three approaches can be described as intercessional orientation. I choose the term "intercessional" advisedly, for it provides both what is potentially most caring and potentially most domineering about business-oriented donors. On the one hand, it connotes an engagement that does what is actually necessary on behalf of another. On the other, intercession connotes interference or a manipulation that forces outcomes that are more willful than helpful. In business philanthropy, both the supportive and domineering potential of its intercessional character arise from the same underlying attribute of agent-animated donors. These strategies possess an overwhelming capacity to generate much care and much dominion.

There are, however, criteria for judgment that can be used by those who themselves engage in intercessory philanthropy and by those who are familiar enough with a particular case to evaluate the relative balance of care and harm. I turn first to the aspects of intercessory philanthropy that advance care and then address the distinctively portentous dysfunctions.

Several propitious opportunities are spawned by agent-animated philanthropy. The first is that it is particularly effective in s*purring creative directions*. When philanthropists recommend or insist on organizational formation and reformation, one goal is to improve a charitable mission in a creative way. In such cases, the intervention can be felicitous, for it offers charities wise organizational suggestions and lowers trepidation about making changes. A second positive outcome deriving from intercessional philanthropy occurs when donors offer sensitive criteria for and insightful appraisals about measuring outputs. High-tech donors make much of producing and measuring charitable outputs. But as many respondents appreciate, they need to recognize that long-term investments in human capital cannot be measured with the same quantitative rigor as short-term material benefits. Being sensitive to this distinction while remaining adamant about the need to formulate and assess performance is a particularly caring exercise of agent-animated philanthropy.

A third expression of care associated with agent-animated philanthropy is knowing when *to step aside and turn a venture over to others*. For instance, one donor who headed a university board felt it her duty to leave the board when someone else could provide the fresh ideas and energy she no longer felt she was capable of offering. She could have stayed on indefinitely, but she realized that different skills were needed to expand the fund-raising efforts she had excelled in starting.

A fourth fruit of intercessional philanthropy occurs when donors and individual beneficiaries *develop a working relationship of mutual respect*. When donors are in direct contact with nonprofit professionals as well as with the individual beneficiaries of a charity, they can learn to understand the cultural differences that separate the business world from the nonprofit world. They also can learn to effectively phrase their advice and frame their assistance so as to hold true to what they believe needs to change without alienating the nonprofit professionals or destroying their own enthusiasm.

Just as intercessional philanthropy can have a salutary impact, it can set in motion several adverse effects that can be described as meddling in or dominating a charity. One such temptation is for activist philanthropists to insist on implementing their views despite countervailing opinions by front-line professionals or community activists. One harmful intercession is to push a pet project that a community may neither need nor want; a second is to sidetrack a worthwhile project. A third way intercessional philanthropists may cross the line from care to dominion is by insisting on an accounting scheme that is too narrow to be effective. Venture philanthropists, especially, are adamant about treating philanthropic funding according to a stakeholder model that stresses the efficient production of outcomes. One pitfall in pursuing this model occurs when donors demand that outputs be measured in a program whose outputs are not known for a long period or are by their nature difficult or impossible to measure. Finally, an equally problematic misapplication of an intercessional logic can occur when charities commence projects merely because they can attract funding and not because the charity and those it serves would benefit. When philanthropic intercession generates not what is needed to be done but what a funder arbitrarily decides to do, an opportunity for care becomes a detriment.

Note that the issue of care and dominion never turns merely on the notion of "welcome" as opposed to "unwelcome" intercession. Certainly it is important to heed what administrators or beneficiaries regard as desirable or undesirable about the engagement of influential donors. And failing to consider the views of beneficiaries is one sure sign of hubris. But what administrators, professionals, or beneficiaries of a charity think (no more than what donors think) ought not be the primary norm for determining care and control. Rather, the criterion is how effective a donor's activities are for producing desirable outcomes—as long as we comprehensively define such outcomes to include not just productive efficiency but also repercussions for organizational ethics, participation, and the quality of goods and services.

The Dialectic of Care and Dominion in Anonymous Giving

In addition to studying the range of strategies used to implement charitable giving, we also studied anonymous giving as an orientation.[3] There are various degrees of anonymity. At one extreme, an intermediary provides a gift so that the donor is not known to anyone; at the other extreme is the case where the donor is known to the development office and charity administrators but no name is credited with the gift in published donor lists. In the course of our research work, we identified aspects of the case for and the case against anonymous giving as enunciated by respondents.

By shielding the recipient from the name and other characteristics of the donor, anonymous giving has the potential to be humane but (and this is surprising) can also end up being manipulative and domineering. Concealment of a donor's identity potentially "destabilizes" the relationship of mutual friendship, accentuating any trajectories toward friendliness or unfriendliness of a contribution. The very same reality—namely, concealment of a donor's identity—has the potential to both heighten and curtail the disproportionate influence of donors when philanthropy is donor led.

Anonymous giving offers donors the opportunity to be philanthropic disciples or demigods in new and telling ways. This is illustrated by the long-running popular television program *The Millionaire,* which aired on Wednesday nights from 1955 to 1960. The 205 episodes of *The Millionaire* followed a stock dramatic formula. Each program began with the billionaire, John Bereseford Tipton, sending his secretary to the door of an unsuspecting beneficiary with a tax-free cashier's check for $1 million. The emissary was not authorized to reveal the donor's name or background and prohibited the recipients from discussing how they came into their windfall. Naturally, the gift turned out to be a boon for some and the ruin of others. Ironically, the show was about the benefactor as much as it about the beneficiary. While the consequences for the recipient unfolded, an insightful viewer could also judge the donor's balance sheet of care and manipulation by keeping tabs on his dramatic and consequential interventions in the lives of others.

The same anonymity that creates potential positive and negative outcomes in the philanthropy of John Bereseford Tipton also occurs in the real-life anonymous giving of New Yorkers Karl and Marta Stempek. The Stempeks report that the hallmark of their anonymous giving is being able to view the handiwork of their beneficence behind what turns out to be a one-way mirror. The secrecy of their gifts, says Karl Stempek, a Columbia University ophthalmologist, enables them to

> thoroughly enjoy being able to see things happen that we are responsible for, without anybody knowing it . . . [and] without the embarrassment or the dissatisfaction that would come from having them be grateful to you. At Christmastime, for example, we've provided funds for families without their knowing where it came from, and we've done it through charities so that their letters of thanks for what they did with it go back to the charity and we aren't known at all in this.

Marta goes on to explain how she and Karl underwrote a struggling artist:

> There is a young fellow . . . who we know in San Francisco who's a talented painter. And we learned that he was having a hard time making ends meet. He has a wife and two children. We arranged through the foundation to make a gift to the University of San Francisco, and they are offering him an opportunity to do a mural for a large sum of money. We can't wait to see the life that we know this fellow

[can make for himself], because he is a friend. You know, he was just delighted to do this; he has no idea who provided the funds. The University of San Francisco said it was provided by some foundation that has offered this opportunity to him. He doesn't know how it happened or why, and we take great delight in the pleasure we know he's going to get from this money and from doing something that [he enjoys].

Despite their wealth, the Stempeks have chosen to live in a working-class neighborhood and to designate their living and dining rooms as office workspaces. My encounter with them in their home offered a portrait of two ethically consistent, humble activists who are profoundly moral in their motivations, work, and philanthropy. Yet it is important to examine how, from their concealed seat of anonymity, they have the potential to construct edifices of both care and dominion. Even for these good people, anonymity can offer a valuable way to both meet the true needs of beneficiaries and be a form of social engineering in the name of knowing what is good for someone else. It would not be bothersome or foreign to the Stempeks to hear me ask whether their anonymous giving is a higher form of friendship or a form of manipulation.

It is easy to note several positive consequences in the anonymous giving of the Stempeks and others we studied. In addressing their rationale for anonymous giving, the Stempeks enunciate two positive consequences of concealing their identity. The first is that they do not want their philanthropy to create a relationship of superordinate to subordinate. The Stempeks "can't bear" to feel superior by making others feel grateful to them. As Marta, founder of the Women's Lives organization in New York says, "I give you something, and you say thank you. You're indebted to me. I can't bear that relationship. That is a dreadful relationship to me; I don't want to be superior to you."

The second conviction, says Marta, referring to her community work with women in poverty, is that "I want to work with these people as equals." "I don't want them to think of me as some rich person who is going to come to their rescue and give them money so they can feel grateful to me and feel that I'm bestowing my funds on them. I don't want that because I want to be friends; I want to be equals; I want to be just at their level." Keeping her contributions secret also affects her relationship with the clients who come to Women's Lives for help. If the clients, who participate with her in a seven-week, three-hour-per-day support group, knew her status as a key donor, it "would totally destroy" her counseling relationship with them. Karl, too, talks of steps to ensure that the unintended consequences of status and privilege do not tarnish the experience of those he helps. He provides minority scholarships for students attending the medical school at which he teaches through anonymous donations in order to keep the recipients from feeling undue deference when they run into him, enroll in his courses, or work with him in clinical settings.

Finally, from the Stempeks' point of view, anonymity makes them more humble and richer human beings and lends their recipients a nobler spirit. In addition to avoiding the corrupting lures of self-aggrandizement, anonymity can serve the instrumental purpose of allowing recipients to focus on using the gift effectively rather than looking back over their shoulder at a donor they might have to cultivate.

Without more knowledge, I cannot say whether the anonymous giving of the Stempeks and others breeds negative consequences. But when it does, several paths make it "unfriendly." First, the anonymity that the Stempeks and others enlist to preserve them from elitism provides a hidden vantage point that allows donors to avoid some of the countervailing pressures of accountability that exist when the funder is as socially exposed as the recipient. Anonymity transposes philanthropy into a nonreciprocal relation in which donors can observe and know their recipients but are themselves shielded from being observed, known, and held accountable.

Second, the element of secrecy may lead to machinations in a manner akin to the mischievous antics of the demigods in Greek and Roman mythology. Leaving their heavenly realm and disguised in human form, these gods enter the world from the outside to shape the fortunes of mortals. The wealthy, as exemplified by the anonymous TV billionaire, the Stempeks, and others, enjoy a similar capacity not only to make a difference in the lives of others but also to make this difference in the way they want and without preparing the recipient for the largesse or receiving input. When shrouded in the cloak of anonymity, donors can readily fall into the temptation of offering help in a way that assuages guilt and grants a sense of efficaciousness without meeting the needs of recipients in a more profound way. For with anonymity comes at least a partial curb on the power of recipients to shape the nature of a gift and the relationships surrounding it.

A third negative consequence of anonymous giving is that it can curtail direct involvement of the donor in intercessional strategies of philanthropy, such as the business-oriented approaches I delineated previously. As entrepreneur and philanthropist Joan Halpern suggests, anonymous giving reduces the intensity of involvement. For her, anonymity would interfere with her ability to carry out hands-on innovation.

In the end, anonymous giving remains spiritually ambivalent. Anonymous giving can introduce reverence for the feelings and needs of the recipient and can provide a unique spiritual opportunity for the giver. "We love being Santa Claus," says Marta Stempek, referring to her and Karl's desire to release recipients from obligations of gratitude. There is something to that. As a friend once remarked, "Santa is the only person who gives you a gift whom you do not have to thank all year." Although not directly accountable to their recipients, the Stempeks hold themselves accountable to a strong egalitarian ethic. Where such normative touchstones are in place, anonymity need not inevitably become an invitation to mischief.

Still, we know that even Santa can fail to confer appropriate gifts. The lack of reciprocity between giver and recipient removes a number of the reciprocal forces that might otherwise forge a better match between gift and need, especially because philanthropy is led by supply. Since the quality of the gift relationship depends so much on the anonymous giver's insight and sensitivity, it is imperative that such donors remain mindful of the range of potentially negative consequences. Being available to help the recipient to prepare for, receive, and work well with the gift; being accountable for what one sets in motion; and being available for direct feedback about how the gift could be better directed all are more difficult for the anonymous donor who wishes to do more than let consequences emerge without counsel.

Conclusion: Opportunity for Self and Others

Generating positive consequences for both self and others is the primary outcome when wealth is used wisely in philanthropy. When used unwisely, it creates an opportunity to be domineering, incompetent, and negligent and can set in motion negative consequences in other ways. This is true for the most actively engaged forms of agent-animated philanthropy as well as for philanthropy that conceals the identity of the donor and curtails a full reciprocal relationship between donor and recipient. I have indicated the noble end of philanthropy to be care or friendship and have discussed philanthropy's supply- or donor-led characteristic and the relationship in various approaches to philanthropy between forces that can bring blessings and curses. Philanthropy is a voluntary relationship of care that requires for its existence and its quality a sensitivity of practical wisdom; the donor most not only want to enter into philanthropy but want to do so in a way that meets the true needs of the recipients. For philanthropy to be a social relation of care, there must be the capacity to meet the needs of others, the moral sensitivity to be aware of such needs, the character to want to do so, and the wisdom to treat others in the way they need to be treated. Today's philanthropists must be vigilant lest they act with all the goodwill of the unfortunate dervish whose philanthropic mission lacked the necessary wisdom to get right the consequences from friendship and care.

Notes

I am grateful to the T. B. Murphy Foundation Charitable Trust and the Lilly Endowment Inc. for supporting the research and writing of this paper.

1. Twelve strategies fall under four rubrics:

Personal Engagement Strategies: donors and beneficiaries have direct personal contact and exchange information with priority given to recipient needs:
1. *Consumption:* donors materially benefit from the organizations to which they contribute
2. *Empowerment:* donors seek simultaneously to enhance their own sense of self-empowerment and to give some active organizational control to beneficiaries
3. *Adoption:* donors attend personally to recipient needs in an ongoing and multi-faceted relationship

4. *Productive*: donors view above-market business relations with employees, suppliers, or consumers as philanthropy

Mediated Engagement Strategies: contact between donors and recipients is mediated by organizations or other individuals though knowledge and concern for recipient needs may be high:

1. *Contributory*: donor gives to a cause with no direct contact with recipient
2. *Brokering*: donors solicit other key donors in their own network
3. *Catalytic*: organizers donate time to mobilize a large number of other donors in a mass appeal

Donor-Oriented Strategies: donors are governed and mobilized by their own circumstances rather than by those of recipients:

1. *Exchange*: giving propelled by mutual obligation within a network of donors
2. *Pro Bono*: giving based on obligations associated with job expectations

Business Strategies: donors focus on using or improving the organizational resources of philanthropy:

1. *Managerial*: efforts focused on improving organizational effectiveness of philanthropic groups
2. *Investment*: philanthropy as raising and applying economic and human capital to achieve discernible outcomes
3. *Entrepreneurial*: hands-on efforts to apply innovative approaches to fulfilling needs

2. All names and identifying information of the respondents here and throughout the text have been changed to preserve the anonymity of respondents and the institutions with which they are associated.

3. This section on anonymous philanthropy is based on Schervish 1994.

References

Aristotle. 1998. *The Nicomachean Ethics*. Trans. David Ross. Rev. J. O. Urmson, and J. L. Ackrill. New York: Oxford University Press.

Dervish, H. B. M. 1982. *Journeys with a Sufi Master*. London: The Octagon Press.

Merton, Robert K. 1949/1968. *Social Theory and Social Structure*. New York: The Free Press.

Provencal, Vernon L. 2001. "The Family in Aristotle." *Animus: A Philosophical Journal for Our Time* 6 (December 24). Available online at http://www.swgc.mun.ca/animus/2001vol6/provencal6.htm.

Schervish, Paul G. 1994. "The Sound of One Hand Clapping: The Case for and against Anonymous Giving." *Voluntas: International Journal of Voluntary and Nonprofit Organizations* 5, no. 1: 15–37.

———. 1998. "Philanthropy." In *Encyclopedia of Politics and Religion*, ed. Robert Wuthnow, 600–603. Washington, D.C.: Congressional Quarterly Inc.

———. 2005. "The Sense and Sensibility of Philanthropy as a Moral Citizenship of Care." In *Good Intentions: Moral Obstacles and Opportunities*, ed. David H. Smith, 139–145. Bloomington: Indiana University Press.

Schervish, Paul G., and John J. Havens. 2002. "The Boston Area Diary Study and the Moral Citizenship of Care." *Voluntas: International Journal of Voluntary and Non-Profit Organizations* 13, no.1: 47–71.

Schervish, Paul G., and Andrew Herman. 1998. *Empowerment and Beneficence: Strategies of Living and Giving Among the Wealthy.* Final Report: The Study on Wealth and Philanthropy. Chestnut Hill, Mass.: Center on Wealth and Philanthropy, Boston College.

Schervish, Paul G., Mary A. O'Herlihy, and John J. Havens. 2001. *Agent-Animated Wealth and Philanthropy: The Dynamics of Accumulation and Allocation among High-Tech Donors.* Chestnut Hill, Mass.: Center on Wealth and Philanthropy, Boston College and Washington, D.C.: Association of Fundraising Professionals.

Toner, Jules. 1968. *The Experience of Love.* Washington, D.C.: Corpus Books.

13 The Foundation Payout Puzzle

Akash Deep and Peter Frumkin

At a time when discretionary public funds for new social programs are limited, many current and future public needs could be addressed through initiatives launched and funded within the nonprofit sector. America's 60,000 grant-making foundations are a small but critical part of the nation's growing nonprofit sector. As a group, private foundations control assets of $600 billion and disburse about $30 billion in grants each year to nonprofit service providers. Roughly half of all foundation grants are made by the 300 largest institutions (Foundation Center 2004). Foundation giving has come to be counted on as a critical early (and often first) funding source for new and innovative projects in the nonprofit sector (Bremner 1988; Karl and Katz 1981; McIlnay 1998; Sealander 1997). Foundation philanthropy continues to grow in size and is expected to explode as the baby boom generation ages and declines. Some estimates have projected a $40 trillion transfer of wealth in the coming decades, with huge amounts flowing into foundations (Schervish and Havens 1998).

Against this backdrop, two separate and narrow debates have raged in recent years about foundation grant-making and investment practices. The first debate has focused on finding ways to improve the way foundations make grants. The second debate has focused on locating the best financial strategy for the investment of endowment assets. However, a more fundamental question has largely been ignored; namely, how much to give now and how much to save for future giving.

Foundations are known for both their endowments and their grants. One of the few regulations all private foundations face is a requirement that each fiscal year they pay out of their endowments at least 5 percent of the average monthly value of their endowment during the previous year. This minimum expected payout includes both grants and administrative expenses associated with operating a foundation. Where did the 5 percent rule come from and what is the logic behind it? During negotiations over the Tax Reform Act of 1969, Congress enacted a set of modest regulations designed to ensure that foundation assets were being productively used for charitable purposes (Freeman 1994). No systematic research lay behind the payout rate, which was originally set at 6 percent, then reduced to 5 percent a few years later. The number remains less a product of economic reasoning than political bargaining that is three decades old.

The 5 percent rate is a lower limit below which foundations cannot go. However, there is no upper limit on how much they can disburse. The decision about how much to pay out in grants is critical because across the entire foundation field, every 1 percent increase in the annual payout rate of all foundations translates into approximately $4 billion in new grant funds for the nonprofit sector. Given the stakes that are at issue, foundations must give serious thought to the question of how much should be given away today and how much should be saved for the future. Pulling at foundations as they deliberate over this complex issue are compelling arguments for a higher payout rate and a strong case for a low payout rate.

This chapter begins with a summary of the arguments on both sides of the payout debate. We then draw on a new dataset on foundation financial management to examine how a group of large and influential foundations has resolved the payout decision over the past twenty-five years. After finding a remarkable convergence in foundation payout behavior, we explore several possible explanations for this behavior. We conclude by exploring policy alternatives to the long-standing 5 percent minimum payout rule and why a revisiting of this 30-year-old public policy is in order.

For and Against the 5 Percent Payout Rule

Because foundations play a visible and important role in the working of the broader nonprofit sector, their behavior is subject to considerable scrutiny. To date, however, discussion of the payout rate has been limited (Nelson 1987; Steuerle 1977). On the one side, a group of progressive grant-makers sympathetic to the nonprofit service community has actively argued for a higher payout rate based on social justice considerations: "Grants are the primary way philanthropy impacts our society. Grants fund the people and organizations at the heart of building communities, alleviating poverty, and creating change. . . . Social change giving is about reaching those that traditional charities often ignore, but who are in the greatest need of help. . . . We call on our colleagues in the philanthropic community to join our effort by increasing their pay-out to include '1% More for Democracy' to support real social and economic change" (Mehrling 1999). On the other side, studies sponsored by or conducted by the foundation trade associations (Demarche 1999; Cambridge Associates 2000; Salamon and Voytek 1989; Salamon 1991) have simply argued that foundations should be allowed to preserve their assets for the future without saying much more about the trade-offs such an approach to giving entails. While admitting that a foundation that spent out an additional 1 percent could have maintained the value of their endowment over the past four decades, these studies point out the undeniable but obvious fact that the less foundations spend today, the more they will have in the future. The inevitable conclusion of the industry is that caution is in order when it comes to changes in policies or practices (Harrison 1999). In order to advance this policy debate beyond these narrow political and self-interested positions, we begin by analyzing the underlying issues on both sides of the payout debate.

Arguments for a Higher Foundation Payout Rate

There are at least five good arguments for high foundation payout rates. They include the possibility of attacking a problem early and before it has become intractable, the desire to achieve greater levels of intergenerational equity, the ability to count on new money entering the field of philanthropy to replace payouts, the need to protect and execute the intent of the donor, and the possibility of diffusing public criticism of foundation avarice by paying out higher levels of grants. We summarize each of these five arguments below.

1. Early intervention: Spending more now will allow
foundations to nip social problems in the bud.

One potent argument for a high payout rate is related to both effectiveness and efficiency. Giving away larger amounts of money today is attractive because it could make it easier for foundations to actually solve social problems within communities rather than merely treat the symptoms of social disorder. The idea of nipping a problem in the bud rather than waiting years for it to fester has strong intuitive appeal, especially since organized philanthropy has for over a century sought to distance itself from charity and almsgiving (Carnegie 1992; Rockefeller 1909). To be effective, foundations need to do preventive giving, which involves intervening before problems become so acute that no amount of foundation funding is likely to have much effect. By getting to root causes and committing large blocks of philanthropic capital in the short run, foundations can in principle avoid having to spend ever-larger amounts of money over longer periods of time. In some fields, such as medical research, funding research today will have considerably more value than funding research 20, 50, or even 100 years from now. Not only will work today to find a cure for a disease such as AIDS help a large number of people, it will also lead to a slowing in the spread of the disease. In New York, feeling that the AIDS issue simply could not wait, Irene Diamond spent most of her large foundation's assets over a ten-year period to fund path-breaking research in a new AIDS research laboratory she created. Her grants played a critical role in supporting the work of Dr. David Ho, who was chosen to lead the new lab and who discovered protease inhibitors, one of the most promising AIDS treatment breakthroughs to date. In cases like this, where problems are likely to grow in the absence of philanthropic interventions, it may be more efficient to act in the present and pay out large amounts of grants in order to tackle a problem aggressively.

2. Intergenerational equity: Generational benefits ought to
roughly equal tax expenditures.

A higher payout rate may also make sense if intergenerational equity is a concern. The whole question of foundation payouts touches on serious tax equity issues, especially given the exponential growth in the size of foundation assets expected in the coming decades. Foundations have long represented one of the few alternatives to paying high estate taxes, which now surpass 50 percent on large estates. When a foundation is created today, the burden of lost tax revenue is borne by citizens today in the form of a tax expenditure. However, for the most part, the benefits of foundation giving do not accrue to the taxpayers that make this expenditure for the establishment of foundations today. By giving the wealthy the opportunity to create a foundation in perpetuity, taxpayers today are in essence being asked to subsidize the welfare of future generations, at a time when many current social needs continue to be unmet. This ever-evolving intergenerational transfer of resources would be unproblematic if each generation made tax expenditures of roughly equal size. This is clearly not the case, however. As demographic waves of different sizes and with different levels of resources age and convey their wealth into foundations, the unequal intergenerational distribution of foundation assets will become pronounced. Just as the burdens and benefits of Social Security are not distributed equally across generations, so too will low foundation payouts in perpetuity create intergenerational inequities. Higher levels of giving may be needed to even out the costs and benefits of foundation giving.

3. Projected growth of philanthropy: New money will enter the foundation field to replace what might be spent.

Higher rates of giving by foundations appear justified by virtue of the fact that new funds will flow into the foundation field as a whole. Money disbursed by foundations may indeed be lost to endowments forever, but new funds are entering philanthropy through bequests to existing foundations and through the formation of new foundations. For foundations pondering whether higher levels of giving will lead to a long-term diminution in the availability of funds, these new institutions offer some reassurance that philanthropy's future is secure. Just in the last five years, three foundations created with technology fortunes have leaped to the top of the list of the largest foundations. As a result of recent infusions of funds, the Bill & Melinda Gates Foundation, The David and Lucile Packard Foundation, and The William and Flora Hewlett Foundation, all relatively new entries in the foundation field, now control almost 10 percent of the assets of the entire field. Other substantial fortunes, including those created by the growing ranks of billionaires, have been pledged to philanthropy, though the funds have not yet arrived at their final institutional resting places. The availability of these new funds for giving in the future should make higher levels of giving today more appealing.

4. Donor intent: Spending more earlier will allow some foundations to fulfill donor desires.

Because foundations often are established in perpetuity, the issue of how best to protect and pursue the donor's philanthropic intent often arises. Sometimes donors leave behind very clear instructions about how they want their fortunes to be used. The challenge of enforcing and implementing the donor's philanthropic agenda is usually not a problem if family members are on the board who knew the donor. Over time, however, as outside directors join the board and as succeeding generations get involved with philanthropy, protecting and pursuing the donor's intent can become difficult. While there is considerable debate over whether philanthropic intent should be enforced at all, for those who are committed to it, higher payout rates are one way to ensure that charitable funds are used appropriately. The desire to carry out a donor's philanthropic agenda has led some foundations to pursue a payout strategy that will eventually lead to the liquidation of assets. Both the Vincent Astor Foundation and John M. Olin Foundation in New York decided to pay out large amounts in order to ensure that the donor or a close friend of the donor was able to maintain control over the funds and apply them to causes that fit the original charitable intent of the founder. While this is an extreme position, many donors have begun to do more of their giving while alive simply because they want to enjoy their giving and see their interests and aspirations fulfilled. For such donors, a higher payout rate represents a tool for ensuring that philanthropic resources are allocated according to their desires.

  5. Legitimacy: A higher payout rate will curtail criticism
  from the nonprofit sector and government.

The legitimacy of the foundation field is at stake in the payout debate. With the huge amounts of money they control, foundations are easy targets for criticism. Criticism from activists within the nonprofit sector has been mounting, and several associations and research groups have raised questions about the generosity of foundations. By paying out the bare minimum required by law, the largest foundations have created conditions not dissimilar to those thirty years ago when the field was first investigated and regulated by Congress. The Tax Reform Act of 1969 contained not just the payout rate but also an excise tax on net investment income, greater disclosure requirements, and a ban on transactions that benefit foundation officers. These measures were enacted because a small number of controversial grants created suspicion and concern about political meddling and mismanagement within the field, concerns that the foundation field failed to address and correct publicly. By paying out grants at a higher rate today, foundations could deflect the mounting criticism of their payout practices and position themselves more effectively as responsible partners within the broader nonprofit sector. In this sense, higher payout rates could be a potent defender of the field's privileges and its long-term independence.

  Arguments for the Current Foundation Payout Rate

  There are at least five good arguments for a lower foundation payout rate. They include the realization that social problems may get worse over time, the uncertainty posed by volatile financial markets, the weight of professional experience and tradition, the appearance on the scene of new problems that cannot now be foreseen, and limitations on the ability of nonprofit service organization to effectively absorb sudden increases in funds. We detail each of these arguments below.

1. Current social problems may get worse.

Some foundations may seek to pay out the minimum required by law in order to conserve their resources for the future when particular social problems may be more acute than today. In areas such as global environmental protection, it is hard to see the problem of sprawl, air pollution, and water quality becoming smaller and less challenging in the future. In fact, some foundations might reasonably argue that these areas are likely to grow substantially in their urgency over time and that careful stewardship of funds today is needed to ensure that large amounts of philanthropic dollars will be available to address these problems in the future. Compounding the issue of exacerbation is the growing perception that many of the most significant human problems cross national boundaries and that philanthropic resources, not public spending, may be needed to address difficult problems that span boundaries and extend into the distant future.

2. Financial markets are uncertain.

Paying out only the bare minimum of 5 percent appears quite defensible in light of the uncertainty of financial markets. Almost all foundations have their assets invested in a mix of stocks and bonds, usually split roughly 60-40 between the two. Although many of the largest foundations have invested more heavily in stocks and have done very well in recent years, memories of foundation financial advisors are long. In the past, there have been fairly prolonged periods of market decline, particularly in the mid-1970s and late 1980s. During the 1970s, the assets of the Ford Foundation dropped precipitously when the free spending policy of its president, McGeorge Bundy, was paired with a down market. Because it is impossible to predict the future of the market, many foundations believe that it is important to pay out the minimum amount to ensure that future volatility will not erode the foundation's endowment. While market declines may hurt foundation endowments in the future, those foundations that pay out less in grants will be able to cope with these declines more easily than those that spend their funds aggressively on grants.

3. Paying out 5 percent is supported by the weight of tradition and professional experience.

Paying out 5 percent is attractive because the practice has the weight of tradition and professional experience behind it. The "5 percent solution" has been endorsed by large numbers of foundation managers and trustees through years of practice. Deviating from this established pattern of behavior exposes foundation managers to considerable risk should the additional funds they wish to expend not achieve their intended purpose. This is particularly problematic given the increased competitiveness in the field of philanthropy over the past three decades and the desire for advancement that accompanies professionalization. For the foundation executive, staying within the confines of the 5 percent payout is simply the safest and surest course of action. Among trustees, who play a critical role in setting payout policy, there is also a strong tendency to defer to tradition. Pushing a foundation to adopt a higher payout than the minimum required by law requires overcoming the strong pull of the duty of care, which directs trustees to preserve foundation assets for the future. The tradition of careful and conservative stewardship argues against breaking the mold and seeking to pay out higher levels of grants. For new entrants to the field, the weight of professional experience and tradition is felt through training and orientation programs that allow newcomers to foundation philanthropy to meet and learn from experienced hands. Given the strong networks within philanthropy that are forged by associations and board interlocks, adopting a conservative 5 percent payout rate is surely appealing.

4. New and unforeseeable social problems may emerge.

For foundations pondering the payout issue, the future needs of society may appear hard to know. Over time, foundations with broad charters may discover that new problems have emerged that will require attention from foundations that today cannot even be foreseen. Many of the largest foundations are established in perpetuity with very broad missions precisely for this reason. The Kresge Foundation, for example, defines its mission as identifying and addressing "at their source, the causes of human suffering and need," while the Rockefeller Foundation simply claims "to promote the well-being of mankind." For foundations with broad purposes established in perpetuity, the idea of spending conservatively in the present seems advisable, since it is impossible to predict what needs will emerge and how critical they will become years into the future. The range of social problems that has emerged over the past century that no one could have predicted is broad enough—from crack cocaine addiction in the United States to flesh-eating bacteria in Africa—that many foundations now spend carefully on grants in order to build their endowment for the next generation of social problems that may emerge in the future but are not obvious today.

5. The capacity of nonprofits is limited.

Spending conservatively on grants today may also appear wise given the limited ability of nonprofit organizations to absorb and use effectively substantially larger amounts of money in a short period of time. The payout decision is not just about the interests and needs of foundations. It has clear practical implications for the broader nonprofit sector, which uses foundation grants to deliver services. For some foundations that are thinking about the question of how to achieve their philanthropic purposes, substantially increasing the flow of grants to nonprofits is not an obviously efficient way to increase a foundation's social impact—especially if smaller, local, and less sophisticated nonprofits lack the infrastructure to direct these additional funds to productive uses. Moreover, there is always the question of whether growth and scale are universally desirable ends; many believe that nonprofit agencies are most effective when they are small and tightly linked to local communities.

Recent Foundation Payout Decisions

Given the compelling nature of the claims on both sides of the issue, one might reasonably expect to find foundation payouts distributed fairly broadly across a spectrum ranging from 5 percent all the way up to much larger numbers. This raises some basic questions: What exactly have foundations done with their assets over time? How have they set their payout rates? What is the connection between asset growth and higher payout rates?

To answer these questions, we have assembled the first comprehensive and reliable database on the management and use of foundation assets. This database contains financial information on 169 foundations from 1972 through 1996. These foundations were randomly selected from among all foundations that reported assets greater than $5 million in 1970 and for which at least ten years of data was available. Unlike other studies that have relied on imprecise aggregate reports based on voluntary surveys, the data in this study was drawn from IRS Form 990PF, the annual reporting form used by private foundations. This data was collected over a two-year period from the IRS, from nonprofit archives across the country where 990PFs are stored, and from the foundations themselves. To supplement this quantitative data, we interviewed thirty-four foundation trustees, presidents, and financial managers about the payout decision-making process.

The data in figure 13.1 shows the average payout rate of this sample of foundations over time. At the beginning of our sample period, private foundations were required to pay out a flat 6 percent of the prior year's endowment value. This was modified in 1976, when the required payout rate was changed to 5 percent of endowment or the investment income of the foundation, whichever was higher. The current payout rate of a flat 5 percent was instituted in 1981. Figure 13.1 reveals that although foundation payout *rates* have responded slightly in response to these adjustments of policy, the payout *policy* of private foundations has remained remarkably stable: they have essentially paid out about the required rate.

Figure 13.2 contrasts investment performance with payout decision across foundations. Each data point in the graph plots an individual foundation's average payout rate against its average return on investments over the 25-year sample period. The most striking feature of Figure 13.2 is the clustering of payout rates around the 5 percent minimum with virtually no correlation between returns and payouts. As a group, the foundations in our sample have earned almost 8 percent annually on their assets while paying out an average of 5 percent.

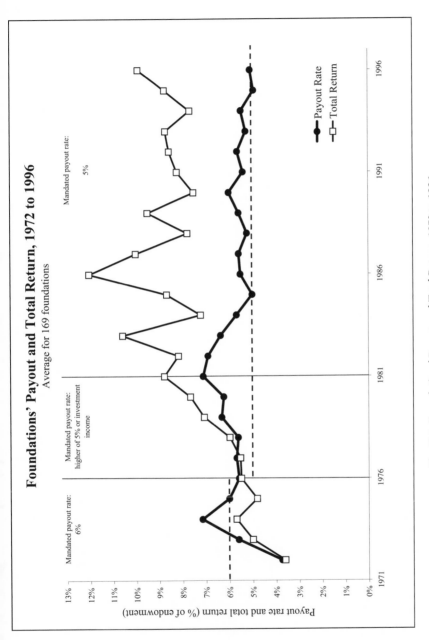

Fig. 13.1. Foundations' Payout and Total Return, 1972 to 1996

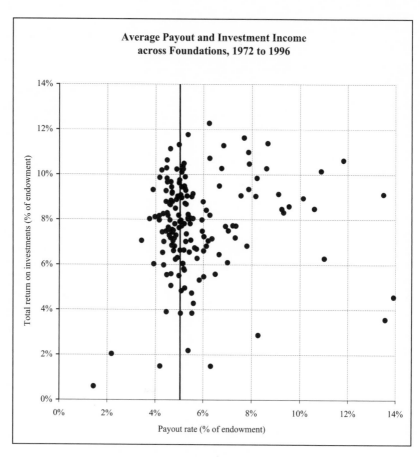

Fig. 13.2. Average Payout and Investment Income across Foundations, 1972 to 1976

The data in these two figures raise the following questions: Given the tremendous diversity of missions and purposes pursued by foundations, why is there such a high level of convergence in the payout rates chosen around the "5 percent solution"? Why do all the arguments for higher payout rates appear to carry so little weight? Are there other considerations, not described above, that foundations weigh when they set a payout rate?

Obstacles to a More Differentiated Approach to the Payout Puzzle

In seeking explanations for the strange convergence of private foundations around a single solution to the payout puzzle, it is tempting to say that the arguments for the minimum rate are simply stronger than those for a higher rate. However, this position does not seem compelling enough to explain the

198 *Akash Deep and Peter Frumkin*

level of homogeneity in foundation behavior that we observe over time. As foundations deliberate over the question of how much they should pay out each year, a set of potentially significant constraints weigh on them. The constraints were aired during a series of focus groups we held to discuss the factors foundation managers weigh when making the payout decision. We met with trustees, presidents, and financial managers in focus groups in Boston, San Francisco, Minneapolis, and New York.

When asked about what obstacles, if any, there were to higher payout rates, one trustee noted that that there is a clear disincentive to high rates of grant spending because it is often very difficult to measure the impact of grants, particularly compared to the rate of return on the portfolio and the growth of the endowment. Faced with committing resources to an activity whose "social return" cannot be precisely quantified or growing an endowment and carefully tracking financial performance, trustees tend to gravitate toward the latter. One trustee explained that it is very hard to understand the claims and arguments of grant-making staff about the effectiveness of grants made by his foundation. On the other hand, the performance of the financial managers is extremely easy to measure with benchmarks and industry averages. This tendency may in part be due to the fact that many trustees come from backgrounds in business and law rather than from nonprofit organizations. Given their stewardship roles, it is hardly surprising that many foundation trustees focus their attention on what they understand and what they can measure. In many foundations, there may thus be an asymmetry in the ability of principals to assess the performance of their grant-making and financial agents. This naturally leads trustees to focus on performing well in the area of portfolio return and asset growth where success and failure are clearly measured.

Another consideration weighing on foundations is the social structure of philanthropy today. Prestige and privilege within philanthropy is accorded to foundations based on the size of their assets and their perceived power. There is therefore a strong impetus to grow the endowment of a foundation as a way to build the visibility of the institution within the national philanthropic community. Large foundations dominate the media presence of philanthropy and bring considerable visibility to their trustees. Moreover, how large the endowment is is usually one of the very first questions foundation trustees are asked when they are introduced to other trustees at conventions and meetings. Because assets are closely correlated to power, trustees admit a tendency toward wanting to grow their foundations. Trustees pursue asset growth and financial performance because the role of boards demands that the trustees watch out for the long-term institutional well-being of the foundation above all else, especially when their status is closely connected to the financial position of the institution they represent.

Size also brings the ability to pay staff higher levels of compensation, which may also influence payout decisions. One recent study found that foundations with endowments of over $1 billion paid their presidents on average $350,000, while foundation with endowments of $100 million only paid their chief executives on average $120,000 (Council on Foundations 2000). A strong correlation between asset size and staff pay introduces an incentive within the staff to go along with the tendency of many foundation boards to pay out close to the minimum required by law. While foundation staff might want to advocate on behalf of higher payout rates so as to have more money to disburse to grantees, staff members also have vested interests in the long-term growth of their foundations. This incentive is especially acute given the professionalization of the field and the emergence of grant-making careers over the past three decades.

Convergence around a 5 percent solution is also a function of the growing weight of professional experience and tradition. Several trustees reported keeping their foundations close to the minimum payout number in part because most other foundations have made this same decision. At some foundations, there is limited time at board meetings to accomplish a long list of administrative functions. Setting time aside for a discussion of the payout question is not a high priority because a simple solution is present, which is to do what foundations have traditionally done. Convergence around a single solution to the payout puzzle thus appears to be a function at least in part of competing priorities within foundations and the perceived presence of field-wide norms. Challenging the field's settled practices requires that foundation trustees work hard not just to change an internal policy but also to demonstrate that there is reason to do something different than other foundations.

The internal logic of foundation decision making is not the only force pushing these institutions toward convergence in payout behavior. Tax policy is driving the unnatural convergence of foundations and depressing foundation payout rates in the process. Current tax policy toward foundations is strangely structured so as to discourage deviations from long-term averages. Foundations that increase their payouts for one or more years above 5 percent then later return to 5 percent are substantially penalized under the existing excise tax policy. This policy makes it hard for foundations to overcome the inertia they face in the payout arena, even when financial returns might tempt them to periodically increase their payout rate.

An excise tax on foundations was first imposed on foundations in 1969 to recover the cost of government oversight of foundations' activities and was set at 4 percent of annual net investment income, which includes interest, dividends, and net capital gains from foundation assets. Over time, the tax generated more income than predicted. In 1978, the excise rate was reduced to 2 percent of net investment income for all foundations, but receipts from the tax still far exceeded the actual monitoring expenses. Thus, in 1984, the Deficit Reduction Act created the current excise tax structure that allows certain foundations to qualify for an even lower tax rate if they exceed their prior five-year average payout rate. It was expected that the two-tier tax structure would provide tax savings and, more important, adequate incentive to foundations to boost spending for charitable activities.

Today, the tax on the net investment income of a private foundation is 2 percent. This excise tax rate is reduced to 1 percent if the foundation's qualifying distributions, as a percent of assets, exceed its average payout over the prior five years. The excise tax rule penalizes the foundation by making it liable to the higher rate of 2 percent if it increases the payout rate by even a small amount in one year then lowers it thereafter. Not only does the higher rate increase the tax liability, it also reduces the rate of growth of foundation assets, thereby substantially reducing the amount paid out in qualifying distributions in the future. The only way for foundation managers to deal with this perverse aspect of the rule is to increase the payout rate only when they are certain that they will be able to sustain the higher payout rate for a long period of time. In the face of large uncertainties on both the financial and grant-making side of foundation activities, this is clearly an onerous burden that few foundation managers are willing to bear. Therefore, it may not be surprising that many foundation managers prefer not to depart from the minimum payout rate even if the current year has experienced a sharp growth in assets or presents exceptional grant-making opportunities. The adverse impact of the two-tier excise tax was noted in the proposed budget of the U.S. government for the fiscal year 2001. One proposal under consideration would reduce the excise tax on private foundation net investment income to a flat rate of 1.25 percent and would repeal the formula for the special reduced excise tax rate for foundations maintaining their historical charitable level of distributions.

Policy Options

In thinking about what public policy toward foundations should be, two objectives seem clear and indisputable. First, public policy should be demanding enough to ensure that foundations use their resources in ways that benefit the public, not just themselves. Second, public policy should be flexible enough to allow foundations to select a payout rate that is strategically aligned with their missions. The existing payout policy fails in both these tasks: Foundations' assets have grown substantially over time, and convergence around the minimum payout rate is widespread. By way of conclusion, we explore the trade-offs required to reform public policy toward foundations.

A first rationale for a minimum foundation payout rate is the encouragement of a steady dispersal of philanthropic funds to the nonprofit community. This rationale flows from the tax-exempt status granted to foundations and the ability of donors who establish foundations to avoid substantial estate taxes. In exchange for their privileged tax status, foundations are required to make disbursements that benefit charitable organizations. The 5 percent flat rate has been only marginally successful in ensuring this transfer, however. Foundations have earned much higher rates of return on their assets over the past thirty years, and many have been able to grow their endowments significantly during this time. Looking beyond the current payout policy, there are several ways to ensure that this transfer of resources is accomplished, ways that would do a more thorough job of moving philanthropic funds into the community.

Perhaps the most obvious alternative is an inflation-adjusted variable payout rate keyed to foundation asset growth or a variable rate keyed to asset growth that is both adjusted for inflation and based on the average rate of return over several years. A variable rate would clearly be more effective than the current flat rate at pushing foundation resources into the nonprofit world—without threatening the ability of foundations to exist in perpetuity. While it would ensure that foundation asset growth is applied to giving, it is not clear that this policy option would be appreciably better than the current flat rate. In large part this is because foundation payout policy should do more than just ensure that funds flow into the nonprofit sector. Public policy needs be flexible enough to encourage foundations to adopt a plurality of payout rates that are strategically aligned with the distinctive missions of individual foundations. While a variable rate would lead foundations to pay out more funds, it would do nothing to encourage foundations to link their grant-making and financial strategies.

This brings us to the second important criteria for judging payout policies; namely, the degree to which the policy encourages foundations to choose a rate that represents the most effective way to accomplish the varied missions defined by foundations. The fact that there is such homogeneity in payout practices would not be troubling if all foundations had identical missions and if 5 percent represented the right payout rate for all foundations at all times. However, it is very difficult to argue that this is the case. In reality, foundations are committed to many purposes and causes. Because missions vary among foundations, the convergence of foundations around a 5 percent payout policy suggests that there may be little or no alignment between the financial and grant-making strategies of foundations. If foundations were indeed matching their payout rates to the nature of their missions and the shape of the social problems on which they are focused, one would expect to find a broad plurality of solutions to the payout puzzle, ranging from very conservative strategies to much more aggressive ones. We therefore hold that the current policy treatment of private foundations is flawed because the convergence it has introduced into the field has made strategic alignment between financial and grant-making strategy hard to achieve.

While many of the possible alternatives to the 5 percent rate are possible, only one of these options would clearly encourage foundations to adopt a payout rate that strategically links mission and payout decisions within foundations. This option is nothing other than the elimination of any and all mandated payout rates. If there were no mandatory payout rate, all foundations would be forced to engage the question of what rate is strategically desirable. It would remove the target and default position that existing policy has created and free foundations to engage the payout decision fully. Eliminating payout regulation would push foundations to think through the payout puzzle more fully. It would also likely lead to a more diverse set of solutions over time as the grip of tradition loosened and foundations began to confront the challenge of making difficult intertemporal trade-offs. Such an approach would not be entirely unproblematic. One clear obstacle to a complete elimination of all mandated minimum rates is that the first rationale for public policy in this field would be difficult to achieve. Foundations might well respond to deregulation by reducing their payouts to levels even lower than those adopted over time. The cost of such a move in political terms would be high, as an increasingly organized and vocal nonprofit service community would surely demand redress.

How then can foundation policy be fruitfully reformed? A clear first step would be the elimination of the excise tax that distorts the incentives in the field. Beyond this obvious but limited first step, the choices become more difficult. On the one hand, adopting a variable payout rate would likely do a better job of ensuring that foundation resources are used for public purposes. On the other hand, abandoning payout regulation entirely might well encourage more pluralism and greater strategic alignment in foundation decision making. In making any change to existing policy, one thing must be kept in mind. Regulating foundation payouts involves tough trade-offs. While it may be necessary for policymakers to choose between either encouraging foundations to increase the scale of their giving *or* allowing these institutions more freedom to pursue their missions, all parties to the search for a solution to the payout puzzle should be clear on one thing. The long-standing 5 percent payout requirement has failed in both these tasks.

Note

The authors gratefully acknowledge the financial support of NewTithing Group and The Bradley Foundation and the research assistance of Yekyu Kim, Jens Christian Niedermeier, Alexander Villanueva, and Jennifer Johnson. We would like to thank Claude Rosenberg, David Scudder, Christine Letts, Mark Moore, and Marion Fremont-Smith for valuable comments on earlier drafts of this chapter.

References

Bremner, R. H. 1988. *American Philanthropy.* 2nd ed. Chicago: University of Chicago Press.

Carnegie, A. 1992. "The Gospel of Wealth." In *The Responsibilities of Wealth,* ed. Dwight F. Burlingame. Bloomington: Indiana University Press.

Cambridge Associates. 2000. *Sustainable Payout for Foundations.* Grand Haven, Mich.: Council of Michigan Foundations.

Council on Foundations. 2000. *Foundation Management Report.* Washington, D.C.: Council on Foundations.

Demarche Associates. 1999. *Spending Policies and Investment Planning for Foundations.* Washington, D.C.: Council on Foundations.

Foundation Center. 2004. *The Foundation Directory.* New York: The Foundation Center.

Freeman, D. 1994. *The Handbook on Private Foundations.* New York: The Foundation Center.

Harrison, C. R. 1999. "It's How You Slice It." *Foundation News and Commentary* (November–December): 32–36.

Karl, B. D., and S. N. Katz. 1981. "The American Philanthropic Foundation and the Public Sphere, 1890–1930." *Minerva* 19, no. 2: 236–270.

Merhling, P. 1999. *Spending Policies for Foundations: The Case for Increased Grants Payout.* San Diego, Calif.: National Network of Grantmakers.

McIlnay, D. P. 1998. *How Foundations Work.* San Francisco, Calif.: Jossey-Bass.

Nelson, R. L. 1987. "An Economic History of Large Foundations." In *America's Wealthy and the Future of Philanthropy,* edited by T. Odendahl. New York: The Foundation Center.

Rockefeller, J. D. 1909. *Random Reminiscences of Men and Events.* New York: Doubleday.

Salamon, L. M. 1991. *Foundation Investment and Payout Performance: An Update.* New York: Council on Foundations.

Salamon, L. M., and K. Voytek. 1989. *Managing Foundation Assets: An Analysis of Foundation Investment and Payout Procedures and Performance.* New York: The Foundation Center.

Schervish, P. G., and J. J. Havens. 1998. "Money and Magnanimity: New Findings on the Distribution of Income, Wealth, and Philanthropy." *Nonprofit Management and Leadership* 8, no. 4: 421–435.

Sealander, J. 1997. *Private Wealth and Public Life.* Baltimore, Md.: Johns Hopkins University Press.

Steuerle, E. 1977. "Pay-Out Requirements for Foundations." In *Commission on Private Philanthropy and Public Needs, Research Papers—Sponsored by the Commission on Private Philanthropy and Public Needs,* III: 1663–1678. Washington: Department of the Treasury.

14 Old Problems, New Solutions: The Creative Impact of Venture Philanthropy

Nick Standlea

Much has been written about venture philanthropy (VP), from its heralded beginnings to the troubled times it fell on after the tech bubble burst to its current state of affairs. However, since venture philanthropy accounts for only 0.2 percent[1] of total dollars given in 2002, one has to ask the question Why all the fuss? We hypothesized that the attention given to VP might be attributed not to VP's actual results in practice but to its creative impact on the philanthropic sector at large. In testing our hypothesis, we found that venture philanthropy has indeed sent ripples though the foundation world by both influencing the practices within traditional foundations and, perhaps more important, by furthering a strategic shift across the philanthropic sector.

In order to answer the question of whether VP has had a creative impact on the philanthropic sector, the GoodWork Project borrowed from the systems model[2] definition of creativity—a tool social psychologists use to assess collective creative impacts or impacts that affect entire domains of knowledge. For the purpose of this study, a creative impact occurs when a new idea or practice, or bundle of ideas or practices, significantly influences the larger body of practitioners in a particular field—in this case, philanthropic foundations, thereby changing the symbolic domain they operate in. We sampled five long-standing influential foundations—William and Flora Hewlett, Rockefeller, Kellogg, James Irvine, and Carnegie—and tracked the degree to which each had adopted six basic practices of venture philanthropy over time. For comparison purposes, we also looked at the Roberts Enterprise Development Fund—a traditional foundation that from 1996 to 2002 transitioned into a venture philanthropy foundation.

In order to assess the degree of influence, we analyzed interviews conducted with foundation executives and program officers; broke down the annual statements and presidential statements each organization had issued in 1996, 1999/2000, and 2002; and analyzed foundation descriptions in independent philanthropy publications. Drawing from these documents, we tracked the bundle of practices that make up venture philanthropy. We tracked VP practices, or references thereto, regardless of whether a foundation's rhetoric referred to the practices as "venture," "engaged," "strategic," or another type of philanthropy. The specific bundle of practices[3] tracked were:

1) Use of Performance Measures
2) Focus on Organizational Capacity-Building
3) Increased Length of Relationships
4) Increased Amounts of Funding
5) Highly Engaged Relationships with Grantees
6) Articulated Risk-Orientation and Exit Strategies

Foundation Case Studies

The three time periods we chose to look at are natural points from which to assess creative impact. The first period, the year 1996, marked the time just before venture philanthropy burst onto the nonprofit sector scene. The second period, 1999–2000, was the height of VP's popularity. Shortly thereafter, the crash of the tech bubble and the subsequent downfall of a number of VP firms took place. The third period, 2002, marks the onset of VP's current phase; it is slightly humbled but focused and resolved to prove that it can be practiced on a large scale. The findings will be presented separately for each of the six foundations we studied.

The Roberts Enterprise Development Fund (REDF)

The REDF case is an ideal starting point for looking at VP's influence across the foundation sector because it was influenced so dramatically by VP that it actually became a venture philanthropy foundation.[4] In Table 14.1, we can easily observe the specific strategic shifts REDF underwent as its structure evolved from a classical model to a VP model. Over the course of 1996 to 2002, REDF developed tools for performance measurement, focused significant resources on capacity-building, increased its average grant size, increased its engagement level with grantees, and developed strategies concerning risk orientation and exit plans. In other words, it engaged in every practice we tracked. This first case will serve as a reference point against which we will check the traditional foundations that have been influenced to a lesser degree.

The William and Flora Hewlett Foundation

1996: The Hewlett case is representative of a number of foundations across the country. In 1996, Hewlett's strategy was based primarily around specific programs; for example, education, the environment, family and community development, and the performing arts. It made no mention of VP ideas or practices such as performance metrics, exit strategies, or commitments to organizational capacity-building. However, there were signs that Hewlett might

Table 14.1. VP Practices of the Roberts Enterprise Development Fund, 1996, 1999–2000, and 2002

Venture Philanthropy Practices	1996	1999–2000	2002
Use of Performance Measures	• Increased outcome-focused evaluation	• SROI analysis • Program grants and capital grants based on business plans • Indices of operational and social outcome success with organizations developed	• SROI analysis through Webtrack and OASIS (Ongoing Assessment of Social ImpactS) performance metrics • Performance measures from 1999–2000 continued
Focus on Organizational Capacity-Building	• Grants • Cash guarantees • Cash flow advances	• Leveraging other resources around cash assistance • Funding for organizational capacity: human capital, overhead, capital requirements, technology, etc.	• Level of nonmonetary support and management assistance equal to dollar value of grants • Financing for organizational infrastructure • Access to business networking opportunities provided
Increased Length of Relationship	• Unknown	• Anticipated: 10 years • Minimum: 5 years	• Anticipated: 10 years
Increased Amounts of Funding	• Mean: $72,500[1]	• Mean: $136,700[2] • Significant core and capital investments support in fund-raising efforts through networking on behalf of enterprise • Portfolio decreased from 10 to 7 between 1997 and 1999	• Mean: $261,000[3] • Funding strategies from 1999–2000 continued

Continued on the next page

Table 14.1. *Continued*

Venture Philanthropy Practices	1996	1999–2000	2002
High Engagement with Grantees	• Met 6 times per year	• Met a minimum of 12 times per year • Ongoing communication and shared decision making	• Provided strategic business development assistance • High engagement strategies from 1999–2000 continued
Articulated Risk Orientation and Exit Strategies	• No formalized strategy concerning risk • No formalized exit strategies	• High managerial risk management through business analyst and Farber interns/fellows • Enterprise and organizational risk management through portfolio diversification • Formalizing specific exit strategies	• REDF may exit a social purpose enterprise expected to generate significant net funding over time, assuming the enterprise can self-finance its continued growth and expansion • Risk orientation practices from 1999–2000 continued

1. Adjusted to 2004 dollars at 2.39% inflation.
2. Adjusted to 2004 dollars at 2.27% inflation.
3. Adjusted to 2004 dollars at 2.27% inflation.

be receptive to innovative philanthropic practices. Its 1996 annual statement noted: "The Foundation considers the nation's habits of philanthropy, individual and corporate, less healthy than they could be, and therefore will be particularly receptive to proposals that show promise of stimulating private philanthropy" ("Statement of Purpose" in The William and Flora Hewlett Foundation 1996, n.p.).

1999–2000: By 1999, the feel and basic focus of the foundation's annual statement had changed dramatically—it focused on organizational objectives rather than on programs. These objectives reflected the foundation's new "investment approach" to philanthropy. The annual report states:

> The business world offers instructive models and guidance for the philanthropic and nonprofit sectors. We can learn from the practices of venture capitalists investing in startups, from "value" investing in more mature companies, and from organizations making internal investments in R&D. As business investments seek economic returns, philanthropic investments seek social returns—the societal benefits that our programs seek to achieve. The business analogy highlights the importance of setting clear objectives and measures of success, considering investments in terms of efficacy, risk, and potential return, assessing a grantee organization's capacity to achieve specified objectives and, where appropriate, helping strengthen its capacity; and measuring the organization's and the foundation's progress toward our shared objectives. (The William and Flora Hewlett Foundation 1999, viii)

From this statement alone, we can see a certain level of influence from venture philanthropy as it touches on three of the six VP practices we tracked: performance measures, focus on organizational capacity-building, and articulated strategies concerning risk orientation and exit strategies.

In an additional reference to performance metrics, Hewlett also states:

> We should strive to define clear objectives and measures of success for each program area and for each grant. . . . We should always specify what would constitute success (or failure) in principle, and should identify milestones on the path to success. Where the Foundation provides general operating support (as distinguished from project-specific funding) to an organization, the success of the grant should be measured in terms of the organization's overall success in achieving its and the Foundation's shared objectives. (ibid.)

The 1999 annual report shows additional evidence that the foundation had thought through VP strategies such as risk orientation and exit plans. It describes itself as "society's risk-taker" and states that "like private investors, foundations can take greater or lesser risks, with concomitant potential yields." It also states that "as an aspect of the evaluation process . . . we must also anticipate exit strategies with respect to failed projects or organizations" (ix, x).

2002: By 2002, Hewlett had embraced a number of VP-based strategies, including a commitment to performance metrics, organizational capacity-building, increased involvement with fundees, and taking on "high-risk" social investments —although they were all now referred to as elements of "strategic philanthropy."

As the president's statement declares, "We think of ourselves as strategic and results-oriented" (The William and Flora Hewlett Foundation 2002, 1).

One year earlier, the president had demonstrated the foundation's commitment to organizational objectives and VP practices such as metrics with the statement that "the foundation's aim of achieving long-term impact on social and environmental problems demands clarity of objectives and the means for achieving them. It also requires systematic assessment of progress toward those objectives and the ability to make mid-course corrections" (The William and Flora Hewlett Foundation 2001, xiv). Additional descriptions of Hewlett's orientation toward performance measures included the statement that "negotiated general operating support is based on an agreed-upon strategic plan with outcome objectives. . . . The funder engages in a due diligence process, which culminates in an agreement about what outcomes the organization plans to achieve, how it plans to achieve them, and how progress will be assessed and reported" (The William and Flora Hewlett Foundation 2002, 2).

Hewlett's president emphasized VP strategies such as long relationships and capacity-building through descriptions of its operations in 2001: "[We are] providing grants of several years duration and of renewing support to high-performing organizations" (The William and Flora Hewlett Foundation 2001, xii). One year later, he noted that "almost 50 percent of Hewlett Foundation's grant dollars are designated for general operating support" (The William and Flora Hewlett Foundation 2002, 1). In addition, Hewlett highlighted its high-level engagement with fundees, stating that the foundation had

> recently made a substantial general operating support grant to a performing arts organization. We expressed some concerns about the viability of the organization's business plan, which led to changes in the plan before the grant was made. (3)

Finally, we can observe a high level of influence from, and commitment to, venture philanthropy in Hewlett's decision to pledge $215,000 to the Seattle Fund to help establish the Social Ventures Partners Cities Plan, a venture philanthropy firm (The William and Flora Hewlett Foundation 2001, 76).

The Rockefeller Foundation

1996: The Rockefeller Foundation did not refer to any VP strategies in 1996; its annual statement that year was primarily program-based. However, Rockefeller describes the nonprofit sector as "entrepreneurial, independent, and innovative," and the president's statement refers to nonprofit relationships as "wellsprings of social venture capital" (Rockefeller Foundation 1997, 4). These statements might lead us to believe that like Hewlett, Rockefeller was a likely candidate to fold VP practices into its own.

1999: Yet by 1999, Rockefeller had become averse to VP strategies. Program officers warned that foundations should be advised against searching for the "magic bullet" that solves societal problems and produces measurable results in too short a time (GoodWork Project 2002). The organization also claimed that although using quantitative measures was becoming increasingly popular in the foundation world, the development and execution of appropriate benchmarks for nonprofits was time consuming and expensive and the final evaluative measures were often thought of as useless and purely subjective (ibid.).

2002: There are no mentions of VP ideas or practices in the 2002 annual statement. As in the statements of years past, its primary focus was specific programs. Rockefeller is the only foundation in this study which appears to have articulated no affiliation to venture philanthropy ideas and practices.

The Kellogg Foundation

1996: As with the other foundations in this study, Kellogg's 1996 annual statement focused on specific grant programs. However, it referred to grant-making as an opportunity to "[build] the capacity of community organizations which have achieved success," hinting at the foundation's openness to VP models (Rockefeller Foundation 1996, 15).

1999–2000: By 1999, Kellogg demonstrated a strong willingness to test venture philanthropy strategies. In Community Wealth Ventures' *Venture Philanthropy: The Changing Landscape*, Kellogg is described as exploring a "collaborative venture fund." In addition, the report stated that they were "very interested in applying [the] venture capital model 'in moderation' to grant-making" and described the foundation as "providing hands-on, capacity-building assistance to grantees" as well as assisting several organizations to work toward long-term sustainability (Community Wealth Ventures 2000, 16).

The foundation's 2000 annual report contains several revealing statements, including a reference to their donors thinking of their contributions as "strategic investments" that would "leverage positive social change." In addition, the president stated that their donors "give from the heart, but believe nonprofits should adhere to effective business practices." The president specifically referred to organizational capacity-building, saying "we've learned that nonprofits cannot operate effectively without proper tools and training. That's why the Kellogg Foundation supports organizations . . . [that] work behind the scenes to strengthen what we call the infrastructure of philanthropy, . . . offer[ing] workshops that build skills in areas such as . . . management . . . and finance . . . [in] the nonprofit sector" (The W.K. Kellogg Foundation 2000, 6, 12)

Interviews at Kellogg also revealed that the foundation had spent significant time and energy thinking about performance measures; one employee stated that "the best evaluation is responsive evaluation . . . designed in response to both the context and the questions being asked." However, not all of Kellogg's staff was convinced that pursuing VP ideas was in the best interest of the foundation. One Kellogg officer cited the naiveté of some venture philanthropists, stating,

They tend to think that, "Well, guys, that worked so well in the Internet business I started, I should be able to apply those same management techniques to social problems." . . . [But often, those business techniques] don't translate easily.

2002: By 2002, Kellogg's disposition toward venture philanthropy had changed considerably—it is difficult to determine whether VP ceased to exert as significant an influence as it had in 1999/2000 or whether the foundation had simply backed away from VP practices, absorbing certain aspects and leaving others behind. Community Wealth Ventures' 2002 report on VP describes several of Kellogg's top lessons surrounding VP: "Don't 'paint yourself into a corner' with the VP rhetoric. Organized philanthropy is challenging, and while there is room for significant improvement, there are no 'magic bullets' [e.g., venture philanthropy] that will solve all the challenges" and:

> Venture-philanthropists will operate more effectively with a better and more disciplined base of knowledge about past organized philanthropic foundations and their approaches. There is too much generalizing going on about mature foundations' practices, for example. Dig deeper and you will find pockets of innovative practice in mature foundations that are quite similar to what VP is articulating as good practice—it may just be "labeled" something different. (Community Wealth Ventures 2002, 176)

In addition, Kellogg seemed to send mixed messages in reference to capacity-building and levels of engagement. The president stated that the foundation "support[s] . . . engagement throughout [its] grantmaking," and Community Wealth Ventures described Kellogg's fund mission as "provid[ing] hands-on capacity-building assistance" (W.K. Kellogg Foundation 2002, 5; Community Wealth Ventures 2002, 176). However, the foundation's 2002 annual statement seems to contradict these claims: "The foundation does not make loans and does not provide grants for operational phases of established programs or capital purposes (purchasing, remodeling, or furnishing of facilities and equipment, or separate budget line items labeled as 'indirect' or overhead costs)" (W.K. Kellogg Foundation 2002, 26).

It should also be noted that there is evidence that Kellogg remained committed to certain VP practices such as performance measures. For example, it focused on further evaluation of "post-grant" periods to assess the effects of grants given. It also gave $100,000 to the establishment of Seattle Ventures Partners in 2001.

In any case, while the degree to which Kellogg adopted venture philanthropy practices is unclear, it is apparent that Kellogg was influenced by venture philanthropy ideas as management clearly wrestled with VP ideas and how they might fit into Kellogg's practices.

The James Irvine Foundation

1996: Like the other classical foundations in our study, The James Irvine Foundation had little to say about venture philanthropy in 1996, focusing instead on specific programs. The only reference to VP ideas in its 1996 annual statement concerned increasing grant size: "These figures represent the Foundation's continuing efforts to reduce the total number of grants while increasing the average grant size, a policy initiated several years ago to better focus our work and to achieve greater impact" (The James Irvine Foundation 1996, 21).

1999–2000: In 2000, The James Irvine Foundation demonstrated that it had been heavily influenced by VP when it launched the James Irvine Innovation Fund. The Innovation Fund was created with the vision of improving the effectiveness of nonprofit organizations and testing new approaches to philanthropy. More precisely, it hoped to identify specific needs in nonprofits and provide access to a full range of outside consultants—including those with expertise in business, evaluation, technology, law, and other areas. With a backing of $6,000,000 and words from management such as "the reluctance or inability of foundations to 'swing for the fences' with unbridled passion to fund the extraordinary is discouraging," it appeared that the foundation clearly believed in venture philanthropy strategies (The James Irvine Foundation 2000, 12).

Yet while creating the Innovation Fund is clear evidence of being heavily influenced by the ideas and practices of venture philanthropy, it is unclear whether the foundation (or at least highly influential members within the organization) ever completely accepted the notion of putting VP ideas to work. For instance, while the fund was given a large amount of capital to work with, it was only staffed by 1.5 full-time workers (Community Wealth Ventures 2000). In addition, several statements from the foundation's president appear to be in opposition to most VP practices. In the 2000 annual statement, the same year the Innovation Fund was created, the president spoke against organizational objectives and performance metrics with the statement that "'hyper-rationalism' and 'managerialism' . . . are taking over the nonprofit sector"; he also said that it is not in the best interest of society to replace a "values-driven, mission-centered approach to philanthropy . . . with a technically-based, efficiency-driven, outcome centered philanthropy" (6). The president claimed that "one of the most pernicious consequences of this rush to proficiency and effectiveness may well be the impulse to avoid—if not eliminate—funding to address big, complicated, messy, seemingly insoluble problems, problems rife with uncertainty, risk, and inefficiency, whose potential for failure is high. . . . A troubling feature of some of the 'new' philanthropy is an enthusiasm to fund projects and activities that are easily quantifiable and visible" (7).

2002: The James Irvine Innovation Fund was closed before the end of 2002. It had administered only $2,000,000 of its initial $6,000,000 principal. Curiously though, just as in 2000, when the Innovation Fund was created and the parent foundation's rhetoric appeared to be at odds with VP strategies, in 2002 when the fund was closed, the rhetoric of the parent foundation seemed to be supportive of VP strategies. This apparent contradiction is likely explained by the arrival of the foundation's new president, James Canales. In the 2002 annual statement, the president referred to high engagement, stating that "the work of our grantees can be enhanced when the Foundation plays a more active partnership role." In addition, he referred to the usefulness of performance metrics, stating that the James Irvine Foundation remained effective by "holding [them]selves to the highest standards of performance and accountability" (The James Irvine Foundation 2002, 2). He also referred to organizational capacity-building, stating that "we believe that organizations best equipped to deliver on their missions are those that invest in the necessary resources to engage in sound organizational planning, to provide ongoing board and staff development, and to develop internal systems that are efficient and effective" (4). He stated that "specific tactics to build organizational capacity of our partners will continue to include: core support grants that include the related costs of a strong organizational infrastructure" (ibid.) Furthermore, in 2002, a "flex fund" was developed to permit the foundation to provide onetime $35,000 grants for the organizational development needs of grantees.

In conclusion, although the James Irvine Innovation Fund no longer exists, the parent foundation was obviously influenced by venture philanthropy practices and ideas.

The Carnegie Foundation

1996: We did not find any references to VP ideas or practices from the Carnegie Foundation in 1996. Their annual statement was program-based, much like the statements of other foundations in this study. However, it should be noted that one year later, in the 1997 annual report, the president posed two strategic questions that demonstrated that the foundation had been influenced to a certain degree by VP ideas and practices. The president's statement referred to performance measures when he posed the important question "How do we evaluate our programs?" He also referred to the VP idea of longer investment periods when he asked "Would we achieve our objectives more effectively if we made fewer grants and larger commitments?" (Carnegie Corporation of New York 1997, 2).

1999–2000: Through 1999, Carnegie continued to generate program-based annual reports. Yet in his personal statement at the beginning of the 2000 annual report, the president also focused on organizational strategies toward philanthropy such as those put forth by "newcomers to philanthropy" who "regard their funds as 'venture capital' " (Carnegie Corporation of New York 2000, 19).

The 2000 annual report reveals that the Carnegie Foundation had clearly been influenced by venture philanthropy. The president referred to high engagement and performance metrics:

> Venture philanthropy brings a welcome new set of strategies to grantmaking. Unlike traditional philanthropies, which make grants to a great many capable organizations with promising proposals, the new philanthropists work intensely with relatively few nonprofit organizations. Traditional foundations fund projects and give free rein to the experts to develop their ideas independently; new founda-

tions often join the boards of directors and may provide day-to-day financial and management support. (20)

He went on to sing the praises of the Roberts Enterprise Development Fund, noting several significant accomplishments and describing its process of using performance measures:

> To determine which philanthropic investments are the most promising, Jed Emerson, a program officer with an M.B.A., analyzes each organization's financial information, social service results and participants' responses on questionnaires. From this analysis comes a bottom line number, called the "Social Return on Investment" that can add efficiency to the foundation's management and investment activities. (ibid.)

In 2000, the foundation also revealed that it had thought through several aspects of the VP model—another clear sign of influence. In the president's statement, he articulated its risk orientation in this way: "We must be fearless about risks, even failure. Unanticipated failure is often to be expected as an inevitable part of the discovery process . . . part of making progress" (19).

2002: In 2002, Carnegie continued to demonstrate that it had been influenced by VP ideas and practices. Carnegie increased its mean grant size from $176,111 in 1996 to $331,759[5] in 2002 (both amounts in 1996 dollars). In addition, Carnegie further committed to the VP notion of capacity-building as it worked to "strengthen the capacity of NP organizations to excel in their work" (Carnegie Corporation of New York 2002, 7). In 2002, Carnegie gave "$175,000 to eGrants.org to develop online donation processing and training service for nonprofits; $300,000 to CompuMentor Project to provide nonprofits with a website for locating technical information and assistance and small grants; and $500,000 to the National Alliance for Nonprofit Management for improving the management and governance of nonprofits" (7).

Analysis across Foundations

Venture Philanthropy Ideas and Practices

As can be seen in table 14.2, the VP practices most widely adopted in our sample foundations were the use of performance metrics and a focus on organizational capacity-building. The table also provides evidence of each of the remaining VP practices we tracked—increases in length of relationships, increases in amounts funded, high engagement with grantees, and articulated risk and exit strategies—in at least two foundations by 2002 (the only exception was "articulated risk-orientation and exit strategies," but this practice was found in both Hewlett and Carnegie in 1999). Preliminary statistical analysis also suggests that the bundle of VP ideas and practices taken as a whole significantly affected our aggregate sample of the philanthropic field.

We would argue that the appearance of the VP ideas and practices found in

Table 14.2. VP Practices across Time, by Foundation

Venture Philanthropy Practices	1996	1999–2000	1999–2000
Use of Performance Measures	Hewlett: – Rockefeller: – Kellogg: – James Irvine: – Carnegie: –	Hewlett: + Rockefeller: – Kellogg: + James Irvine: – Carnegie: +	Hewlett: + Rockefeller: – Kellogg: + James Irvine: + Carnegie: +
Focus on Organizational Capacity-Building	Hewlett: – Rockefeller: – Kellogg: + James Irvine: – Carnegie: –	Hewlett: + Rockefeller: – Kellogg: + James Irvine: – Carnegie: –	Hewlett: + Rockefeller: – Kellogg: –/+ James Irvine: + Carnegie: +
Increased Length of Relationship	Hewlett: – Rockefeller: – Kellogg: – James Irvine: – Carnegie: –	Hewlett: – Rockefeller: – Kellogg: – James Irvine: – Carnegie: –	Hewlett: + Rockefeller: – Kellogg: – James Irvine: – Carnegie: +
Increased Amounts of Funding	Hewlett: – Rockefeller: – Kellogg: – James Irvine: + Carnegie: –	Hewlett: – Rockefeller: – Kellogg: – James Irvine: + Carnegie: –	Hewlett: – Rockefeller: – Kellogg: – James Irvine: + Carnegie: +
High Engagement with Grantees	Hewlett: – Rockefeller: – Kellogg: – James Irvine: – Carnegie: –	Hewlett: – Rockefeller: – Kellogg: – James Irvine: –/+ Carnegie: –	Hewlett: + Rockefeller: – Kellogg: – James Irvine: + Carnegie: –
Articulated Risk Orientation and Exit Strategies	Hewlett: – Rockefeller: – Kellogg: – James Irvine: – Carnegie: –	Hewlett: + Rockefeller: – Kellogg: – James Irvine: – Carnegie: +	Hewlett: + Rockefeller: – Kellogg: – James Irvine: – Carnegie: –

Key: Plus signs (+) indicate the appearance of a VP idea or practice; minus signs indicate the absence of VP ideas or practices.

table 14.2 in combination with the amount of anecdotal references to VP ideas and practices found in the former five case studies demonstrates that venture philanthropy has likely influenced the traditional foundations we sampled to a significant degree. Thus, according to our definition, VP seems to have had a creative impact on these foundations. The fact that the rise of VP practices and ideas in these classical foundations directly correlates with the rise of venture philanthropy further suggests the validity of our claim (as seen in table 14.2, there was no direct evidence of VP practices or extensive discussion of VP ideas in 1996). Because we chose the foundations, other than REDF, without prior knowledge of VP influence, we also believe it would be reasonable to assume that results of this study could be extrapolated to reflect a general impact on the field at large of traditional foundations.

Bringing Management to Philanthropy

However, perhaps the most interesting result of this study is not that VP has had a creative impact, but how and in what capacity it has had the greatest impact. As we hypothesized at the beginning of this study, VP has influenced classical foundations by causing them to think through, and in several cases employ, VP practices such as performance metrics, capacity-building, increased grant sizes, and so forth. Yet we did not anticipate that venture philanthropy might have had an even larger, though not easily observable, effect on the philanthropic sector by providing a bridge between philanthropy and *management*.

As Peter Drucker outlined in 1974 in *The Practice of Management,* management theory rests on the structure of the Management by Objectives philosophy, or MBO. The basic elements of MBO include:

- All organizations start with their mission statement.
- From the mission statement, objectives are derived.
- From the objectives, smaller goals are set and performance metrics are created and used to measure the success or failure of achieving these goals and objectives.
- Changes, if necessary, are then either made to practices to achieve objectives and goals or to the specific objectives and goals themselves.

During our analysis it became clear that the rise of VP was directly correlated with an increase in articulated objectives (as seen in table 14.2). That is, even foundations who rejected the tenets of venture philanthropy as applicable to their particular foundational mission shifted the focus of their rhetoric to organizational strategy—or management by objectives. In 1996, there was little to no discussion of "objectives" that directly stemmed from mission statements or measurements with which to assess the achievement of objectives among any of the foundations we studied. Instead, the foundations all issued program-based statements. Yet by 2002, all of the foundations, save Rockefeller, used their annual statements to delineate their overall organizational strategy along with, or in the context of, the descriptions of their programs.

The language these statements used also indicated a shifting away from program-based thinking toward management theory. Numerous statements issued by foundations we studied directly referred to practices and ideas based in MBO:

- "The foundation's aim of achieving long-term impact on social and environmental problems demands clarity of objectives and the means for achieving them. It also requires systematic assessment of progress toward those objectives and the ability to make mid-course corrections" (The William and Flora Hewlett Foundation 2002, xiv).
- "We've learned that nonprofits cannot operate effectively without proper tools and training. That's why the Kellogg Foundation supports organizations . . . that build skills in areas such as . . . management" (W.K. Kellogg Foundation 2000, 12).
- "A key part of our strategic planning initiative has been a review of the Foundation's mission and goals, last revisited by the Board of Directors in 1986" (The James Irvine Foundation 2002, 2)

Conclusions

For years, philanthropists and foundation officers have acknowledged the lack of standard principles and practices, or at the very least, a sharing of best practices, as a problem in philanthropy. As a head of a prominent philanthropy organization notes, "Philanthropy's amazingly fractured . . . it's a fractured cottage industry . . . [and it] is still as random as it was 100 years ago" (Good Work Project 2002). We believe this problem stems from the philanthropic sector's resistance to using the breadth of knowledge contained in the management discipline. In 1974, Drucker stated that "the service institution does not differ much from a business enterprise in any area other than its specific mission . . . [and] it faces very similar challenges to make work productive and the workers achieving" (Drucker 1974, 135). However, the nonprofit sector has never completely bought in to MBO—the building blocks of management— because it has always viewed management theory as a tool of business rather than a tool of organizations. As Drucker—a champion of nonprofit organizations himself and author of *What the Nonprofits Are Teaching Business*—observed of charitable organizations in 2000: "[They] are not so much mismanaged as nonmanaged. . . . They believe spending money produces results. Their strength is that they have a clear focus. Their weakness is that they do not define results" (Thomsen and Balda 2002, 16).

Yet for perhaps the first time in the last 100 years, many major philanthropic organizations *are* attempting to achieve social ends by using the organizational tools that have served wealth-creation entities so well. Segments of the foundation sector are beginning to realize that management encompasses all organizations—and while they define results very differently from private sector organizations, they are still better able to achieve their desired results by employing management by objectives.

We contend that this shift has been at least in part fueled by the ideas and practitioners of venture philanthropy. While it is possible that other forces have ushered management tools into the traditional foundations, it is difficult to ignore the correlation between the rise of objective-based thinking and the rise of venture philanthropy from 1996 to 2002. At a minimum, VP has provided another voice in the ongoing dialogue about the importance of using management tools and establishing standardized "good practices" for the sector.

It should also be noted that we agree with the argument that the individual pieces of VP are really nothing new to philanthropy. Business moguls as early as Rockefeller and Carnegie[6] tried to bring business ideas to the philanthropic sector, which led to Carnegie's much-quoted statement that it is easier to make money than it is to give it away. However, we would argue that the venture philanthropists of today actually do bring a different framework to the table than the business moguls of the past because their private-sector ideas are grounded not just in business but also in *management*—a discipline of knowledge that did not exist in Carnegie's and Rockefeller's time.

Finally, we return to our original question: Since venture philanthropy only constitutes a sliver of total giving in the philanthropic sector, what's all the fuss about? The fuss is about VP's larger cultural and creative impact on philanthropy. It is directly impacting the way foundations go about doing what they do. Venture philanthropy is acting as a conduit between nonprofit organizations and the wealth of knowledge that resides in the management discipline—an impact that may help propel the nonprofit sector to achieve social results that have never been seen before.

Notes

1. According to a report by Venture Philanthropy Partners, venture philanthropy grants totaled $50 million in 2002, making up only 0.2 percent of all foundation grants (Community Wealth Ventures 2002, 10).

2. For more on the Systems Model, see Csikszentmihalyi 1996, 27–36.

3. Taken from Letts, Ryan, and Grossman (1997) and the Philanthropy Phase I interviews for the GoodWork Project.

4. Although the foundation has changed its name and now uses "REDF" exclusively, because it was known as "Roberts Enterprise Development Fund" during much of the period of this study, I refer to that name here.

5. Actual average grant was $379,365. This figure has been discounted to 1996 dollars at 2.26 percent.

6. Andrew Carnegie established the Carnegie Corporation of New York in 1911 with

$125 million. John D. Rockefeller founded the Rockefeller Foundation in 1913 with $35 million.

References

Billitteri, T. 2000. "Roberts Fund Puts Venture Philanthropy to the Test." *The Chronicle of Philanthropy,* June 1.

Brest, P. 2002. "In Defense of the 'Effective Philanthropy' Approach." *The Chronicle of Philanthropy,* September 19.

Brower, B. 2001. *The New Philanthropists and the Emergence of Venture Philanthropy.* Washington, D.C.: CSIS Press.

Carnegie Corporation of New York. 1996. *Annual Report 1996.* New York: Carnegie Corporation of New York.

Carnegie Corporation of New York. 1997. *Annual Report 1997.* New York: Carnegie Corporation of New York.

——. 1999. *Annual Report 1999.* New York: Carnegie Corporation of New York.

——. 2000. *Annual Report 2000.* New York: Carnegie Corporation of New York.

——. 2002. *Annual Report 2002.* New York: Carnegie Corporation of New York.

Community Wealth Ventures. 2000. *Venture Philanthropy: Landscape and Expectations.* Washington, D.C.: Venture Philanthropy Partners.

——. 2001. *Venture Philanthropy 2001: The Changing Landscape.* Washington, D.C.: Venture Philanthropy Partners.

——. 2002. *Venture Philanthropy 2002: Advancing Nonprofit Performance through High-Engagement Grantmaking.* Washington, D.C.: Venture Philanthropy Partners.

Csikszentmihalyi, Mihaly. 1996. *Creativity: Flow and the Psychology of Discovery and Invention.* New York: HarperCollins Publications.

Davis, L., and N. Etchart 2001. "Venture Philanthropy: The Black Sheep in Wolves Clothing." Excerpted from "Venture Philanthropy: The Rise of New Philanthropy in the Old World." *Philanthropy in Europe* (Spring).

Drucker, P. F. 1954. *The Practice of Management.* New York: Harper & Row.

——. 1974. *Management: Tasks, Responsibilities, Practices.* New York: Harper & Row.

Eisenberg, P. 1999. "The 'New Philanthropy' Isn't New—or Better." *Chronicle of Philanthropy,* January 28.

GoodWork Project 2002. Unpublished Philanthropy Phase 1 Interviews.

Gose, B. 2003. "Cornering a Franchise on Giving." *The Chronicle of Philanthropy,* August 21.

——. 2004. "Supporters Say Venture Philanthropy Still Thrives, Even if Reach Is Limited." *The Chronicle of Philanthropy* 17, no. 1. Available online at http://www.nesst.org/COPVenturePhilanthropySummitOCT2004.htm.

The James Irvine Foundation. 1996. *The James Irvine Foundation Annual Report 1996.* San Francisco: The James Irvine Foundation.

——. 1999. *The James Irvine Foundation Annual Report 1999.* San Francisco: The James Irvine Foundation.

——. 2000. *The James Irvine Foundation Annual Report 2000.* San Francisco: The James Irvine Foundation.

——. 2002. *The James Irvine Foundation 2002 Annual Report.* San Francisco: The James Irvine Foundation.

Letts, C. W., W. Ryan, and A. Grossman. 1997. "Virtuous Capital: What Foundations Can Learn from Venture Capitalists." *Harvard Business Review* (March 1): 36–44.

Rockefeller Foundation. 1997. *1996 Annual Report.* New York: Rockefeller Foundation.

———. 2000. *1999 Annual Report.* New York: Rockefeller Foundation.

———. 2001. *2000 Annual Report.* New York: Rockefeller Foundation.

———. 2003. *2002 Annual Report.* New York: Rockefeller Foundation.

Sievers, B. 1997. "If Pigs Had Wings." *Foundation News & Commentary* 38, no. 6: 44–46.

Thomsen, M., and J. Balda. 2002. "The Next Society: A Conversation with Peter Drucker about the Future." *The Flame* 3 (Spring): 13–17.

Tuan, M. 1998. "The Roberts Enterprise Development Fund: A Case Study on Venture Philanthropy." San Francisco: The Roberts Enterprise Development Fund.

Vesper Society. 2001. *Principles and Practices of Venture Philanthropy: Do They Fit Your Human Service Organization?* A report of workshops. San Francisco: Vesper Society.

W.K. Kellogg Foundation. 1996. *W.K. Kellogg Foundation 1996 Annual Report: Capitalizing on Diversity.* Battle Creek, Mich.: W.K. Kellogg Foundation.

———. 1999. *W.K. Kellogg Foundation 1999 Annual Report: Leadership: It's Time.* Battle Creek, Mich.: W.K. Kellogg Foundation.

———. 2000. *W.K. Kellogg Foundation 2000 Annual Report: The Many Faces of Philanthropy.* Battle Creek, Mich.: W.K. Kellogg Foundation.

———. 2002. *W.K. Kellogg Foundation 2002 Annual Report: Together We Grow.* Battle Creek, Mich.: W.K. Kellogg Foundation.

The William and Flora Hewlett Foundation. 1996. *1996 Annual Report.* Menlo Park: The William and Flora Hewlett Foundation.

———. 1999. *1999 Annual Report.* Menlo Park: The William and Flora Hewlett Foundation.

———. 2000. *2000 Annual Report.* Menlo Park: The William and Flora Hewlett Foundation.

———. 2001. *2001 Annual Report.* Menlo Park: The William and Flora Hewlett Foundation.

———. 2002. *2002 Annual Report.* Menlo Park: The William and Flora Hewlett Foundation.

15 Ethical Standards in Philanthropy

Jenni Menon Mariano and Susan Verducci

In June 2004, the United States Senate Finance Committee held a hearing on charitable giving. Chairman Chuck Grassley opened the proceedings with the following statement:

> Today the Finance Committee considers a very serious matter—ensuring that charities keep their trust with the American people. We will hear testimony today that is troubling. The testimony we will hear will suggest that far too many charities have broken the understood covenant between the taxpayers and nonprofits— that charities are to benefit the public good, not fill the pockets of private individuals. (Grassley 2004)

The following September, a paper based on a series of public surveys questioned whether there was any trust with the American people left to keep. Paul C. Light's "Fact Sheet on the Continued Crisis in Charitable Confidence" detailed the decline in the public's view of the credibility of charities since the summer preceding 9/11 (2004). The report articulates public doubts regarding the ability of charities not only to meet their fiduciary responsibilities but to spend their dollars wisely, run their programs well, and be fair in the decisions they make.

Recovering the trust of the American people and boosting the credibility of philanthropy before the government takes regulatory action is foremost in the minds of many working in philanthropy. This chapter outlines a burgeoning effort that may not only help keep external regulation at bay but, more important, may move the field toward recognizing and mitigating the unintended harms articulated in this volume.

We recommend the creation and adoption of a set of national ethical standards for professionals in the field of philanthropy. Two types of standards interest us: the first focuses on field-wide standards such as accountability, and the second type centers on personal standards such as humility. A third type of standard, institutional, follows from field and personal standards. Institutional standards consist of best practices and are tailored to the particular missions, strategies for giving, and types of foundations in organized philanthropy. They are generated by the interaction of field-wide and personal standards with the demands and styles of individual foundations. Although this latter type of standard is critically important, it lies beyond the scope of this chapter.

Our recommendations derive from the GoodWork Project (GWP). Our experience in studying a number of established fields such as journalism, genetics, theater, and higher education combined with data collected directly from the study of exemplary workers in the field of philanthropy indicates that national ethical standards are becoming increasingly necessary. In this two-part chapter, we articulate the need for these standards and draw directly from our philanthropy data to discuss personal standards that our exemplars have told us are clearly indicated but have been fundamentally neglected.

Part I: Standards

Every domain the GWP has studied except philanthropy has a clear code of widely accepted ethical standards. These standards are snapshots of what the respective field holds to be valuable, both operationally and morally. They serve as reference devices and navigation aids to help workers make their way toward good work. Although some standards may not be consistently realizable, they can be instrumentally useful. Visions of excellence can pull people or a field toward positive outcomes. They can impact decision-making by organizing, prioritizing, and motivating actions and by providing means of appraisal. A set of national ethical standards for philanthropy can act as means by which the field can navigate the well-known complexities of the giving world.

State of Standards in the Field of Philanthropy

The field of organized philanthropy currently lacks a single set of widely accepted ethical standards. Certain historical facts and beliefs about philanthropy have allowed it unprecedented freedom from social, governmental, and legal regulations. The laws governing philanthropy provide only certain minimal standards pertaining to governance issues such as payout and conflict of interest. These requirements are notable for their narrowness.

Paul Brest of The William and Flora Hewlett Foundation confirmed the GWP findings on the state of standards in an interview in *Philanthropy*.

> I don't think this is a field with any significant professional standards.... It is only a bit of an exaggeration to say it's a field held together by a section of the tax code.... (N.a. 2004)

Similarly, the former president of another leading foundation remarked:

> The interesting thing about foundations is that there is no klieg light shining on us. There's no accreditation board, there's no required self-study that is part of any accreditation.... We basically are responsible for self-policing in this domain.

Still another president told us:

> [T]here is a quality of softness about this foundation business and criterialessness. So it would be a hard place to get a self-regulatory mechanism.... In the foundation world, there's no core set of principles.

Current Standards

Although there is no set of widely accepted ethical standards, there have been scattered efforts to create, disseminate, and talk about standards since the late 1970s. These movements are located in professional organizations (such as the Council on Foundations [CoF] and Independent Sector [IS]), in peripheral nonprofit endeavors (such as the Center on Global Ethics), in regional associations of grantmakers (such as the Minnesota Council on Foundations), in affinity groups (such as Disability Funders Network), and in individual foundations (such as the Charles Stewart Mott Foundation).

The most notable efforts to create standards have come from the CoF and IS. In June, 1980 the CoF developed its first set of standards, the "Statement of Principles and Practices for Effective Grantmaking" (hereafter referred to as "the Statement"). Two years later, the Council required all members to subscribe to the content of the Statement. There are currently six basic categories of standards: clear goals and procedures, legal knowledge; accountability, addressing change, diversity, and constructive relationships. These standards are a mix of procedural guides and ethical principles and are revisited and updated periodically (Council on Foundations 2004).

Ten years after this first major effort, IS developed a set of standards for the entire nonprofit field, including the philanthropic community (Independent Sector 2004a). The current version consists of a prototype that outlines general ethical principles that can be tailored to fit individual organizations. The basis of this code is a statement of values shared by members: commitment to the public good; accountability to the public; commitment beyond the standards set by law; respect for the worth and dignity of individuals; inclusiveness and social justice; respect for pluralism and diversity; transparency, integrity, and honesty; responsible stewardship of resources; and commitment to excellence and maintaining the public trust. These values translate into eight ethical principles: personal and professional integrity, clarity of mission and purpose, governance, legal compliance, responsible stewardship, openness and disclosure, program evaluation, inclusiveness and diversity (Independent Sector 2004a).

Troubles with Standards

The history of the development of standards has not been simple, nor has it been peaceful. These and other efforts have generated (and continue to generate) wide and heated debate. A number of significant problems with standards in philanthropy are well documented in their history and in the current conversation.

First, the extent to which these efforts reach the majority of foundations is unclear but most likely minimal. For example, although the CoF requires members to subscribe to its standards, the number of member organizations is but a small fraction of the total number of foundations in operation.

There's 50 or 60,000 foundations in America. Around 3,000 of them publish an annual report. So, you know, 57,000 of them, who I assume are all non-[CoF] members, are non-transparent. So are those twelve principles effective for everybody? They are effective for the Council's membership. 'Cause that's the only [group] they represent.

Second is the matter of enforceability. One critic doubted the effectiveness of the standards even for members of the CoF.

[T]he twelve standards [from the CoF] are toothless. . . . To have teeth, you have to have enforcement. I mean they might as well abolish [the Statement] for all the good it does.

The CoF itself has acknowledged trouble with enforceability. Eugene Struckhoff, CoF president during the development of the first set of standards, recalled:

It was always our objective to have a set of principles and practices for members and others. The only trouble was that there was no enforcement mechanism—no way to make certain foundations were living by that standard. In terms of true value—how can you set up enforcement? Compliance is completely voluntary. (John 2000, 2)

Even the IS standards were at one time titled "Obedience to the Unenforceable" (Independent Sector 2004b). None of the standards in organized philanthropy are binding in a systematic manner. Nor is it clear how any standards could become binding in the absence of accrediting bodies or governmental regulation.

Third, and perhaps most important, what belongs in any set of standards is debated. Although there is much overlap among the examples of standards available, many worry that the creation of widely accepted standards might constrain the autonomy and freedoms the field values highly. Therefore, concern about what is included permeates the field. This became evident in the development of the CoF's standards. In response to a particular statement regarding diversity, a group of members split off from the organization to form the Philanthropy Roundtable. One of those who seceded and went on to become a foundation president argued that the CoF "smuggled in content" in this statement to achieve its own political agenda.

This is what actually led to our falling out with the CoF; they tried to provide something of a definition of the public interest. And then there would be an obligation for foundations that accepted that.

Others believe that content is necessary in order for the standards to be meaningful. As the head of a watchdog organization noted in a discussion of current efforts to develop standards,

I consistently walk out of discussions of accountability because usually the ground rules of accountability are if we're going to discuss accountability, we're talking about how to report our funding, how well we do with our 990s, how we can improve our 990s, and what should we do regarding annual reports—and not standards of accountability in terms what are you doing in society and how do you stack up to the value of the tax exemption that you all exist under. And I find . . . the surgical excision of content as a matter of accountability to be the gaping hole here.

Finally, leaving issues of reach, enforcement, and content aside, consensus on the necessity for national standards does not exist. As articulated above, conversation on field-wide ethical standards is divided and heated. Although some believe there is a compelling warrant for field-wide standards, others believe this is not the case. Some believe that such standards would be a step toward governmental regulation, while others believe they are protection against the same. Still others articulate that standards are best taken care of within individual organizations and by individual workers. Further, many see standards as connected to the professionalization of philanthropy, a topic that a number of our subjects see as problematic.[1]

Warrant for Standards

The majority of the exemplary workers we interviewed, however, believe the field will soon move to a place where it will need a set of common ethical standards. When asked if he saw the lack of field-wide standards as a problem, one program officer said,

> Maybe. If you'd asked me eight years ago, I'd have said, "I don't think so." And now I think maybe. If you ask me in five years, I'll say, "Yes." It has to do with the growth in philanthropy. It is moving, in its growth in just sheer numbers, to a point where it probably will need some attention to issues like any other profession. I remember a long time ago studying, I think Greenwood . . . who studied the emergence of professions. . . . [H]e developed the six or eight key elements of a profession, and one of them was a code of ethics. And that at some point, when you are large enough and there is a standard of practice that becomes generally acceptable, one needs to capture those in terms of a code of ethics. And I think that if you looked at philanthropy today, you probably have most of Greenwood's elements. But maybe not that one.

There are reasons other than the anticipated growth in the field to be interested in creating a set of ethical standards. It would make transparent to the general public the philosophical and ethical underpinnings of the field. This effort might improve the field's credibility. Standards can promote self-regulation, even if they do not guarantee it. Moreover, they can protect the field from the abuses that have captured the American public's attention and threatened philanthropy's reputation. National ethical standards could also create a sense of consistent expectations across the field, despite the diversity of organizations, individual missions, and strategies for giving. Given the field's rapid growth, they could serve as a means to acculturate and train newcomers, a method of transmitting wisdom gleaned from years of discussion and the practice of philanthropy. Finally, as mentioned above, these principles can be used as a framework for determining institutional best practices.

IS recognized a further powerful warrant for creating ethical standards. It opens its standards with this statement: "As a matter of fundamental principle, the nonprofit and philanthropic community should adhere to the highest ethical standards because it is the *right thing to do*" (Independent Sector 2004b, 2; emphasis added). Vaclav Havel, although speaking on a different topic, concurs: "Work for something because it is good, not just because it stands a chance to succeed."

Regardless of the fact that a warrant for ethical standards clearly exists, the troubling issues of reach, enforcement, and content remain. Each can be addressed to varying degrees of satisfaction. Issues of content can be addressed most effectively. These issues derive from belief in the fundamental philanthropic value of freedom.[2] In the GWP, we frequently heard about the importance and value of pluralism in donor intent. We also heard about the importance of aligning the diverse methods of giving with these intents. Discussing Congress's support of philanthropy through granting tax incentives, one interviewee said,

> [Congress's] view is that the public interest would be served by a lot of people trying to do a lot of different things. And the attempt to define one particular public interest would defeat that. I think the idea was [that] there are a lot of conceptions of the public interest. And people work that out and fight that out in a lot of different ways. We have elections and we have a marketplace and we have all these donors out there who are trying to do it as best they can but in different ways and for different ends.

A president of a foundation reiterated this:

> I happen to be one who likes very much the broad possibility for philanthropy. I don't think that there is one way to do philanthropy, nor do I think that there is one purpose for philanthropy. I think that philanthropy really is enormously strengthened by the pluralism that is represented within it. I think it's enormously strengthened by the diversity that is possible.

It is generally believed that the field is founded on, and strengthened by, the principles of freedom from constraint and pluralism of aims and means. Many worry that any set of national standards can function to constrain these freedoms.

The first step in addressing these concerns is to separate ethical standards from best practices. The ethical standards we recommend consist of principles. Although some principles may be interpreted as practices, they are not the same. Take for example the diversity practice in the CoF standards that originally catalyzed a group of its members to leave the association. What was contested pertained to the original version of the following: "We reflect this diversity in multiple ways, such as through our grantmaking, through membership on our boards, committees, staffs and advisors, and through our business practices" (Council on Foundations 2004). It was the particular framing of the practices of honoring diversity that was contested; the principle remained valued, as can be seen in the following statement from the president of the group that broke away from the CoF. In his official response to the 2004 Senate hearings mentioned above, he characterized the field as diverse and advocated that it should stay that way.

> The Philanthropy Roundtable strives to preserve the freedom and philosophical diversity of the philanthropic sector. Freedom thrives under conditions of robust debate, competition and exchange of ideas. Freedom thrives when there are standards of excellence and vigorous watchdog groups monitoring performance. (Meyerson 2004)

Principles are not the same as best practices. They are not as directive as practices. They can be sensitive to particular contexts and are somewhat open to individual and institutional interpretation. We recommend that philanthropy's national standards be based on ethical principles for this reason. Best practices follow from the interpretation of these principles in each institutional setting and make up a foundation's own set of standards; essentially, the principles provide the framework for best practices. For example, if an agreed-upon field-wide ethical principle is "transparent and honest communication with grantees," institutions are free to determine what respecting this standard might look like given their own particular circumstances. Conditions that might impact the practice of the principle include the approach to giving (i.e., venture or more traditional), the relational model used (i.e., parent, partner, or sponsor; see Verducci, chapter 6 in this volume), and mission, to name a few. Although we believe that best practices cannot be specified across the field, ethical principles can (and should) be.

Organized philanthropy may be unique in having to surgically separate principles from best practices. The standards of other professions we have studied in the GWP, including journalism and law, possess mixtures of principles and practices. This fact, coupled with the reality that most people working in philanthropy come from other fields,[3] may have made it difficult for the field to generate a compelling and widely accepted set of standards. Recommending that the field leave the task of generating best practices to individual institutions respects and protects the philanthropic values of pluralism and freedom.

The problems of reach and enforcement are more difficult to address than those of content. The field of philanthropy is remarkably insulated, and not just from forces such as the market and government. Philanthropists and foundation personnel are insulated from each other as well; they are remarkably nontransparent. Although efforts to collaborate have increased and groups of grantmakers now meet at conferences and through affinity groups, partnerships, and tight collaborations are usually found only between the nonprofits and the grantmakers that fund them, if they are found at all.

In light of the insularity and isolation of philanthropy and the resulting problems with creating standards, it can be helpful to look for solutions in a different field with many of the same characteristics as philanthropy. As a result of the first amendment, journalism is a field with minimal legal restrictions. It also lacks accrediting bodies. Further, journalists and their organizations are notoriously independent from each other. Journalism, however, differs from philanthropy in that it has a set of standards that are remarkable in terms of reach and self-regulation. In the 1950s, the Radio-Television News Directors Association (RTDNA) created and disseminated a formal set of standards that govern the behavior of journalists in the absence of government regulation or regulation by professional associations. Its effectiveness can be seen clearly in the cases where reporters have stepped outside the standard's boundaries. The backlash against Jayson Blair at the *New York Times* and Stephen Glass at *The New Republic* for "making up" news was swift and devastating for both the individuals involved and the organizations they worked for. Although journalists are not bound by the RTNDA code in any legal sense, the field itself accepts the values underlying this code of ethics and regulates accordingly. The code acts as the conscience of the field.

Philanthropy does not yet have a common conscience. It leaves it to the government to enforce any breach of its narrow laws, and the government is notoriously spotty in pursuing these cases. To ensure the development of ethical standards that might function like those of journalism, there needs to be a coalition of people from across the sector—from foundations with no formal staff to those with many, from those that fund single issues to those that have multiple areas of interest, from those that fund a certain political position to those that fund the antithetical point of view, from those who are members of professional associations to those that have never been affiliated with anything. This coalition must work across differences to develop ethical principles that articulate the underlying values of the field. Its members must also work within their own networks to establish the importance of the standards. The scattered conversation on standards must become more coherent, more consistent, and more inclusive. Unless foundations and grantmakers feel they are part of a common body, there is no reason to embrace standards, let alone enforce them.

The conversation may, however, need to be reframed to highlight certain aspects of the warrant and address the attendant issues. We suggest a move away from discussion of the fear of government regulation and regaining public trust toward construction of a set of principles aligned with the basic and shared mission of the field: to do good in the public interest as stewards of public monies. This mission assumes, as in the medical profession, that the "do no harm" principle is necessary for good work. Reframing the conversation on ethical standards to ameliorate potential harms forces those working in the field to shift their focus from questions of effectiveness and efficiency to questions such as How does our work contribute directly to the public good? and Can our work cause harms, and if so, how?

Part II: Personal Standards

The basis for any principle included in ethical standards should address and ameliorate the potential harms articulated throughout this book. It may also be helpful to formulate particular standards more directly from the empirical data we have collected. Exemplary workers in philanthropy have compensated for the lack of field-wide standards and external regulation by developing personal standards. In talking with them about what ought to be in philanthropy, as well as what is, we came to understand some personal standards these exemplars hold and think that others should hold. In this second section of the chapter, we emphasize and detail personal standards not only because of their presence in our data but also because of support that can be found for them in the field of social science, the way they can be used in the development of field-wide standards, and their relative neglect in the examples of standards currently available.

Humility, honesty, commitment, communication, and cooperation are principles that exemplary workers have employed in various ways and can be used as a resource for the development of field-wide standards. However interpreted, each of these principles cultivates good relationships between those who work in foundations and those who work in nonprofits; they build the trust, respect, and openness to growth that fosters success. All of these principles also support learning, creating environments where critical and effective evaluation can take place. For the individual, humility is a guard from ego; it equips him or her to participate constructively in building relationships and develop an openness to learn from mistakes and from the knowledge of others. Honesty (and its institutional counterpart—transparency) fortifies foundations' credibility with grantees and the American public; it strengthens the trust between these parties and reflects a dedication to truth. Commitment helps workers remain fully engaged in their work in the face of frustration and boredom and helps them have a long-term as well as a short-term vision of the impact of the projects they support. Communication and cooperation guard against isolationism and allow people to learn from the mistakes of others.

Defining "Authentic" Humility: What It Is and What It Is Not

The late John Gardner, longtime activist and visionary, described his experience in the foundation world in this way: "I think we grope our way, and if we don't grope our way with humility we are crazy." A word of clarification is needed here, however. Humility can certainly have negative associations, conjuring up images of self-deprecation, low self-esteem, or an underestimation of one's abilities (Tangney 2000). As other authors in this volume point out, what is paraded as humility may sometimes in fact be a false sort of modesty. Yet humility in its most authentic form is positive. We therefore use the terms "authentic," "real," and "true" humility to emphasize its positive meaning and to distinguish it from false humility and its various negative connotations. Recent social science research shows that most people think that humility is a positive trait (Exline and Geyer 2004), and other researchers suggest that humility may be beneficial in a variety of professional circumstances (i.e., Bridges, Ware, Brown, and Greenwood 1971; Collins 2005; Colby and Damon 1994; Emmons

1999, 171–172; Weiss and Knight 1980). We draw on the work of philosophers and psychologists in defining real humility not as self-disgust, low self-regard, or low self-confidence (Emmons 1999; Peterson and Seligman 2004; Templeton 1997) but rather as a forgetting or transcending of the self, a sort of high-mindedness (Pieper 1966, 189, 191) that allows a person to focus on the needs of others. Authentic humility moderates ego, performing a self-regulatory function and providing a protection from emotional and behavioral excesses such as arrogance and self-loathing (Peterson and Seligman 2004, 431).

Implications of Humility for Philanthropy

Within philanthropy, authentic humility alleviates the difficulties in personal relationships that arise from the power differential that exists between nonprofits and the foundations that fund them. Many subjects cited this power dynamic as a source of tension. One grantmaker likened the "tricky" relationship that exists between foundation officers and their grantees to that of a professor and a graduate student, where as a graduate student "there wasn't much you could do to diminish your professor's reputation, but your professor had an enormous control over your outcomes and reference letter and whether your dissertation would be approved and so on."

Clearly this dynamic can be an uncomfortable source of tension, and the problems it creates can be substantial. One such dilemma is a lack of trust between foundations and nonprofits. Another is lack of respect on the part of foundation officers for personnel of nonprofits. Yet another is a hesitancy on the part of nonprofits to be candid about their difficulties; this leads to a sense of frustration on their part. It also does not allow the nonprofits or the foundation to critically evaluate the programs of the nonprofits. "What happens in the process, oftentimes, in managing that relationship, is that you don't have honesty and you don't have candor," says one foundation's executive. "You don't have mutual trust and oftentimes you don't have mutual respect."

How does humility operate as a personal standard to build and restore trust and respect between nonprofits and foundations? One way is that it protects foundation officers from letting the power associated with the money they give away go to their heads. It accomplishes this by giving them a balanced sense of perspective about the importance of their work and their role in that work. It guards them against exercising a sense of superiority over the people they fund, which they admit is no small challenge: there is a tendency for officers to confuse their position with who they are and what they are. Says one foundation executive, "I think one of the things that probably makes me effective at this work is that I take all of this with a *huge* grain of salt. You know, when I go downstairs and climb in my car, I'm like the guy that's driving out of this place right next to me."

Good foundation officers believe that in order to do good work one must "never think it's your own money." One subject shared the mantra he constantly repeats to himself: "It's not our money. It's not our money." As he said, "We put on our pants one leg at a time just like everybody else. And we're employees and we draw a paycheck, and we ought not to have any confusion about whose money this is." This sentiment was shared by other subjects, such as one board member who said, "If I had a group of them [foundation people] to educate, what would I say to them, until they were sick of hearing it? 'It's *not* your money.'"

Foundation officers use the perspective proffered by authentic humility to build professional relationships when they fairly attribute success where it is due rather than grabbing the credit for themselves. They appreciate the contributions of others and feel grateful for what others around them have to give. One prominent donor acknowledged his own part in the success of his work but admitted that other people are the source of many of the solutions he finds: "I come up with [solutions to problems] all the time," he says. "But stored away in my brain is all of that information that I've learned from everybody else. Obviously whenever I need information on a specific subject that I'm weak in, I avail myself of all the sources."

This attitude was echoed by many more of our interviewees. One said, "It's important to get the best advice you can from all the people out there who do what it is that you're interested in helping. Then try to shape a program that takes the very best of what you've heard and then invite people to participate in it." According to this grantmaker, "being a good listener" is also what makes a foundation's work good. One person suggested that good foundations understand their role in that they "start with the proposition that it is not all about them . . . it's all about the others." A good foundation celebrates the work of others. One executive believes good work in philanthropy is not about being "turfy or power-bound" by giving money but about being willing to share credit as well as information. He rejects the idea that "you have power because you give the illusion of it" and asserts that "you can certainly achieve respect and power by giving it up" and by "putting what you have to give in perspective of what other people have to give." Another officer said: "I was always lucky. I surrounded myself with all people who were brighter than I was, and that's very important. I'm bright enough to figure out who they are, and that was always useful." She attributes her success to others: "It's luck, luck, luck to be able to participate in something really worthwhile with people who are so talented." When we asked another executive what makes his work good, he told us this: "So much of it is dependent on the work of other people. You're really only as good as the work of your grantees. They're the ones who actually do the work."

Perspective also suggests that officers avoid an over elevated sense of their own or their foundations' importance. One grantmaker characterized arrogance and foundations fooling themselves and society into thinking that they are making a bigger impact than they really are as the two "dark sides" of philanthropy. In the words of an executive: "Philanthropy doesn't really do much. It supports the good work of others." He added, "Its role should be kept in perspective."

True humility facilitates an openness to new ideas and advice that come from outside the foundation. Said one subject: "You need a foundation that's accessible, open. I call it the open door and the listening ear—a door you can come in through and some foundation officer who listens." This kind of openness means that foundation officers show trust in their grantees. The same subject described himself as "a listener" and as someone who puts his trust in the ability of the people he is working with and for: "I think you can go far in assuming that talent is out there, the judgment is out there, and that you can gather it around you and learn from it." In his work he has always "thought of myself as an observer, a student, trying to understand, not trying to run anything."

Humble foundation officers soak up information from outside sources, always looking for knowledge in different places, including from others in the foundation world. They are consequently engaged in a learning process, seeking "multiple inputs from all over the place." A humble attitude makes one flexible; one welcomes criticism and evaluation so that it may lead to new knowledge, movement, and growth, and diminish one's fear of failure. Failure is seen not as a personal threat or a threat to the foundation but as an asset to facilitate improvement. Many subjects found that they were able to avoid an attitude of perfectionism and adopt a developmental approach to their work. One grantmaker takes it for granted that some programs are simply just not going to succeed but says that "you learn a lot from something not working." Some failures are "kind of important" in this regard, so she doesn't "write them all off as big mistakes." In fact, she asserts that being open to ideas and advice from others creates an environment where it is difficult to make bad mistakes, because in the process relationships are built and strengthened and knowledge is ultimately shared and gained: "You're getting a lot of good people to talk to each other about a project. At least you've built some bridges."

It is clear that the personal and institutional effects of real humility in the foundation world are closely related. It is difficult to speak about them separately, since so much of what a foundation is, how it is perceived, and the work it does depends on how its officers conduct themselves. However, it is clear that the missions of foundations and how their officers understand those missions are shaped by humility. One person told us that doing good philanthropy means involving others' input about where money should go, thereby avoiding using philanthropic monies to advance one's own agenda. He believed that is bad work to press one's own agenda without the input of others, because this reflects an arrogant know-it-all attitude that is detrimental to the work. There is a natural tendency in a foundation to begin to think that all the wisdom and knowledge is lodged within it and that doing philanthropy is just a matter of going out and finding people who will support the answers the foundations have already reached. For this subject, the worst practice is when people use what appears to be philanthropy as "a means of advancing, by the systematic use of money, their own agenda." It is important to "guard against this tendency to serve your own ego or your own purposes." He said, "A lot of ailments come from people thinking that they don't need to consult." Another subject said: "I don't think it's good for a foundation from its ivory tower to decide what's needed. And then to seek someone . . . who will agree with that and take money to do it." Rather, good philanthropy means finding the best people out there and funding what they want to do. She takes a humble attitude in this regard; for the sake of her own education, she asks grantees to "let me know what you do with this money. And let me know what more you need." Foundation staff should be "more learners than teachers," yet presently most are "much more teachers than learners." A second grantmaker believes that foundations can do great harm when they suggest that they know better than nonprofits what they should be doing.

Implications of Honesty for Philanthropy

Honesty is a less controversial term than humility. It is seen as positive. It is one of the characteristics our subjects in the field of philanthropy mentioned most frequently as necessary for accomplishing good work. Like true humility, honesty plays an important role in building trusting relations with grantees and grantseekers. In the foundation world, honesty means having candor, being trustworthy in one's dealings, and having personal and institutional integrity.

These qualities are painfully missing in philanthropic practice, according to our interviewees, but dishonest acts are not always overt. For instance, many subjects mentioned that funders can be indirect and evasive in their interactions with grantseekers and grantees, "leading people on" to believe that they will give or renew grants. Some foundations may break promises to their grantees and hide reasons for rejecting a grant. However, being candid is critical because, as one board member and executive emphasized, "This is public money."

Subjects recommended being "up front" about the foundation's desires and goals even if it means turning down applicants. People need to be clear and honest with each other, even when things aren't working as planned. For example, a grantee should never be led to believe that a grant is a done deal until it has been officially passed. And in order to do this, individuals are often required to develop discipline in their communications with grantees and their foundation co-workers. One subject admired a colleague's candidness: "She has no problem saying 'No' or being clear about when something is coming from her authority as president." Some grantees were said to sacrifice personal integrity for the "survival" of the organization. Integrity is an antidote in this respect because it helps eliminate conflicts of interest and values.

Institutional transparency assists with good work by encouraging critical examination. One recipient said: "It is the cloaking of foundation decision making in a toga of respectability, where the toga prevents any kind of critical examination, that has to be changed. That's a big change." One example of this would be the acknowledgement of failures as well as successes. Transparency requires admission of failures too.

Some of our interview subjects said that they were troubled by pressure to maintain confidentiality in foundation work instead of seeking transparency. There is a conflict between how much and what information one is obliged to disclose to other grantors and the field and the degree to which one has the obligation to protect the confidentiality of the grantees. The responsibility to be transparent was seen as applying to one's own person and to foundations themselves. One subject said that a responsibility even exists *between* foundations to be transparent.

Implications of Commitment for Philanthropy

Another host of potential standards make up what could be termed commitment. Being committed was one way many subjects described attributes of their mentors in philanthropy. This involves having a deep care and passion for one's job, the enthusiasm to engage deeply in one's work and with those one works with, and the wherewithal to stick wholeheartedly with a project until it succeeds.

Implicit in commitment is an attitude of constancy and sustained engagement. Lack of engagement and low interest in a grant after making it was mentioned as two qualities of bad philanthropists. One recipient we interviewed described a situation in which this happened: "He gave us the grant and then he just sort of never really took the grant seriously." "I tell every new person who comes into this field with new money asking What should I do? that you've got to care passionately about things," said one subject. Two others said that instilling passion in new philanthropists was the best thing a mentor could do.

An inherent dilemma in philanthropic work is how to maintain enthusiasm and passion when the work becomes mundane, routine, and even boring. As one executive admitted: "The fact is this is really hard, bone wearying, sometimes not very interesting work." Grantmaking can sometimes lead to burnout and stagnation because the time, effort, and volume of work required does not often have projected results. A by-product of burnout is that program officers can become distant or disengaged from their work. Good workers in the field need to be aware of this tendency and exercise determination to overcome it when it arises—to wait out and persevere through the inevitable bad patches of frustration and refuse to disengage from the work.

Commitment to a long-term vision or goal, to seeing projects through to their end, is a strategy that may allow staff to avoid giving in to the need for immediate results that is so common in the field. Admittedly, the movement toward quick measurable results is positive in many respects in that it is an attempt to evaluate. However, many subjects suggested the need to approach this emphasis with caution. The full impact of a grant may sometimes take years—a period which, all too often, grantmakers are not willing to wait through. People want to "find the magic bullet," or a solution that can take care of the problem instantly. However, the reality is that "it's not that easy to move that fast in the foundation world." As one recipient said: "You're not going to change something in one or two years. It's going to take seven to ten years to really build any kind of institution or to change the culture. You have to get people who are used to operating differently and it requires fairly constant and significant and systematic interventions on the part of third parties." Another recipient suggested that longer-term core support would decrease the need to raise money all the time. Others talked about how this sort of support would actually allow organizations to focus more on their programs.

Implications of Communication and Cooperation for Philanthropy

Adopting positive attitudes toward communication and cooperation are further candidates for standards in the field. Communication and cooperation may extend to relationships between foundations, between foundations and grantees, and between foundations and the general public. Collaboration was frequently mentioned as a component of good work and was typically referred to in four ways:

- As occurring between advisors, consultants, nonprofits, grant recipients, and experts in the field and taking place at the levels of strategy development, program development, grantmaking, or grant evaluation;
- As a convening of separate grantees and grantseekers to share their work and/or engage in joint initiatives;
- As foundation encouraging nonprofits to partner with government and business; and
- As occurring within and between foundations.

In spite of overwhelming support for collaboration among our interview subjects, however, it is important to note that when cooperation means official collaboration between foundations, some in the field are cautious. This caution is not unwarranted. William Schambra (2005) notes the very real dangers of collaboration between foundations, including the danger that smaller, newer, or local philanthropists (i.e., donors or foundations) will be intimidated by bigger and more established institutions. Such partnerships are hardly ones of equals, and original ideas these smaller initiatives bring can be thwarted.

> Like most philanthropy buzzwords, "collaboration" sounds unobjectionable. When it means [that] foundations with common purposes should bring some coordination to their efforts, it is reasonable and benign. But when it tends to suppress or constrain promising new modes of giving in America, it unwittingly serves a philanthropic establishment that seeks desperately to re-establish its professional authority in a world that is, to them, frighteningly recalcitrant and disordered. (4–5)

What the majority of our subjects recommend, however, is not out of line with what Schambra is cautioning against. They promote a wisely conceived sense of cooperation that is characterized by a more open communication and exchange between the participants in the field. They praise a healthy sense of individualism yet point out that all too often this tendency goes overboard. It becomes "autonomy run amuck," where everyone is "doing their own thing." Indeed, some subjects characterized foundation work as too individualistic. It is common practice for foundations to act individually on issues that in fact demand collective action and conversation.

Communication and cooperation may be antidotes for the characteristic isolation in the field. Although strides have been made in changing the isolationist mindset prevalent in foundations, there is still a need for increased communication and cooperation between foundations and their grantees. There is a tendency to become disconnected from the field while working in a foundation: "The longer you are in a foundation, no matter how hard you try, you get further and further away from what's going on on the ground." Many current strategies result in isolation. These include donors creating barriers against partnership with others and foundations not sharing what they do with other foundations. Such strategies may lead to redundancy in the foundation world.

As a solution to isolation, more intragrantee communication was recommended as a way to increase public support and generate more effective grantmaking.

> Sometimes there ought to be reports, sometimes there ought to be convening, sometimes there ought to be action-oriented long-term projects where we bring several grantees together and say, "You guys all . . . have pieces of the same problem. Why don't you—with our money—why don't you work together and see if we can't make something really huge happen."

Many of our subjects felt that communication and sharing is not just a cordial activity that people engage in but a serious responsibility. Specifically, they believe that one has a responsibility to disseminate what one has learned from successes and failures. One subject said, "We mess up. We learn some lessons from messing up, and maybe other people won't mess up quite the same ways if we get our lessons out there." Another opinion is that foundations have a responsibility to share information with each other and have open communication in order to advance the field as a whole, rather than working as individual units: "When institutions aren't functioning well, as well as they should, there's a set of responsibilities to do that, to contribute to the sector beyond grantmaking."

Fortunately, collaboration has been increasing between funders who share common goals and interests. One person mentioned that there is more collaboration now than when she first entered the field. At one time, collaboration was a rare thing. The increasing use of collaborative learning in the philanthropic world is slowly building an accumulated wisdom about grantmaking that may lead to more effective and positive grantmaking in the future. "Teaming up" and partnering with other individuals and organizations is an effective way to learn about such experiences of success and failure and about the efforts of other foundations. Two subjects said grantees are an excellent source of information and insight that is not often utilized by foundations. Another subject mentioned how young staff members can offer fresh perspectives and energetic and innovative solutions to problems that seasoned veterans should learn from. One subject felt that methods and strategies for grantmaking could grow from contact with other theoretical frameworks than the ones currently used in the field of philanthropy.

No single individual in the field is capable of adequately dealing with the diversity of individuals, interests, issues, and challenges in philanthropic work. Subjects felt that the ability to collaborate and have an excellent network of experts in the field and in related fields, within (and outside) one's foundation, and in nonprofits was a valuable and necessary skill: "You want people to be on a team, so you have to be a team player." In addition, they felt that the ability to delegate responsibility to others is necessary because of the overwhelming workload. The staff and president must work well with the trustees, and the grantmaker must have a good network within and outside the foundation.

Greater accountability in the field may also be achieved through more communication and cooperation between foundations and the people they work with. Educating the general public about foundations can be important in this regard. Increased public awareness would also put pressure on the press to pay better attention to foundations. Two subjects said that communication between philanthropic researchers and policymakers was also needed if foundations are to have the broad effect most strive for.

Cooperation also has implications for evaluation. Our subjects spoke about specific desirable strategies they adopt in the methods and processes they use to evaluate their work that draw on principles of open communication. They spoke about how conducting site visits and facilitating open discourse with nonprofits and communities effectively gathers qualitative information about the progress and outcomes of grants. These methods can help estimate impact. Many saw using resources outside the foundation as an effective and informative strategy for evaluating the work of foundations and nonprofits. Creating a panel of "outside," or nonfoundation, personnel provides expert opinions and measurements on grant progression; these experts can suggest courses of action that will enable them to highlight strengths and correct problems of grants. Subjects also said that forming "informal networks" of people who are directly affected by the grant can be extremely beneficial in evaluating the success or failure of a grant.

In the absence of deliberate and active collaboration between foundations, the dissemination of knowledge and research is difficult. This deficit continuously poses a problem for foundations. Smaller foundations often have effective and innovative strategies for dealing with universal difficulties, yet they are unheard of because of their size and lack of reputation. Further cooperation should help this situation by building an infrastructure that could help foundations and workers just starting out learn the best strategies and tactics for grantmaking.

Conclusion

The need for a set of field-wide ethical standards in philanthropy is becoming increasingly clear. Personal standards, such as humility, honesty, commitment, communication, and cooperation, can inform the development of these standards. In turn, these standards can be translated into best practices within institutions; individuals and organizations must determine how to interpret and manifest these standards in the multiple contexts in which they find themselves. Ethical principles can take effect differently across situations, depending on the complexity of a situation, how the individual principles are prioritized, the individuals and organizations involved, and changing social contexts. This fact presents a challenge to the philanthropic community on two fronts. The first is to do the relatively easier work of identifying the highest ethical standards for their field's practice. Here we have offered five such standards derived from our empirical work, but many others may be relevant to the field. The second, more difficult, challenge is the effort that each individual and institution must expend to consistently adhere to such standards. From this point of view, how professional philanthropists respond to the ethical challenges inherent in the field need not be "standardized" in the pejorative sense of the word. These ethical standards can act as navigation aids, not rules. The experience of the exemplary workers in philanthropy discussed in this chapter, however, show that what *is* possible is a creative engagement with such standards. Actively applying these standards even on an individual basis is a promising solution to the very real problems philanthropists and grantmakers encounter in their work. Imagine what could be accomplished with the application of field-wide standards.

Notes

1. See Horn and Gardner, chapter 5 in this volume.
2. See Reich, chapter 2 in this volume.
3. See Horn and Gardner in this volume.

References

Bridges, C. M., W. B. Ware, B. B. Brown, and G. Greenwood. 1971." Characteristics of the Best and Worst College Teachers." *Science Education* 55: 545–553.

Colby, A., and W. Damon. 1994. *Some Do Care: Contemporary Lives of Moral Commitment.* New York: Free Press.

Collins, J. 2005. "Level 5 Leadership: The Triumph of Humility and Fierce Resolve." *Harvard Business Review* 83, no. 7/8: 136–146.

Council on Foundations. 2004. "Recommended Principles and Practices for Effective Grantmaking." Available online at http://www.cof.org/Content/General/Display .cfm?contentID=156&menuContainerName=&navID=0.

Edie, J. A. 2000. "Principles and Practices: A Retrospective." *Council Columns* 19, no. 10 (October): 2–3. Available online at http://www.cof.org/files/Documents/Building%20Strong %20Ethical%20Foundations/Council_Columns_Principles_Practices_Retrospectives.pdf.

Emmons, R. A. 1999. *The Psychology of Ultimate Concerns: Motivation and Spirituality in Personality*. New York: Guilford Press.

Exline, J. J., and A. L. Geyer. 2004. "Perceptions of Humility: A Preliminary Study." *Self and Identity* 3, no. 2: 95–114.

Grassley, C.. 2004. "Opening Statement, Hearing on Charitable Giving, June 22, 2004." Available online at http://finance.senate.gov/hearings/statements/062204cg.pdf.

Independent Sector. 2004a. "Statement of Values and Code of Ethics for Nonprofit and Philanthropic Organizations." Available online at http://www.independentsector .org/members/code_main.html.

———. 2004b. "Obedience to the Unenforceable: Ethics and the Nation's Voluntary and Philanthropic Community." Available online at http://www.independentsector.org/ PDFs/obedience.pdf.

Light, P. C. 2004. "Fact Sheet on the Continued Crisis in Charitable Confidence." Available online at http://www.brook.edu/views/papers/light/20040913.pdf.

Meyerson, A. 2004. "Response to Senate Finance Committee Discussion Draft." *Philanthropy* 18, no. 4. Available online at http://www.philanthropyroundtable.org/ prtofficialresponse.htm.

N.a. 2004. "Know Where You're Going: An Interview with Hewlett President Paul Brest." *Philanthropy* 18, no. 1: 10–13, 28. Available online at http://www.philanthropyroundtable .org/magazines/2004/january/Paul%20Brest%20Interview.htm.

Peterson, C., and M. E. P. Seligman. 2004. *Character Strengths and Virtues: A Handbook and Classification*. New York: American Psychological Association.

Pieper, J. 1966. *The Four Cardinal Virtues: Prudence, Justice, Fortitude, Temperance*. South Bend, Ind.: University of Notre Dame Press.

Schambra, W. A. 2005. "One Cheer for Collaboration: Beware a Foundation Establishment Eager to Smother Innovative Local Giving." *Philanthropy* 19, no. 2. Available online at http://www.hudson.org/index.cfm?fuseaction=publication_details&id=2805.

Tangney, J. P. 2000. "Humility: Theoretical Perspectives, Empirical Findings and Directions for Further Research." *Journal of Social and Clinical Psychology* 19, no. 1: 70–82.

Templeton, J. M. 1997. *Worldwide Laws of Life*. Philadelphia, Pa.: Templeton Foundation Press.

Weiss, H. M., and P. A. Knight. 1980. "Information Search and Problem-Solving Efficiency." *Organizational Behavior and Human Performance* 25 (April): 216–223.

Concluding Thoughts

Mihaly Csikszentmihalyi

The volume you are reading provides a good illustration of how quickly human behavior becomes complicated. Giving money away for good causes appears on the surface to be a simple act with clear motives and outcomes. Yet at second glance, it becomes evident that things are not as obvious as they seem.

Actually, it would be surprising if things were simpler. Human behavior is, after all, the result of contradictory impulses inherited from randomly linked genetic instructions, which in turn must be reconciled with values inherited from the culture and with the norms and laws of society. The combinations are practically endless. Philanthropic behavior is no exception: it can originate from any combination of selfish greed and selfless ideal and can result in outcomes that are either life enhancing or amount to just another form of greed.

What we now call philanthropy takes three rather different forms. The oldest and still most prevalent form is that of "charity," which applies to members of a community when they voluntarily redistribute resources to avoid severe inequalities. Such practices have roots in the division of labor and food of social insects (where the notion of "voluntary" hardly applies) and is clearly present in ethnographic descriptions of various practices by which tribal leaders redistribute grains and other resources to those in need. This function became centralized with the advent of large-scale farming about 10,000 years ago in the great temples of Egypt and Mesopotamia, where the clerical elite was charged with the management of surplus. Ever since, charity has had many different guises, and not without engendering controversy. As some of the previous chapters point out, charity has often been held to task for providing a safety valve that prevents the disadvantaged from pursuing more permanent and thorough social change.

The second and more recent form that philanthropy takes is that of investing resources in public projects outside the market. What we now consider the greatest accomplishments of art—from the music of Bach to the statues, frescoes, and cathedrals of the Renaissance—would not exist if wealthy patrons had not decided to use some of their resources to enrich the common environment with the most beautiful artifacts human skill could produce. This kind of cultural philanthropy is still vigorous, supporting orchestras, ballet, opera, and the visual arts. In addition, the sciences have come to rely on private donors and foundations for the pursuit of basic research and its applications. If resources were not invested in beauty and knowledge, life would obviously be so much less worth living. Yet cultural philanthropy can also be misused to create a genteel pseudo-artistic aura which only serves to bolster the superiority of the donors and their friends without helping the rest of the community in any meaningful way.

Finally, the third and most recent form of philanthropy is the support of initiatives aimed at social justice—helping individuals, organizations, and communities overcome obstacles to the realization of their own goals. While one might argue that giving of this kind was not unknown in former times, usually the beneficence was top down, doled out according to conditions set by the donor. Under the influence of social entrepreneurship and venture philanthropy, however, the beneficiaries are increasingly expected to be involved in the setting of goals and procedures to an extent that makes this form of giving qualitatively different from earlier ones.

Given all this complexity, how are we to understand philanthropy? This volume begins to focus on the most urgent issues. Some are philosophical and strategic, but most are focused on the practical question What is good work in philanthropy and how can the harms of giving be avoided?

The most basic ontological question has to do with the origins, or the "prime mover," of the impulse to give. As the chapters by Schervish and Percer describe, the values and ideologies of donors can generally be seen as the "causes" of giving. However, Reich suggests that who gives how much to what purpose is also strongly influenced by the fiscal laws societies enact to regulate philanthropy. From that point of view, philanthropic giving is explained by taxation rather than motivation.

More disturbing is the possibility that giving resources away might do more harm than good. The central theme of this book is how to prevent this from happening. The list of mistakes is daunting. Thoughtless giving can harm the recipient or it can harm society by withdrawing taxable funds from the common purse and allocating them instead to special interests that may or may not help society at large. It can even harm the giver's interest. For instance, Laura Horn describes how faith-based agencies sometimes downplay their spiritual mission in favor of social goals that are more attractive to funders. However, such short-term tactics can undermine the ultimate purpose of the organization.

The main thrust of the book is not about actual givers but about the profession that has evolved to mediate between donors and recipients. The growth of this profession adds another layer of complexity. "Philanthropoids"—as they are sometimes not-so-gently called—have their own values and agendas that, consciously or not, may diverge from those of the donors and those of the recipients.

The peculiar pressures these professionals work under are amply documented in the chapter by Horn and Gardner and James and Marshall. Susan Verducci reviews the various kinds of relationships—parenting, partnering, sponsoring—philanthropists typically have with the recipients they support. Recent changes that the influx of social entrepreneurs (Barendsen) and venture philanthropists (Standlea) have brought to the art of giving, update the historical trend. So does

Deep and Frumkin's analysis of the increasing tendency for foundations to liquidate their assets in one final burst of flamboyant generosity.

So what can be learned from this book? In some respects, knowledge about the ins and outs of giving is unlikely to bring fundamental changes in how much money individuals will part with or in their reasons for giving it away. This will continue to be determined by personal values, laws, and economic conditions regardless of what we know or do not know about them. However, the knowledge that arises from studies like the ones reported here ought to be very useful to the practice of philanthropy and help establish it on principles based on theory and systematic empiricism.

Figure C.1 presents a much-simplified and schematic model of what a domain of philanthropic giving might encompass. The professionals in this domain would have to be familiar with the personal, cultural, and social forces that shape donors' intent. They would have to know how to interpret such intent in changing times, taking into account new laws, mores, and opportunities that bear on the intent.

Next, the professional ought to be able to identify the most effective vehicle for meeting the intent of the donor (or of the foundation). Having decided on the recipient most likely to carry on good work in line with that intent, the professional needs to establish the kind of relationship that best serves the conduct of the work, what model would fulfill mutual expectations, and the means by which performance is to be evaluated.

At each of these steps, the philanthropic professional can either exercise due diligence or hope for the best. The second of these choices is unlikely to result in good work and has the potential of actually causing harm.

Obviously this schema is only tentative, but as the preceding chapters indicate, the knowledge to fill it out is beginning to accumulate. At this point, as the other writers in this book have shown over and over, there are many ways to undermine the good that giving is expected to achieve. Effective generosity is a difficult art. To the many good suggestions contained in the previous pages, let me add one close to my own heart: make sure that how you evaluate giving is consistent with the intent of your grant.

Accountability and evaluation are useful and admirable goals, but they can become counterproductive when applied in a mindless fashion. If the interest of a foundation is to increase the production of widgets, it makes sense to evaluate the success of a widget-making training intervention by the number of widgets produced. Even when the effects of a project to decrease the incidence of unwanted pregnancy in an inner city are to be assessed, it makes sense to use clear quantitative measures of success.

The danger is that if quantifiability of outcome becomes a ruling dogma, many potentially excellent projects will never be allowed to start. The work of the Curies with radiation took many years to show practical results in the area of health. Would the merchant families of Verona who built the many lovely bridges in the city have gone ahead with their project if the results of their generosity had to be verified by focus groups? And where will the next major tech-

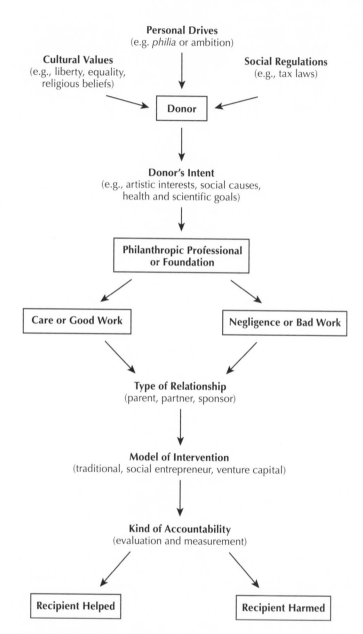

Fig. C.1. A Schematic Model of the Philanthropic Process

nological breakthroughs come from when even such wildly successful research institutes as Bell Labs are closing? The insistence on immediate results, on precisely measurable outcomes, can be carried to pathological extremes that are signs of a lack of confidence and hope, of a short-term horizon, rather than signs of rigor and accountability.

To point out such threats is a sign not of pessimism but of faith in a better future. I think I can speak for all of the authors in this volume when I say that although they often focus on potential harms in the practice of philanthropy, they do so because when giving involves good work, it enhances our lives enormously. And by pointing out pitfalls to avoid in this complex endeavor, we hope to improve, even if by the slightest amount, the effective deployment of human generosity.

Contributors

Lynn Barendsen is a project manager at the GoodWork Project. She completed graduate work in American literature at the University of Chicago and Boston University. She has published articles on African American and regionalist literatures and young social and business entrepreneurs. With Wendy Fischman, she has developed the GoodWork Toolkit, a set of materials designed to encourage good work.

Mihaly Csikszentmihalyi, a leading authority on the psychology of creativity and optimal experience, is the C. S. and D. J. Davidson Professor of Psychology at the Peter F. Drucker and Masatoshi Ito Graduate School of Management at Claremont Graduate University and Director of the Quality of Life Research Center. He is also emeritus professor of human development at the University of Chicago, where he chaired the department of psychology.

William Damon is Professor of Education at Stanford University, Director of the Stanford Center on Adolescence, and Senior Fellow at the Hoover Institute on War, Revolution, and Peace. His books include *Good Work: When Excellence and Ethics Meet* (2001, with Howard Gardner and Mihaly Csikszentmihalyi) and *The Moral Advantage: How to Succeed in Business by Doing the Right Thing* (2004). He is currently working on projects aimed at fostering excellent and ethical work in journalism, business, higher education, and philanthropy.

Akash Deep is Associate Professor of Public Policy specializing in finance at Harvard University's John F. Kennedy School of Government. His expertise lies in financial risk management, infrastructure finance, and the management and regulation of banks and financial institutions.

Peter Frumkin is Professor of Public Affairs and Director of the RGK Center for Philanthropy and Community Service at the Lyndon B. Johnson School of Public Affairs, University of Texas at Austin. He is the author of *On Being Nonprofit* (2002) and *Strategic Giving* (forthcoming).

Howard Gardner is the Hobbs Professor of Cognition and Education at the Harvard Graduate School of Education and co-principal investigator of the GoodWork Project. He is the author of many books, including *Frames of Mind* (1983), *Creating Minds* (1993), *Making Good* (2004), and *Changing Minds* (2004).

Laura Horn has been a researcher on the GoodWork Project at Harvard University since 2002. She has a B.A. in psychology from Amherst College.

Carrie James is a project manager at the GoodWork Project at Harvard University. Her work focuses on the Project's studies of philanthropy, higher education, and medicine. Carrie has a M.A. and Ph.D. in Sociology from New York University.

Leslie Lenkowsky is Director of Graduate Programs at the Center on Philanthropy and Professor of Public Affairs and Philanthropic Studies at Indiana University. From 2001 to 2003, he served as chief executive officer of the Corporation for National and Community Service, a position to which he was appointed by President George W. Bush.

Paula Marshall is a project manager at the GoodWork Project at Harvard University. Her work focuses on philanthropy, theater, and law. Paula has an Ed.M. from Harvard University.

Jenni Menon Mariano is a doctoral candidate at the Stanford University School of Education in the field of Psychological Studies and a research assistant at the Stanford Center on Adolescence. Her research looks at positive and moral development in young people, including the development of purpose in adolescence.

Sarah Miles is currently a doctoral candidate in psychological studies in education at Stanford University. In addition, she holds an M.S.W. from the University of Pennsylvania and has taught bilingual fifth grade.

Liza Hayes Percer is a postdoctoral fellow at the National Writing Project in Berkeley, California. She received her M.A. and Ph.D. in Arts Education at Stanford University. During her tenure on the GoodWork Project, she was involved in research on professionalism in genetics, higher education, and philanthropy.

Rob Reich is Assistant Professor of Political Science at Stanford University and the author of *Bridging Liberalism and Multiculturalism in American Education* (2002). He is currently at work on a book about ethics, public policy, and philanthropy.

Tanya Rose is a doctoral student at the University of Colorado, Boulder, in Educational Foundations, Policy and Practice. Prior to her graduate studies, she was a research assistant at the Stanford Center on Adolescence. She has a master's degree in education from Stanford University and has worked as a high school teacher.

Paul G. Schervish is Professor of Sociology and Director of the Center on Wealth and Philanthropy at Boston College and National Research Fellow at the Indiana University Center on Philanthropy. He is senior advisor to the John Templeton Foundation and to the Wealth & Giving Forum. He has served as

Distinguished Visiting Professor of Philanthropy at the Indiana University Center on Philanthropy and as Fulbright Professor of Philanthropy at University College, Cork, Ireland.

James Allen Smith is the Waldemar A. Nielsen Professor of Philanthropy at Georgetown University. He has spent more than twenty years working in foundations, including The Twentieth Century Fund, the Howard Gilman Foundation and the J. Paul Getty Trust. He is the author of *The Idea Brokers: Think Tanks and the Rise of the New Policy Elite* (1991) and other books and articles on civil society and philanthropy.

Nick Standlea holds an M.B.A. from the Peter F. Drucker and Masatoshi Ito School of Management at Claremont Graduate University. He is a writer and entrepreneur as well as a part-time research associate at the Quality of Life Research Center in Claremont, California.

Thomas J. Tierney is the former chief executive of Bain & Company and currently serves as Chairman of the Bridgespan Group, Bain's nonprofit affiliate.

Susan Verducci is Assistant Professor of Humanities at San Jose State University. As a research associate at the Stanford Center on Adolescence, she managed the GoodWork Project in Philanthropy.

Index